CAT + GAMER

VOLUME 1

Story and art by **Wataru Nadatani**

Translation by **Zack Davisson**
Lettering and retouch by **Susie Lee** and **Studio Cutie**

DARK HORSE MANGA

TABLE OF CONTENTS

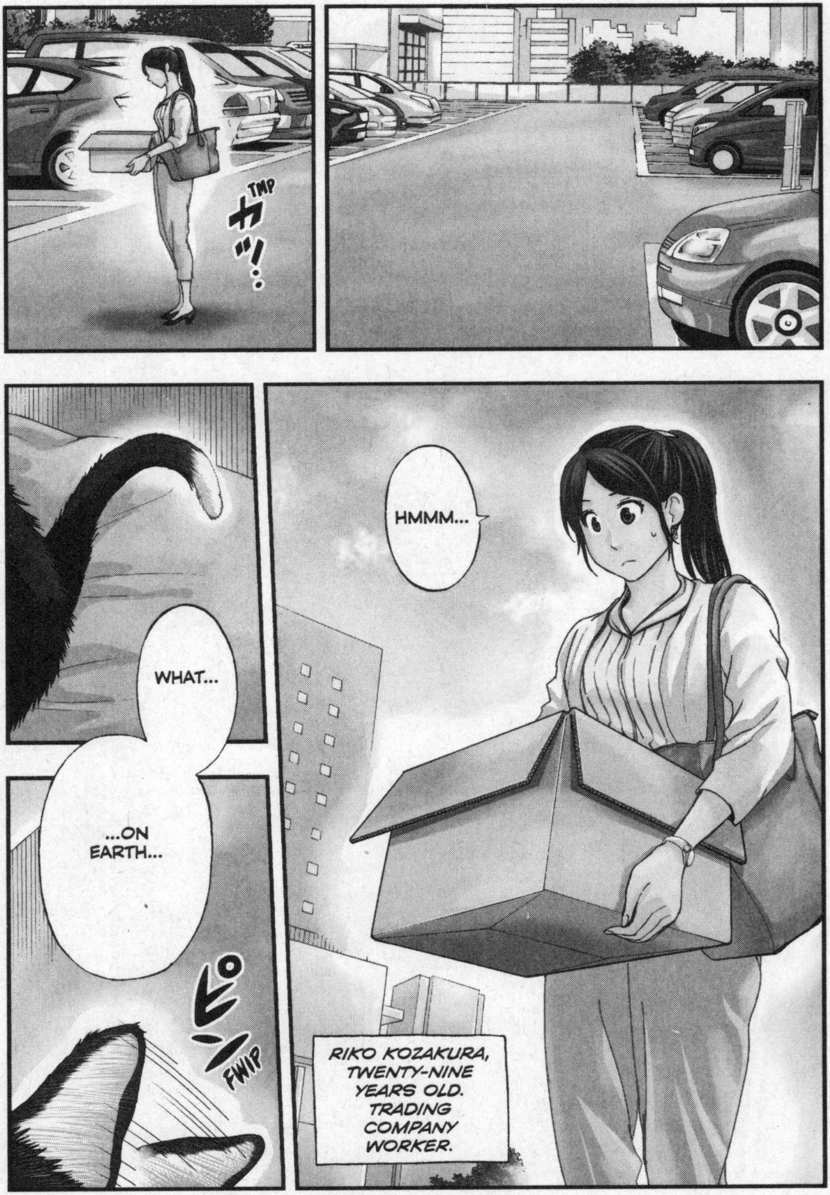
TMP
HMMM...
RIKO KOZAKURA, TWENTY-NINE YEARS OLD. TRADING COMPANY WORKER.
WHAT...
...ON EARTH...
FWIP

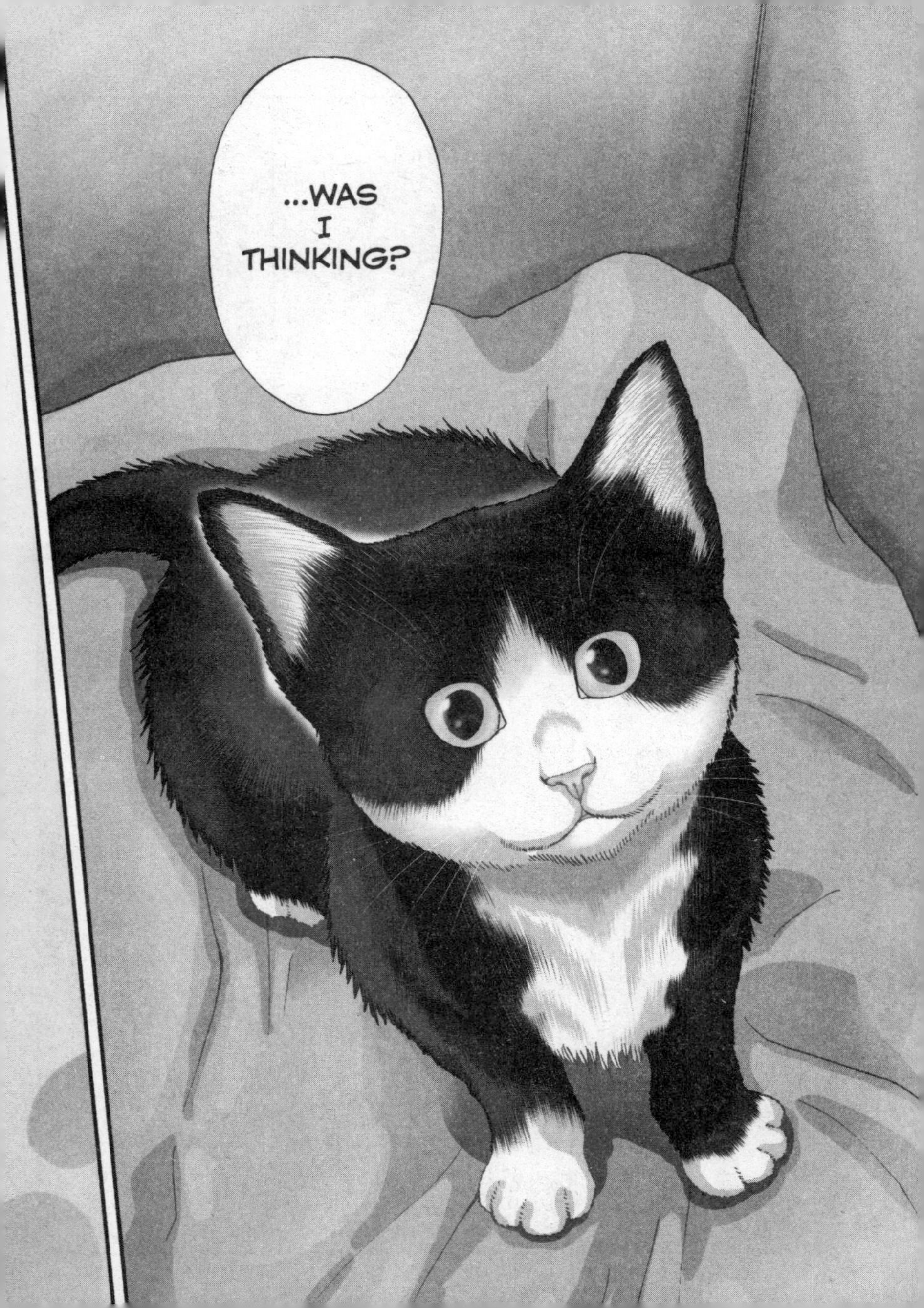
...WAS I THINKING?

Chapter 1: Zero Overtime

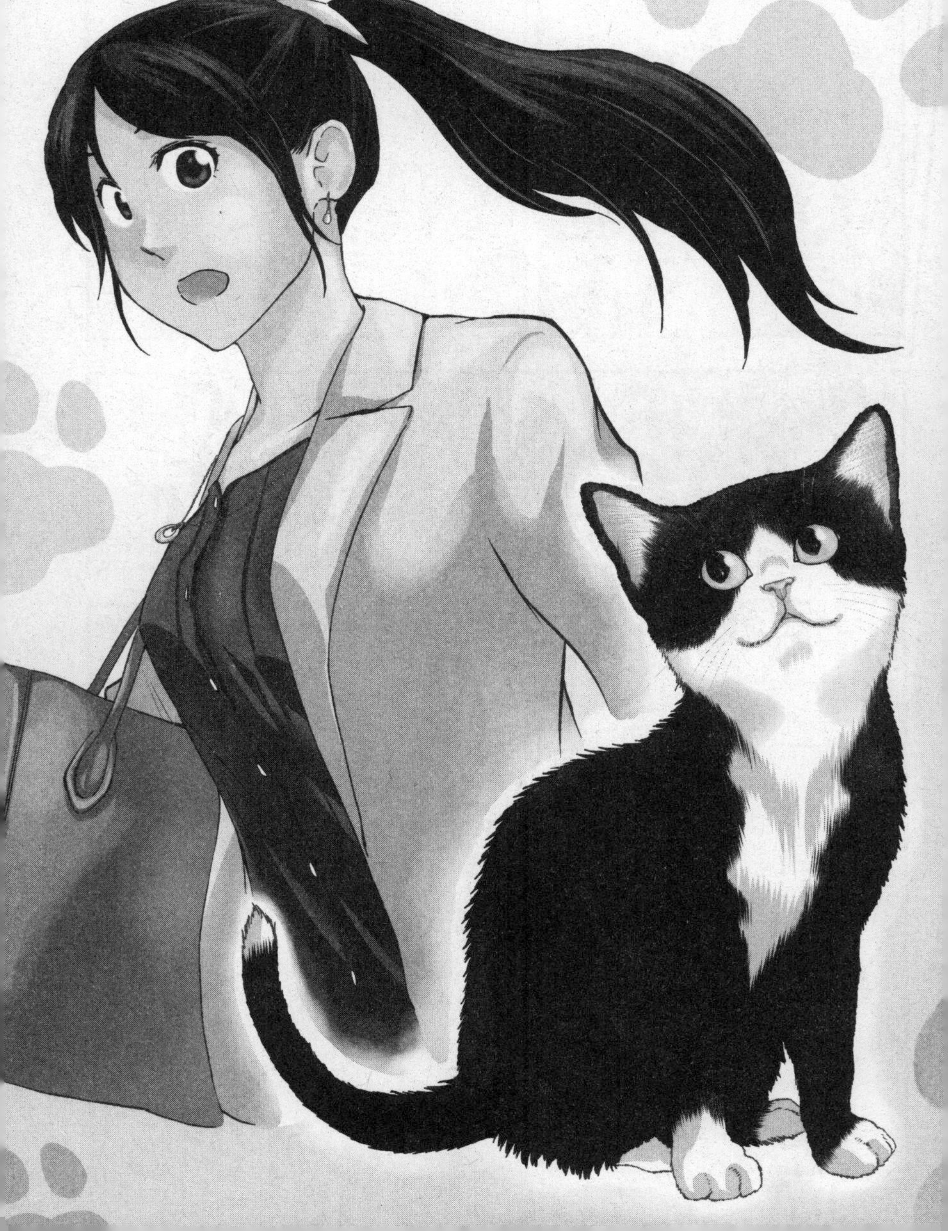

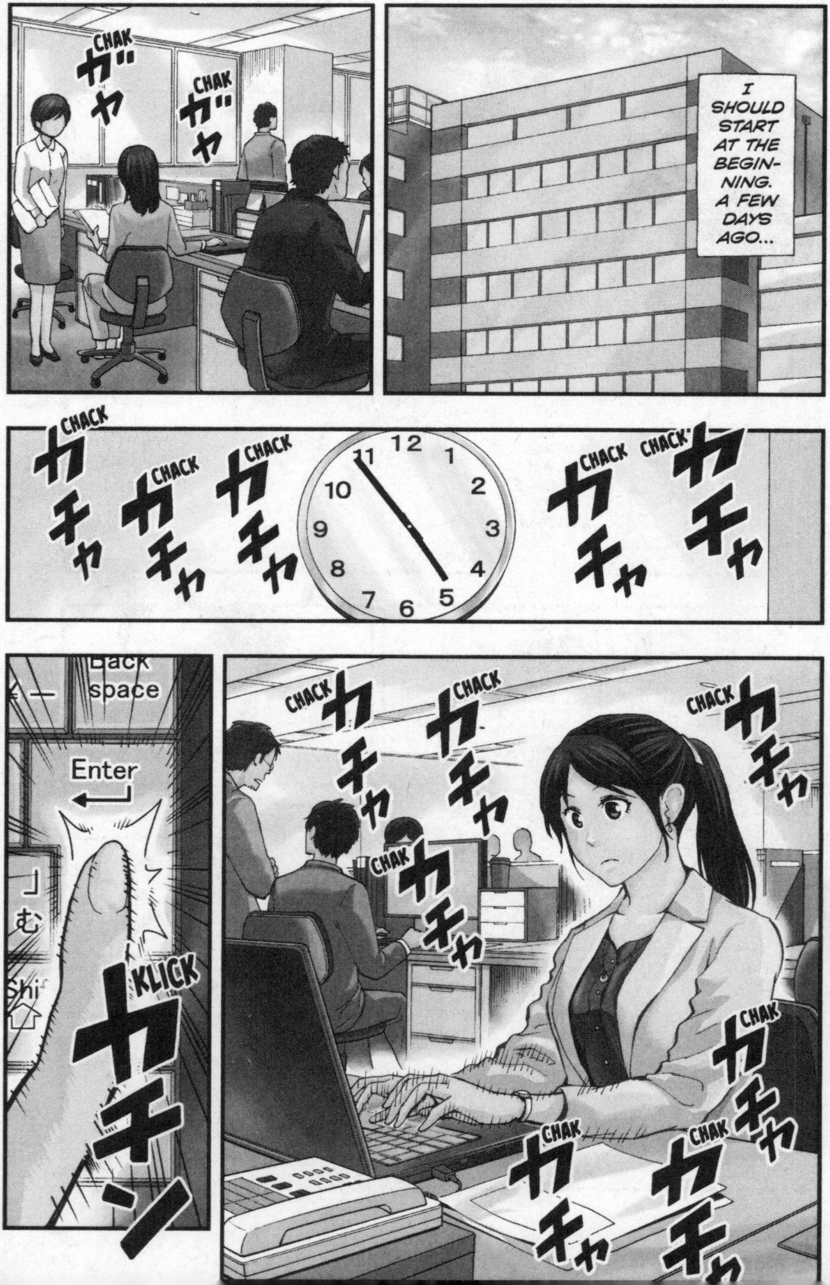

I SHOULD START AT THE BEGINNING. A FEW DAYS AGO...
CHAK ガヤ
CHAK ガヤ
CHACK カチャ
CHACK カチャ
CHACK カチャ
CHACK カチャ
CHACK カチャ
CHACK カチャ
CHACK カチャ
CHAK カチャ
CHACK カチャ
CHAK カチャ
CHAK カチャ
CHAK カチャ
Back space
Enter
KLICK カチーン

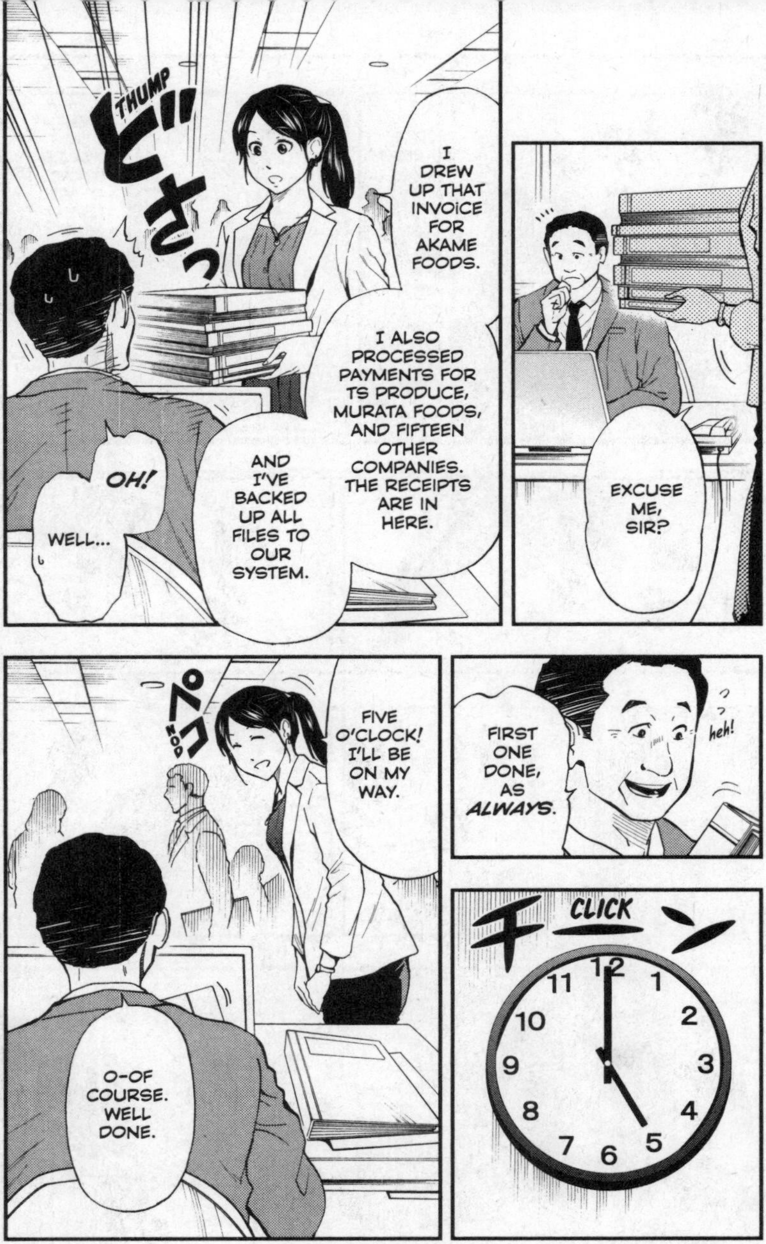
EXCUSE ME, SIR?
I DREW UP THAT INVOICE FOR AKAME FOODS.
どさっ
THUMP
I ALSO PROCESSED PAYMENTS FOR TS PRODUCE, MURATA FOODS, AND FIFTEEN OTHER COMPANIES. THE RECEIPTS ARE IN HERE.
AND I'VE BACKED UP ALL FILES TO OUR SYSTEM.
OH!
WELL...
heh!
FIRST ONE DONE, AS ALWAYS.
チーン
CLICK
FIVE O'CLOCK! I'LL BE ON MY WAY.
ぺこっ
NOD
O-OF COURSE. WELL DONE.

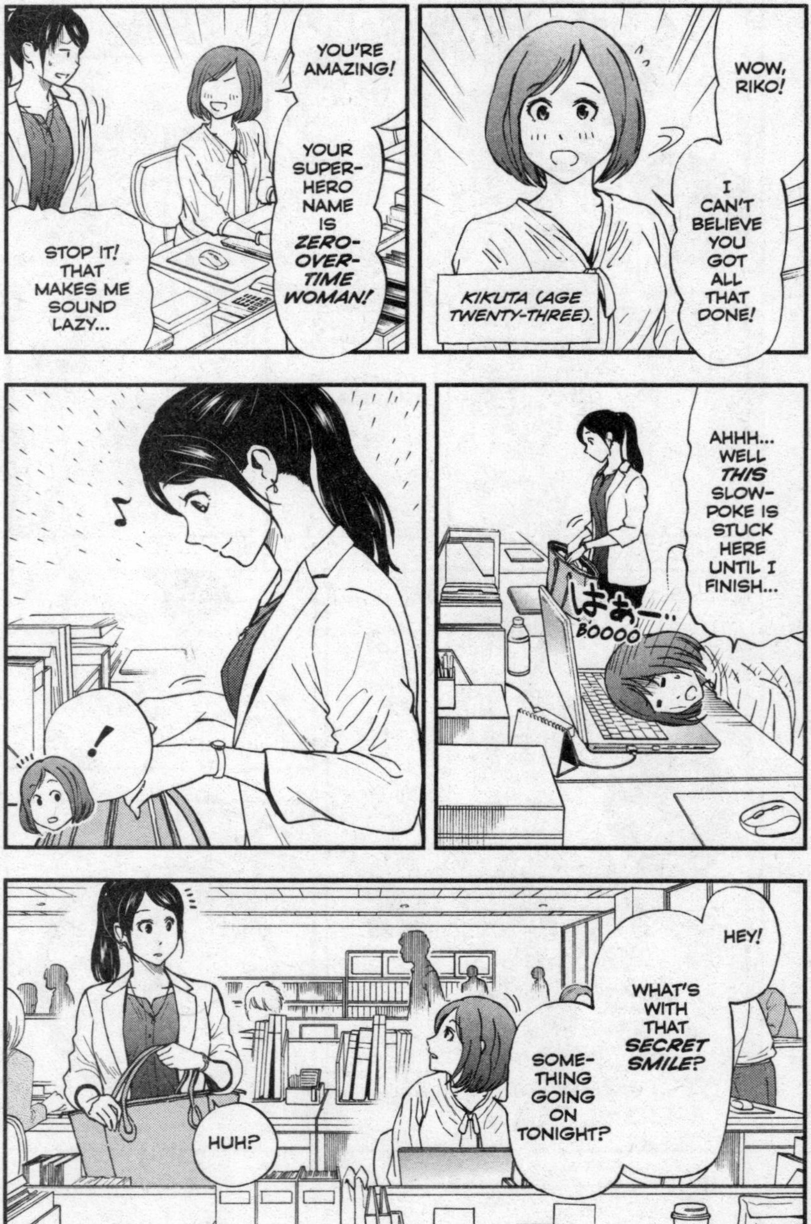
WOW, RIKO!
I CAN'T BELIEVE YOU GOT ALL THAT DONE!
KIKUTA (AGE TWENTY-THREE).
YOU'RE AMAZING!
YOUR SUPER-HERO NAME IS ZERO-OVER-TIME WOMAN!
STOP IT! THAT MAKES ME SOUND LAZY...
AHHH... WELL THIS SLOW-POKE IS STUCK HERE UNTIL I FINISH...
はぁー…
BOOOO
!
HEY!
WHAT'S WITH THAT SECRET SMILE?
SOME-THING GOING ON TONIGHT?
HUH?

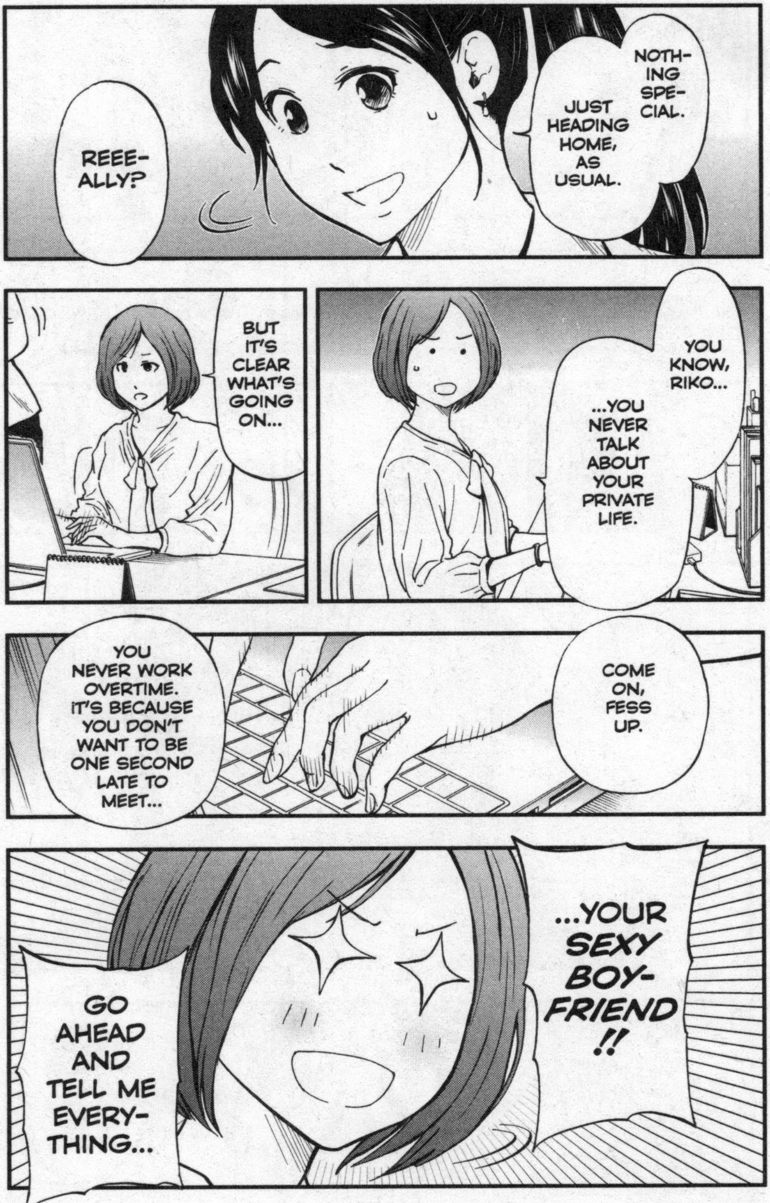
NOTHING SPECIAL.
JUST HEADING HOME, AS USUAL.
REEEALLY?
YOU KNOW, RIKO...
...YOU NEVER TALK ABOUT YOUR PRIVATE LIFE.
BUT IT'S CLEAR WHAT'S GOING ON...
COME ON, FESS UP.
YOU NEVER WORK OVERTIME. IT'S BECAUSE YOU DON'T WANT TO BE ONE SECOND LATE TO MEET...
...YOUR SEXY BOYFRIEND!!
GO AHEAD AND TELL ME EVERYTHING...

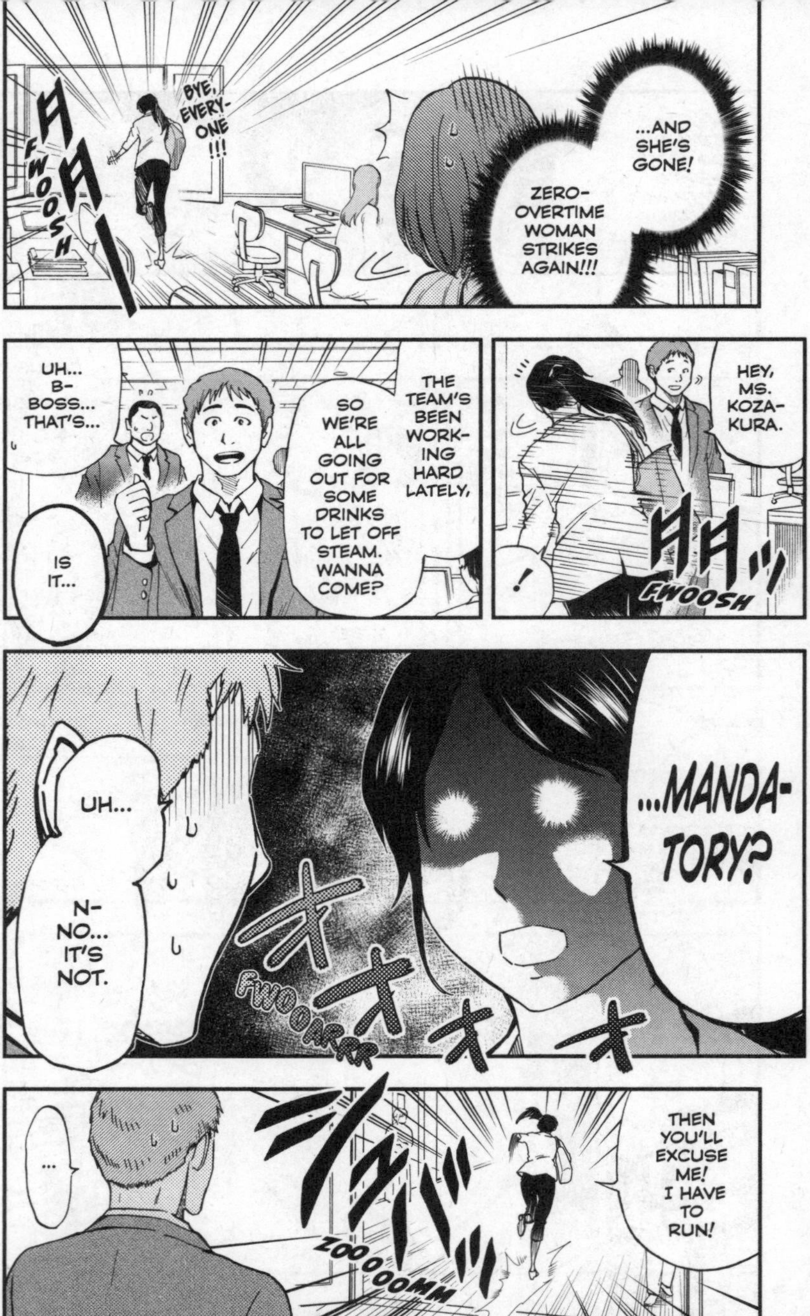
...AND SHE'S GONE!
ZERO-OVERTIME WOMAN STRIKES AGAIN!!!
BYE, EVERY-ONE!!!
FWOOSH
HEY, MS. KOZA-KURA.
!
FWOOSH
THE TEAM'S BEEN WORK-ING HARD LATELY,
SO WE'RE ALL GOING OUT FOR SOME DRINKS TO LET OFF STEAM. WANNA COME?
UH... B-BOSS... THAT'S...
IS IT...
...MANDA-TORY?
UH...
N-NO... IT'S NOT.
FWOOARRR
THEN YOU'LL EXCUSE ME! I HAVE TO RUN!
ZOOOOOMM
...

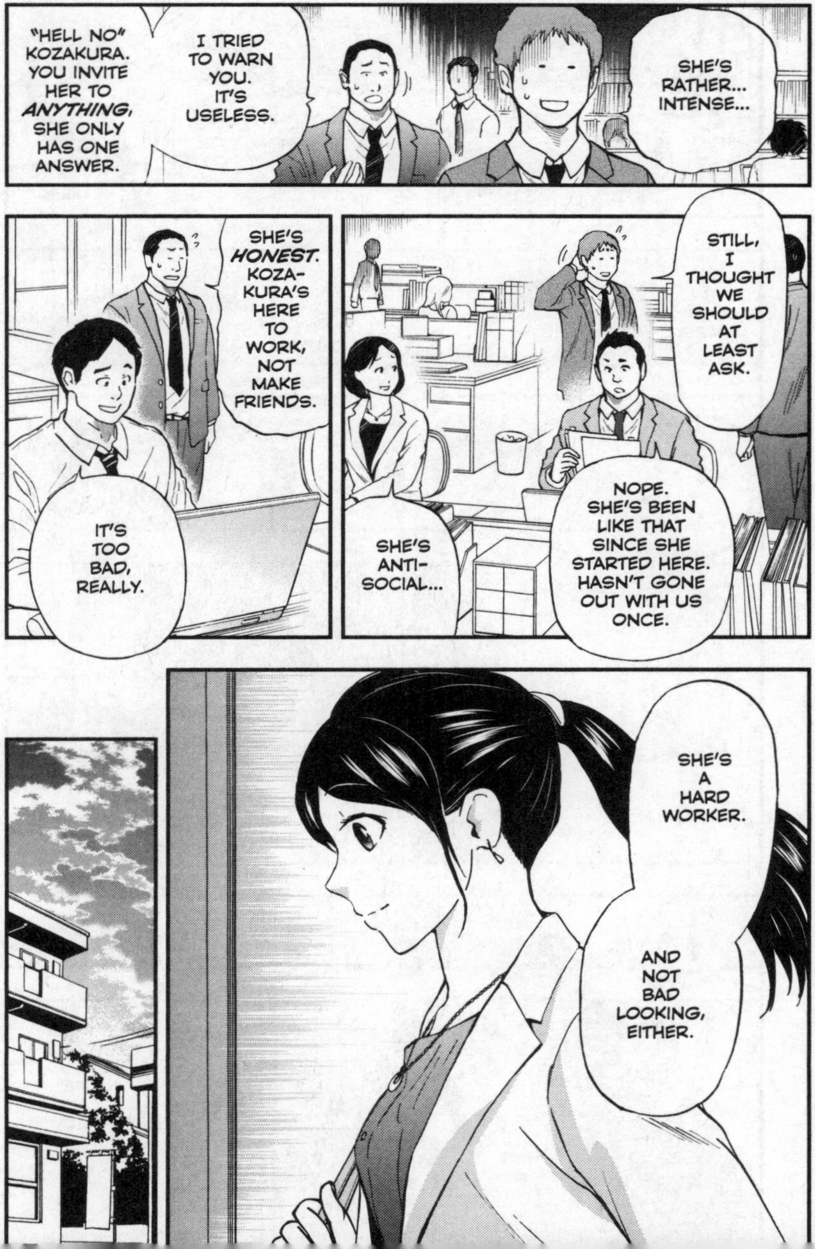
SHE'S RATHER... INTENSE...
I TRIED TO WARN YOU. IT'S USELESS.
"HELL NO" KOZAKURA. YOU INVITE HER TO *ANYTHING*, SHE ONLY HAS ONE ANSWER.
STILL, I THOUGHT WE SHOULD AT LEAST ASK.
NOPE. SHE'S BEEN LIKE THAT SINCE SHE STARTED HERE. HASN'T GONE OUT WITH US ONCE.
SHE'S ANTI-SOCIAL...
SHE'S *HONEST*. KOZA-KURA'S HERE TO WORK, NOT MAKE FRIENDS.
IT'S TOO BAD, REALLY.
SHE'S A HARD WORKER.
AND NOT BAD LOOKING, EITHER.

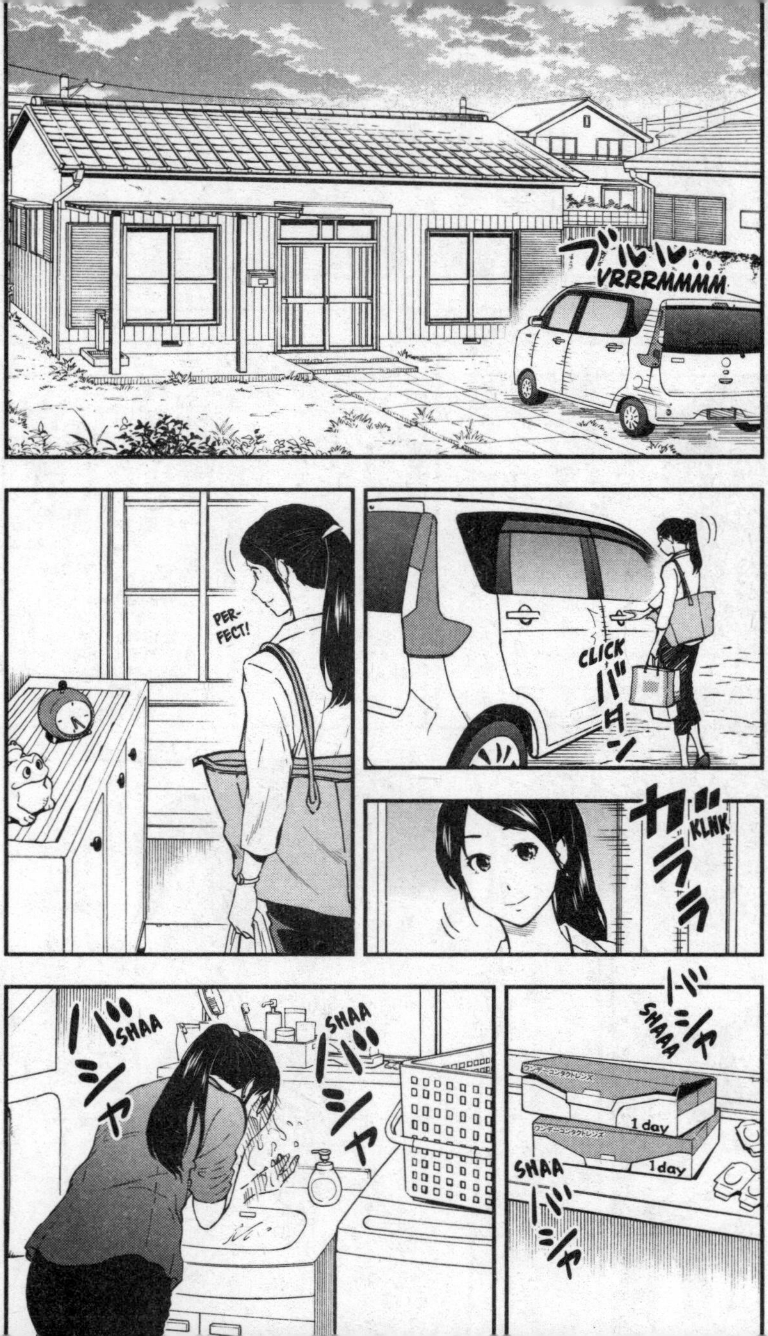

ブルル..
VRRRMMMM
CLICK
バタン
ガララ
KLNK
PER-FECT!
バシャ
SHAAA
ワンデーコンタクトレンズ
1 day
ワンデーコンタクトレンズ
1 day
SHAA
バシャ
SHAA
バシャ
SHAA
バシャ

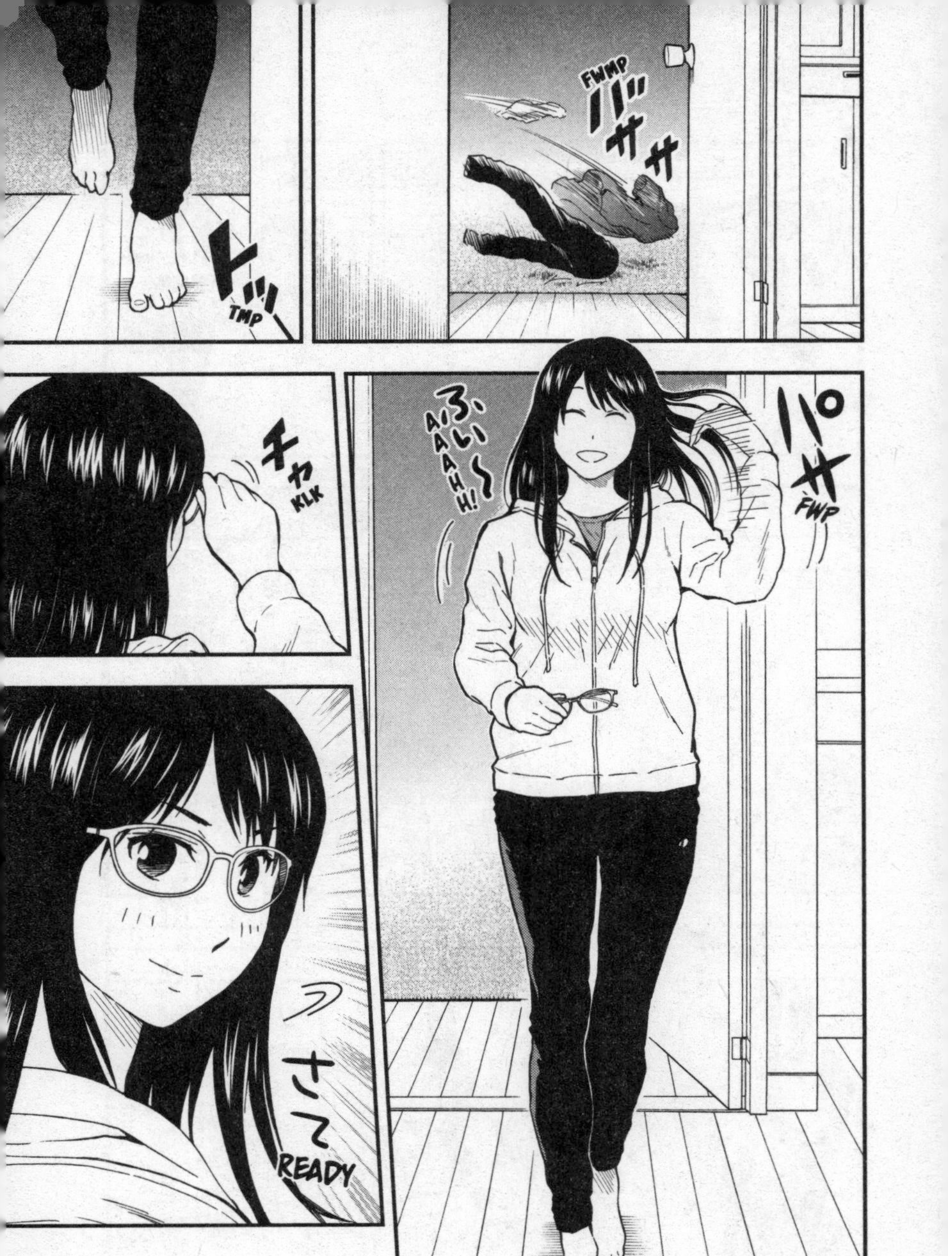

バサッ
FWMP
トッ
TMP
パサ
FWP
ふぃ～
AAAAHH!
チャ
KLK
さて
READY

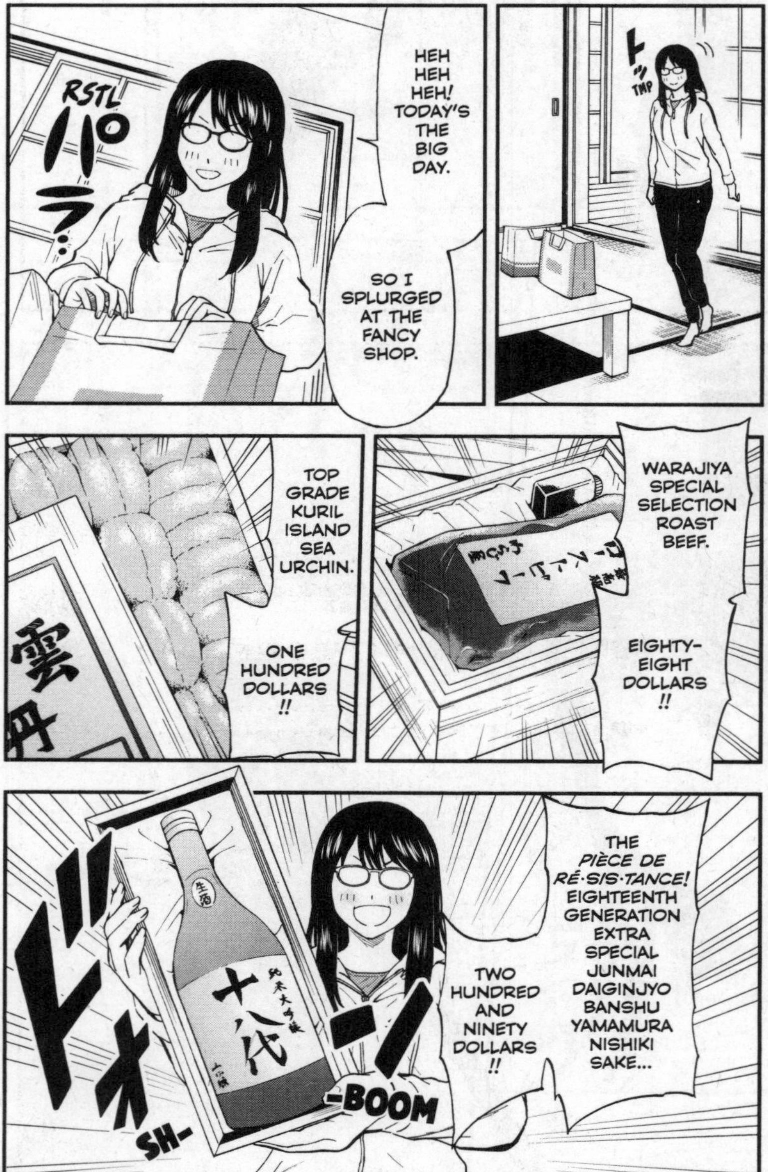

TMP
RSTL
HEH HEH HEH! TODAY'S THE BIG DAY.
SO I SPLURGED AT THE FANCY SHOP.
WARAJIYA SPECIAL SELECTION ROAST BEEF.
EIGHTY-EIGHT DOLLARS !!
TOP GRADE KURIL ISLAND SEA URCHIN.
ONE HUNDRED DOLLARS !!
THE *PIÈCE DE RÉ·SIS·TANCE!* EIGHTEENTH GENERATION EXTRA SPECIAL JUNMAI DAIGINJYO BANSHU YAMAMURA NISHIKI SAKE...
TWO HUNDRED AND NINETY DOLLARS !!
SH- -BOOM

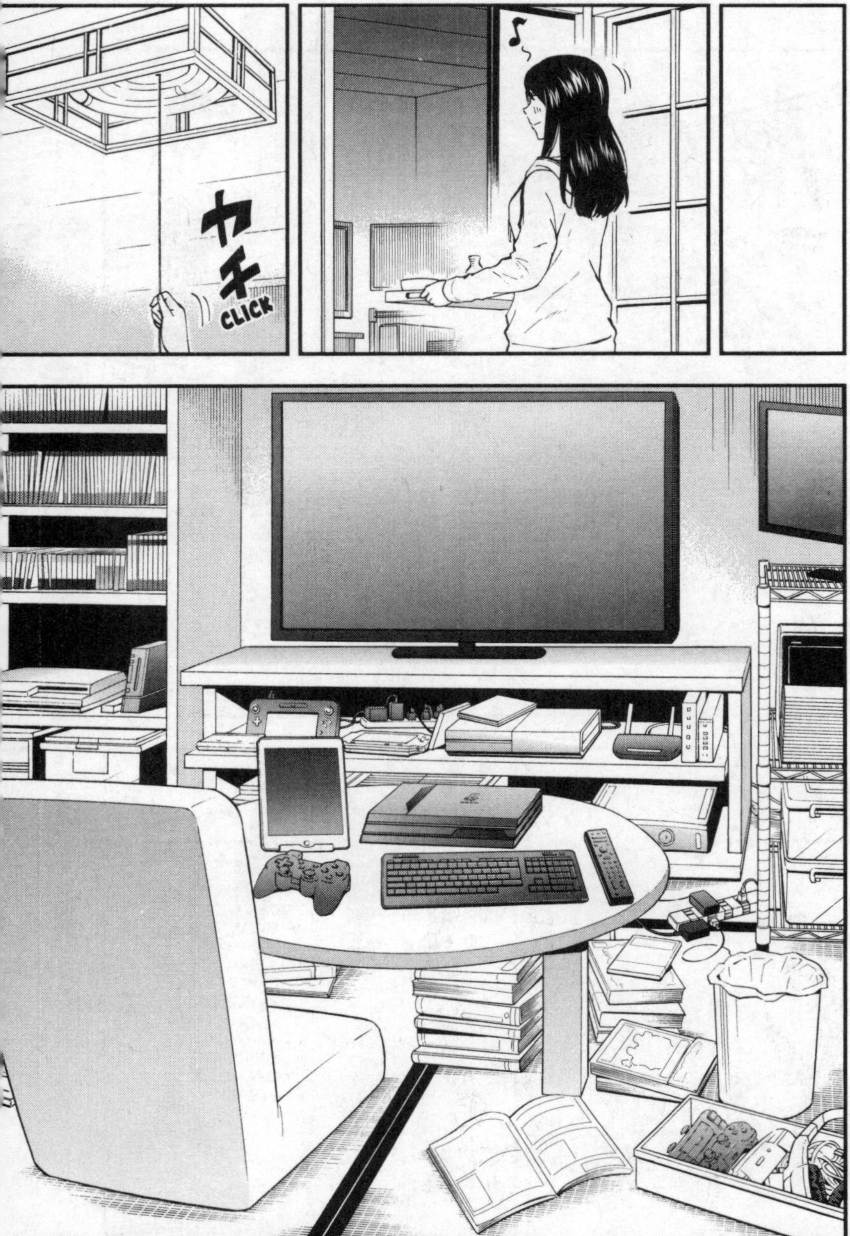

♪
カチ
CLICK

BAMM

BWAM

BOOM

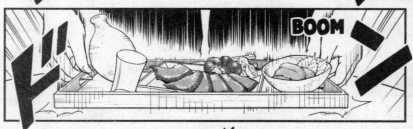

SKNCH

GAME...

...ON!

PIIP

Neo Dragoon

NEW GAME
CONTINUE
OPTIONS

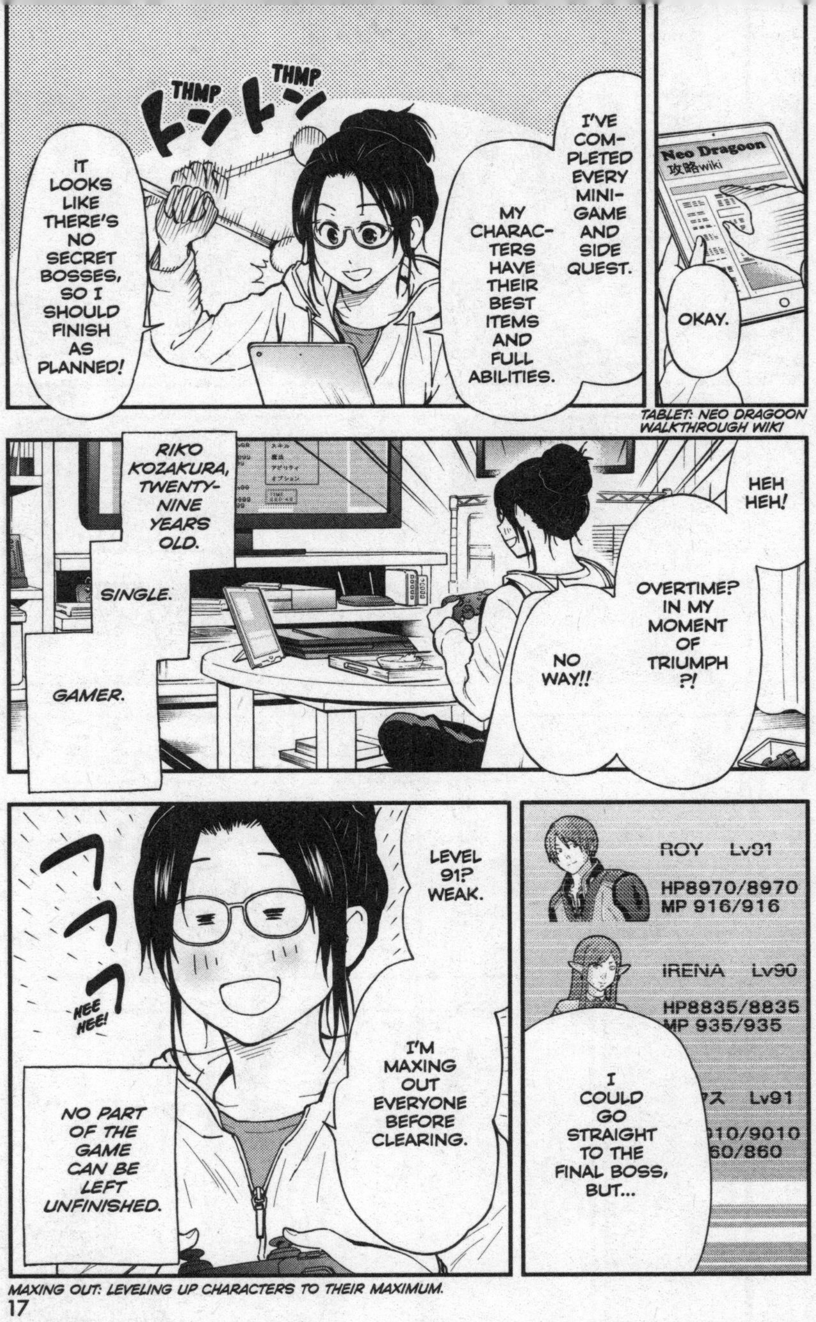
Neo Dragoon
攻略wiki
OKAY.
TABLET: NEO DRAGOON WALKTHROUGH WIKI
I'VE COMPLETED EVERY MINI-GAME AND SIDE QUEST.
MY CHARACTERS HAVE THEIR BEST ITEMS AND FULL ABILITIES.
THMP THMP
トントン
IT LOOKS LIKE THERE'S NO SECRET BOSSES, SO I SHOULD FINISH AS PLANNED!
HEH HEH!
OVERTIME? IN MY MOMENT OF TRIUMPH?!
NO WAY!!
RIKO KOZAKURA, TWENTY-NINE YEARS OLD.
SINGLE.
GAMER.
ROY Lv91
HP8970/8970
MP 916/916
IRENA Lv90
HP8835/8835
MP 935/935
I COULD GO STRAIGHT TO THE FINAL BOSS, BUT...
LEVEL 91? WEAK.
I'M MAXING OUT EVERYONE BEFORE CLEARING.
HEE HEE!
NO PART OF THE GAME CAN BE LEFT UNFINISHED.

MAXING OUT: LEVELING UP CHARACTERS TO THEIR MAXIMUM.

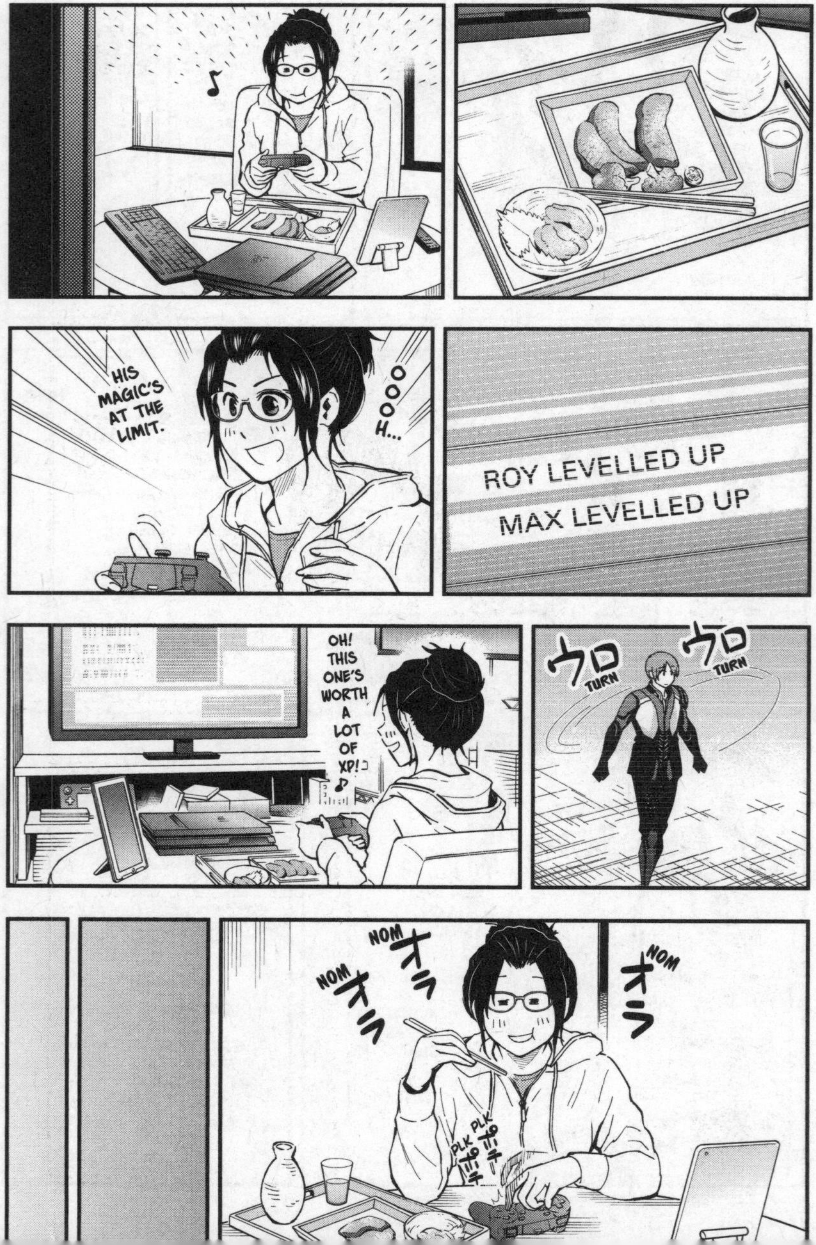
♪
ROY LEVELLED UP
MAX LEVELLED UP
OOOH...
HIS MAGIC'S AT THE LIMIT.
ウロ TURN
ウロ TURN
OH! THIS ONE'S WORTH A LOT OF XP! ♪
オラ NOM
オラ NOM
オラ NOM
ポチ PLK
ポチ PLK

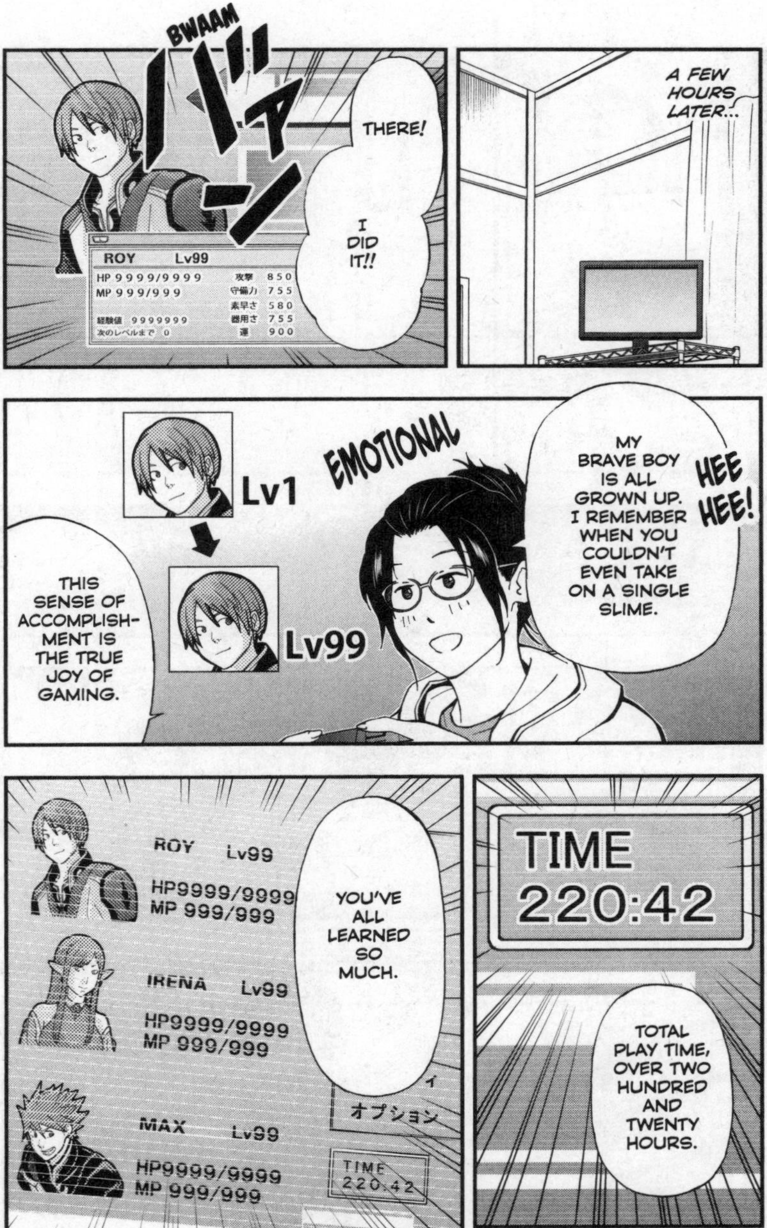
A FEW HOURS LATER...
BWAAM
THERE!
I DID IT!!
ROY Lv99
HP 9999/9999
MP 999/999
経験値 9999999
次のレベルまで 0
攻撃 850
守備力 755
素早さ 580
器用さ 755
運 900
MY BRAVE BOY IS ALL GROWN UP. I REMEMBER WHEN YOU COULDN'T EVEN TAKE ON A SINGLE SLIME.
HEE HEE!
EMOTIONAL
Lv1
Lv99
THIS SENSE OF ACCOMPLISHMENT IS THE TRUE JOY OF GAMING.
TIME 220:42
TOTAL PLAY TIME, OVER TWO HUNDRED AND TWENTY HOURS.
YOU'VE ALL LEARNED SO MUCH.
ROY Lv99
HP9999/9999
MP 999/999
IRENA Lv99
HP9999/9999
MP 999/999
MAX Lv99
HP9999/9999
MP 999/999
オプション
TIME 220.42

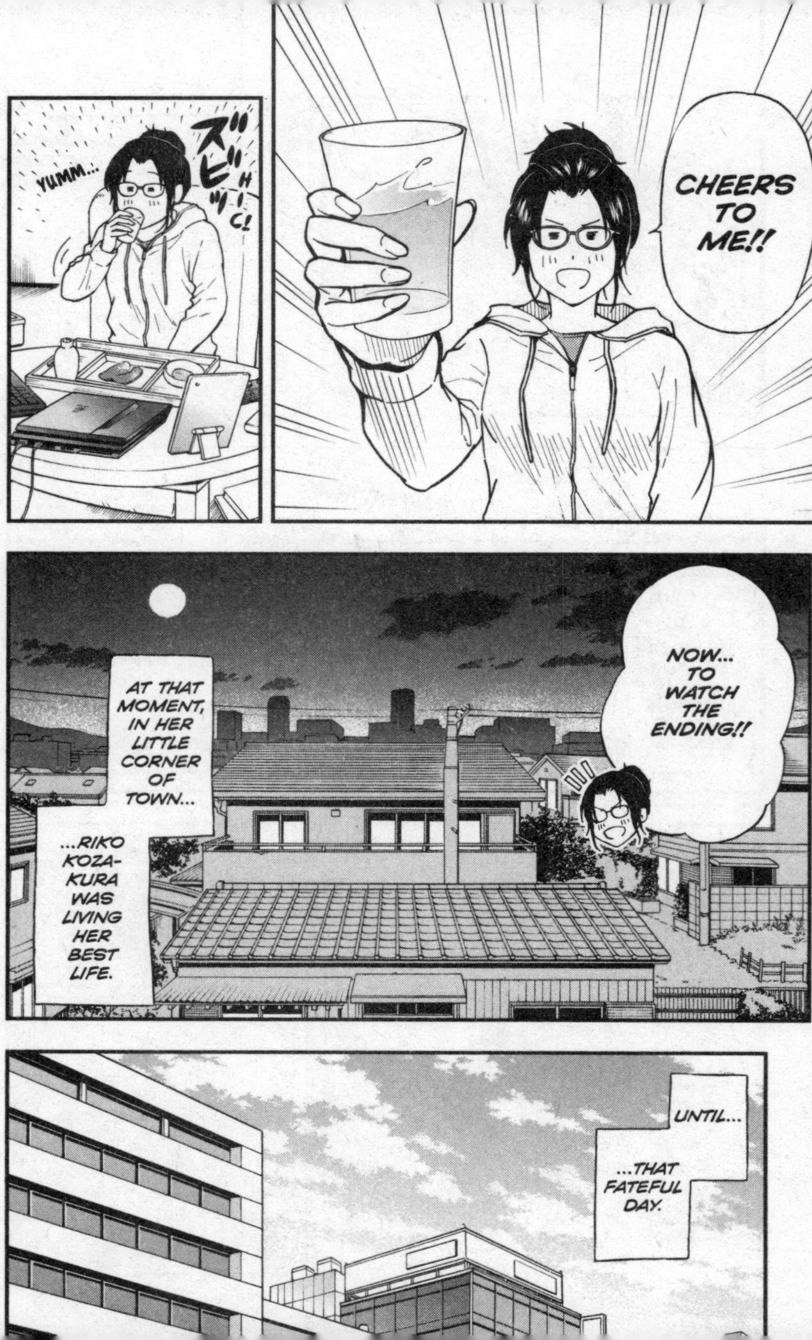
CHEERS TO ME!!
ズビッ
HIC!
YUMM...
NOW... TO WATCH THE ENDING!!
AT THAT MOMENT, IN HER LITTLE CORNER OF TOWN...
...RIKO KOZA-KURA WAS LIVING HER BEST LIFE.
UNTIL...
...THAT FATEFUL DAY.

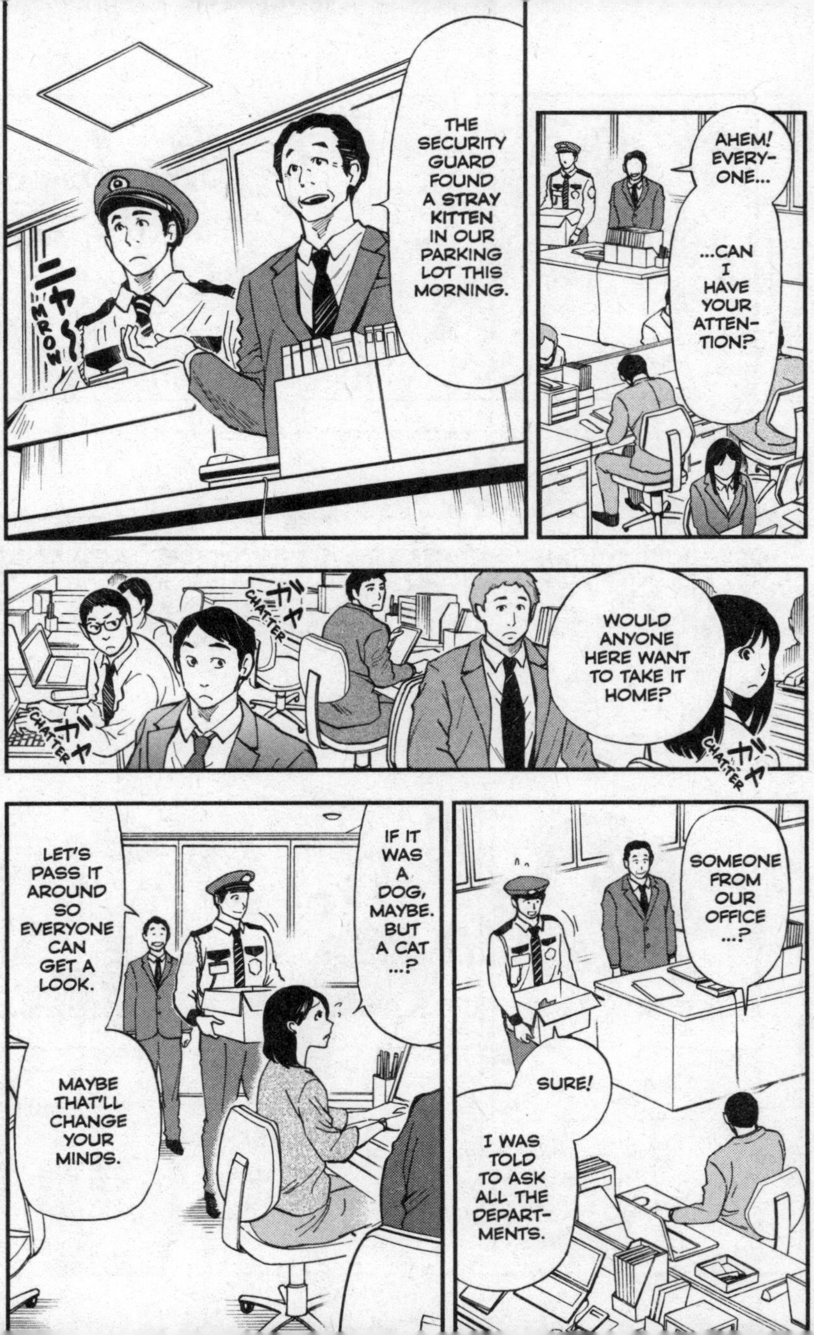
AHEM! EVERYONE...
...CAN I HAVE YOUR ATTENTION?
THE SECURITY GUARD FOUND A STRAY KITTEN IN OUR PARKING LOT THIS MORNING.
ニャ~ MROW
WOULD ANYONE HERE WANT TO TAKE IT HOME?
ガヤ CHATTER
ガヤ CHATTER
ガヤ CHATTER
ガヤ CHATTER
SOMEONE FROM OUR OFFICE ...?
SURE!
I WAS TOLD TO ASK ALL THE DEPARTMENTS.
IF IT WAS A DOG, MAYBE. BUT A CAT ...?
LET'S PASS IT AROUND SO EVERYONE CAN GET A LOOK.
MAYBE THAT'LL CHANGE YOUR MINDS.

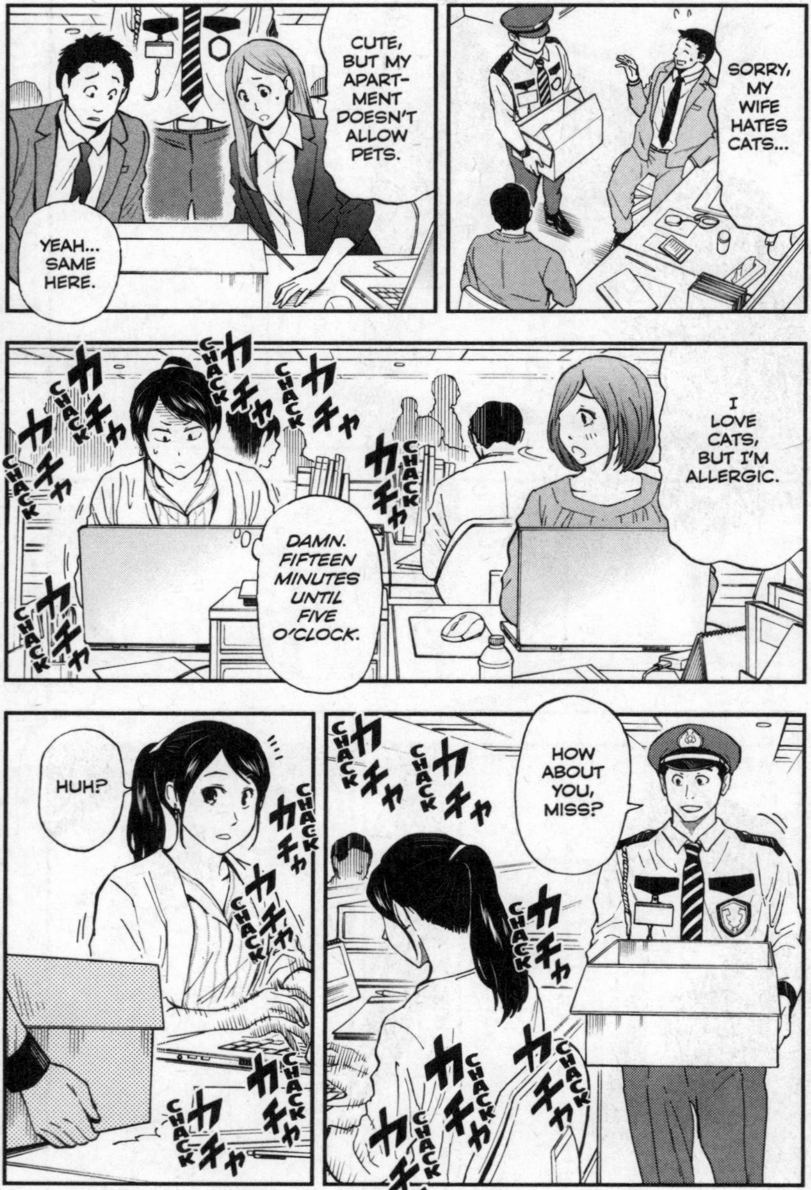
SORRY, MY WIFE HATES CATS...
CUTE, BUT MY APART-MENT DOESN'T ALLOW PETS.
YEAH... SAME HERE.
I LOVE CATS, BUT I'M ALLERGIC.
カチャ CHACK カチャ CHACK カチャ CHACK
DAMN. FIFTEEN MINUTES UNTIL FIVE O'CLOCK.
カチャ CHACK カチャ CHACK
カチャ CHACK カチャ CHACK
HOW ABOUT YOU, MISS?
カチャ CHACK カチャ CHACK カチャ CHACK
HUH?
カチャ CHACK カチャ CHACK カチャ CHACK

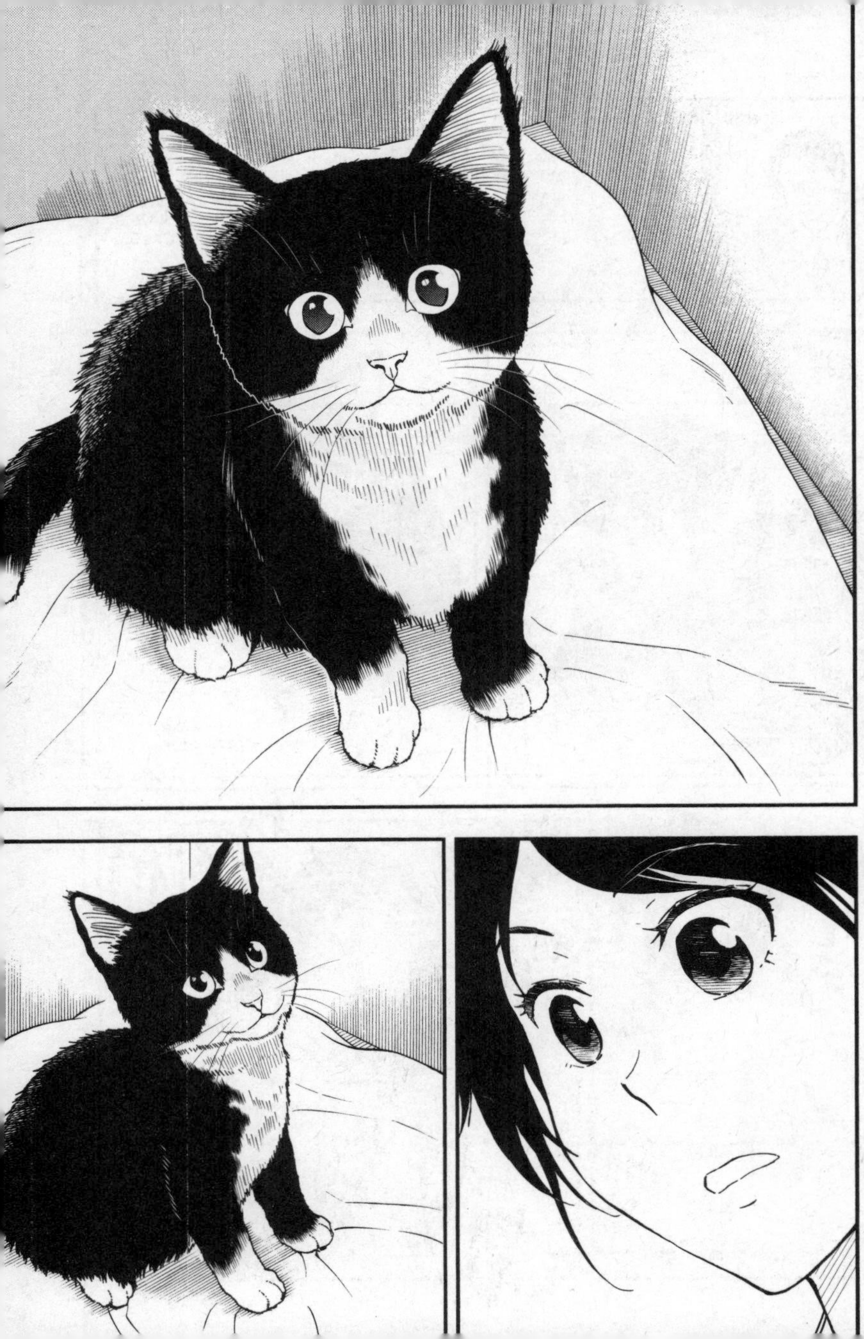

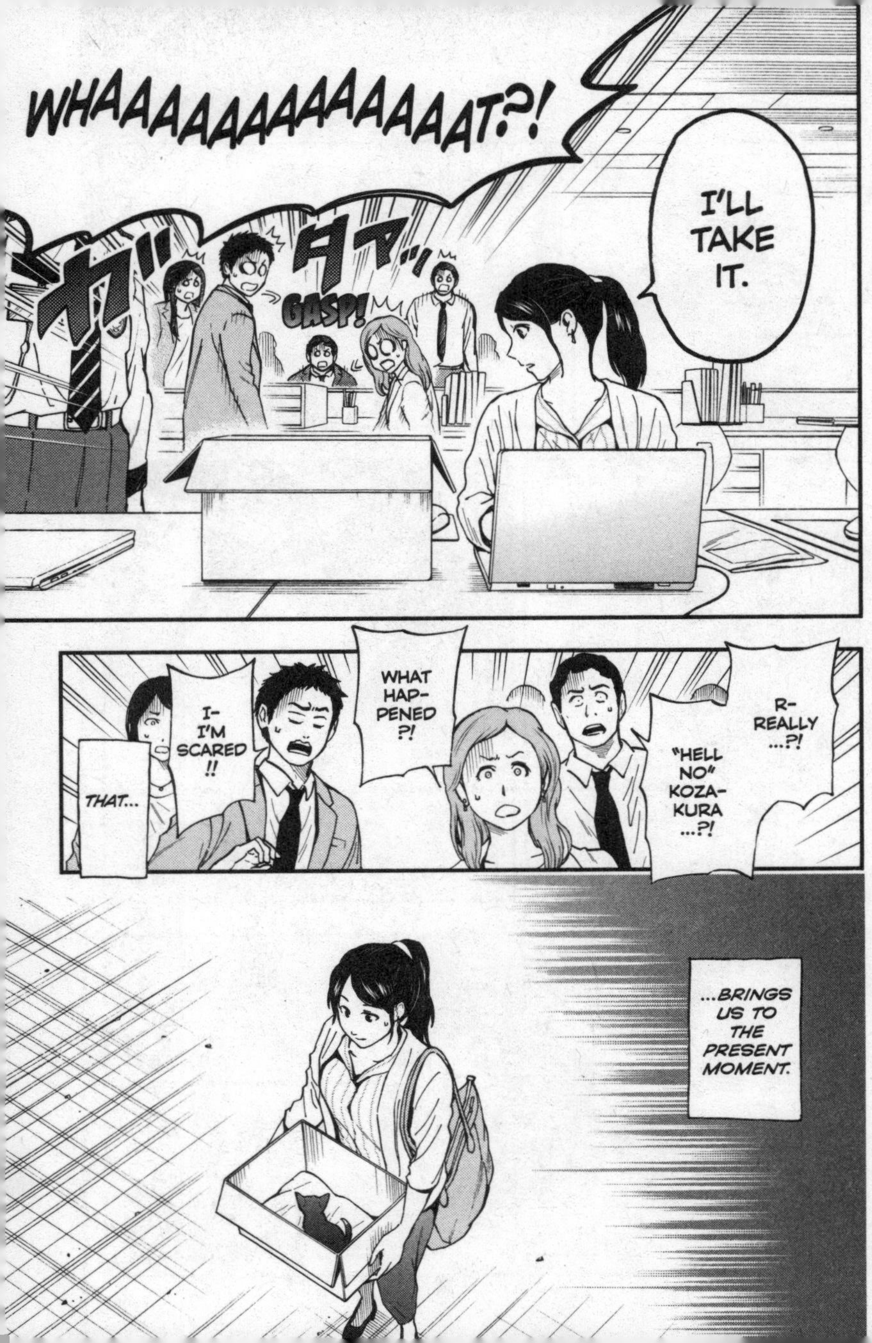
I'LL TAKE IT.
WHAAAAAAAAAAAAT?!
GASP!
R-REALLY ...?!
"HELL NO" KOZAKURA ...?!
WHAT HAPPENED ?!
I-I'M SCARED !!
THAT...
...BRINGS US TO THE PRESENT MOMENT.

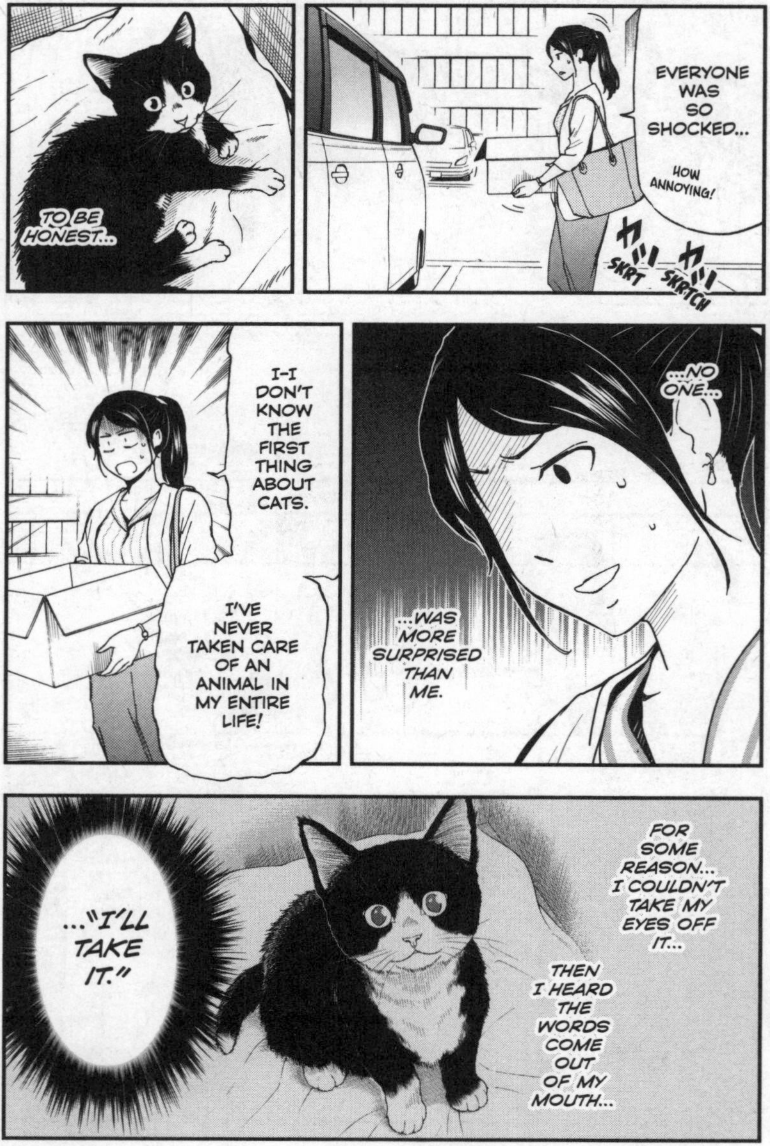
EVERYONE WAS SO SHOCKED...
HOW ANNOYING!
SKRT
SKRTCH
TO BE HONEST...
...NO ONE...
...WAS MORE SURPRISED THAN ME.
I-I DON'T KNOW THE FIRST THING ABOUT CATS.
I'VE NEVER TAKEN CARE OF AN ANIMAL IN MY ENTIRE LIFE!
FOR SOME REASON... I COULDN'T TAKE MY EYES OFF IT...
THEN I HEARD THE WORDS COME OUT OF MY MOUTH...
..."I'LL TAKE IT."

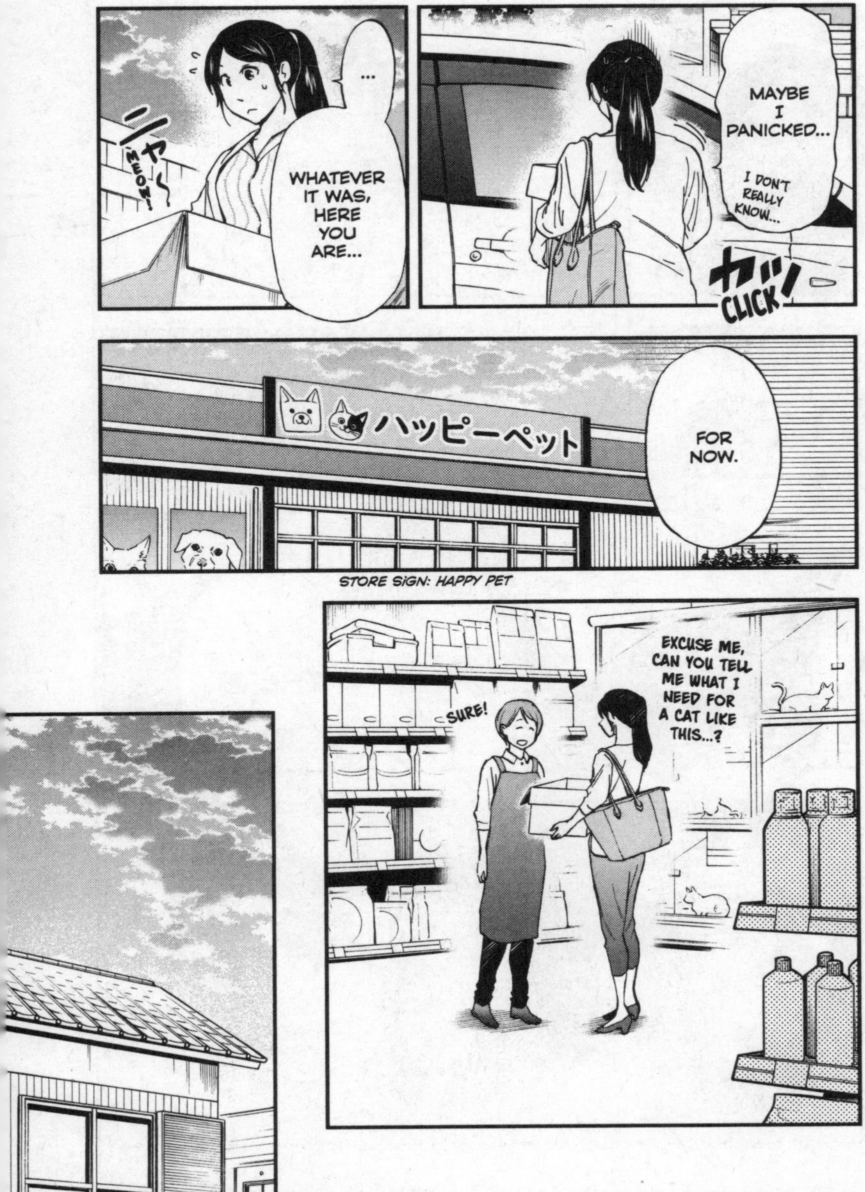
MAYBE I PANICKED...
I DON'T REALLY KNOW...
カッ
CLICK!
...
WHATEVER IT WAS, HERE YOU ARE...
ニャ～
MEOW!
FOR NOW.
ハッピーペット
STORE SIGN: HAPPY PET
EXCUSE ME, CAN YOU TELL ME WHAT I NEED FOR A CAT LIKE THIS...?
SURE!

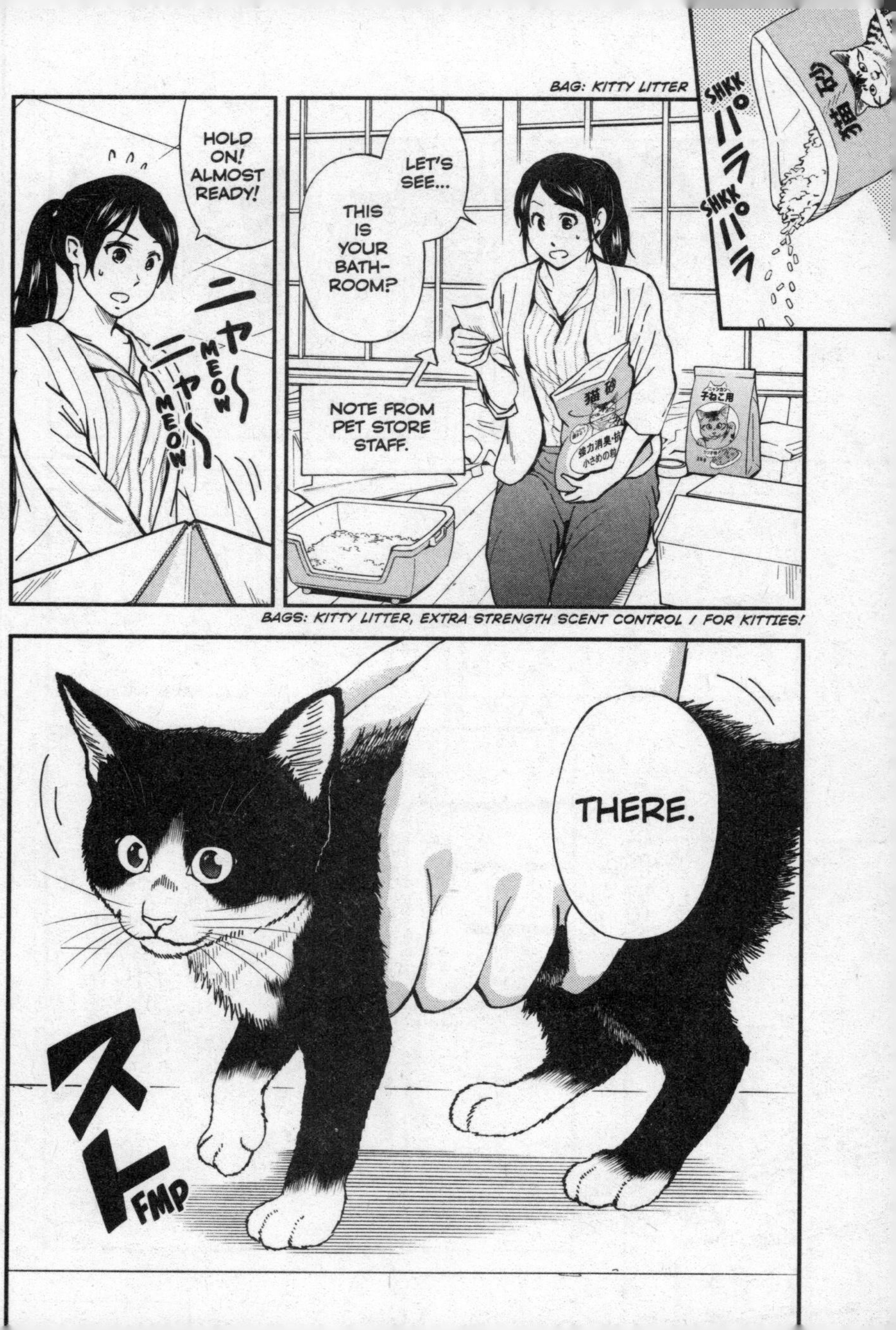
BAG: KITTY LITTER
パラ SHKK
パラ SHKK
猫砂
LET'S SEE...
THIS IS YOUR BATH-ROOM?
NOTE FROM PET STORE STAFF.
猫砂
強力消臭・抗
小さめの粒
子ねこ用
HOLD ON! ALMOST READY!
ニャ〜 MEOW
ニャ〜 MEOW
BAGS: KITTY LITTER, EXTRA STRENGTH SCENT CONTROL / FOR KITTIES!
THERE.
スト FMP

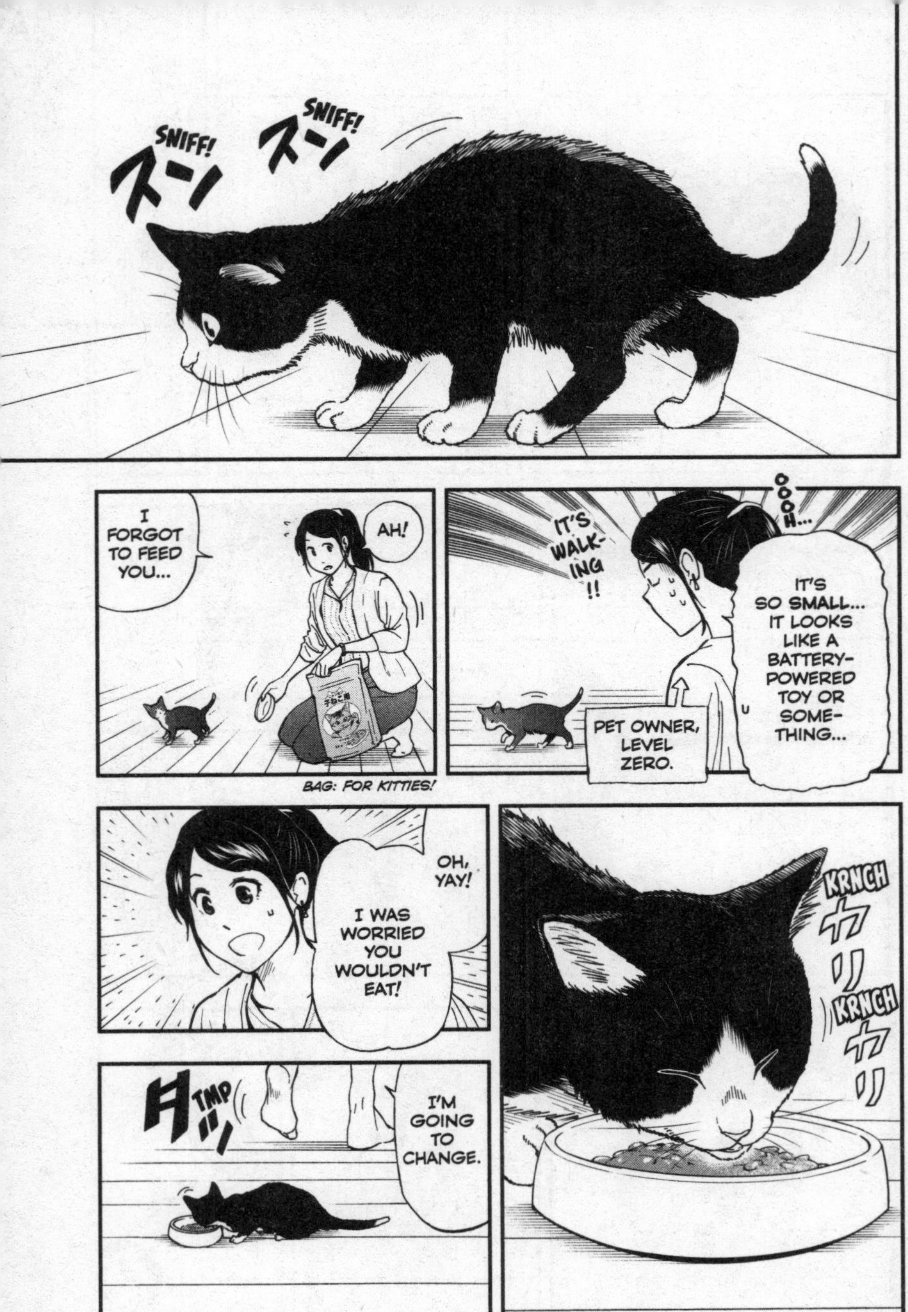
SNIFF!
スーン
SNIFF!
スーン
OOOOH...
IT'S WALKING!!
IT'S SO SMALL... IT LOOKS LIKE A BATTERY-POWERED TOY OR SOMETHING...
PET OWNER, LEVEL ZERO.
AH!
I FORGOT TO FEED YOU...
BAG: FOR KITTIES!
KRNCH
カリ
KRNCH
カリ
OH, YAY!
I WAS WORRIED YOU WOULDN'T EAT!
TMP
I'M GOING TO CHANGE.

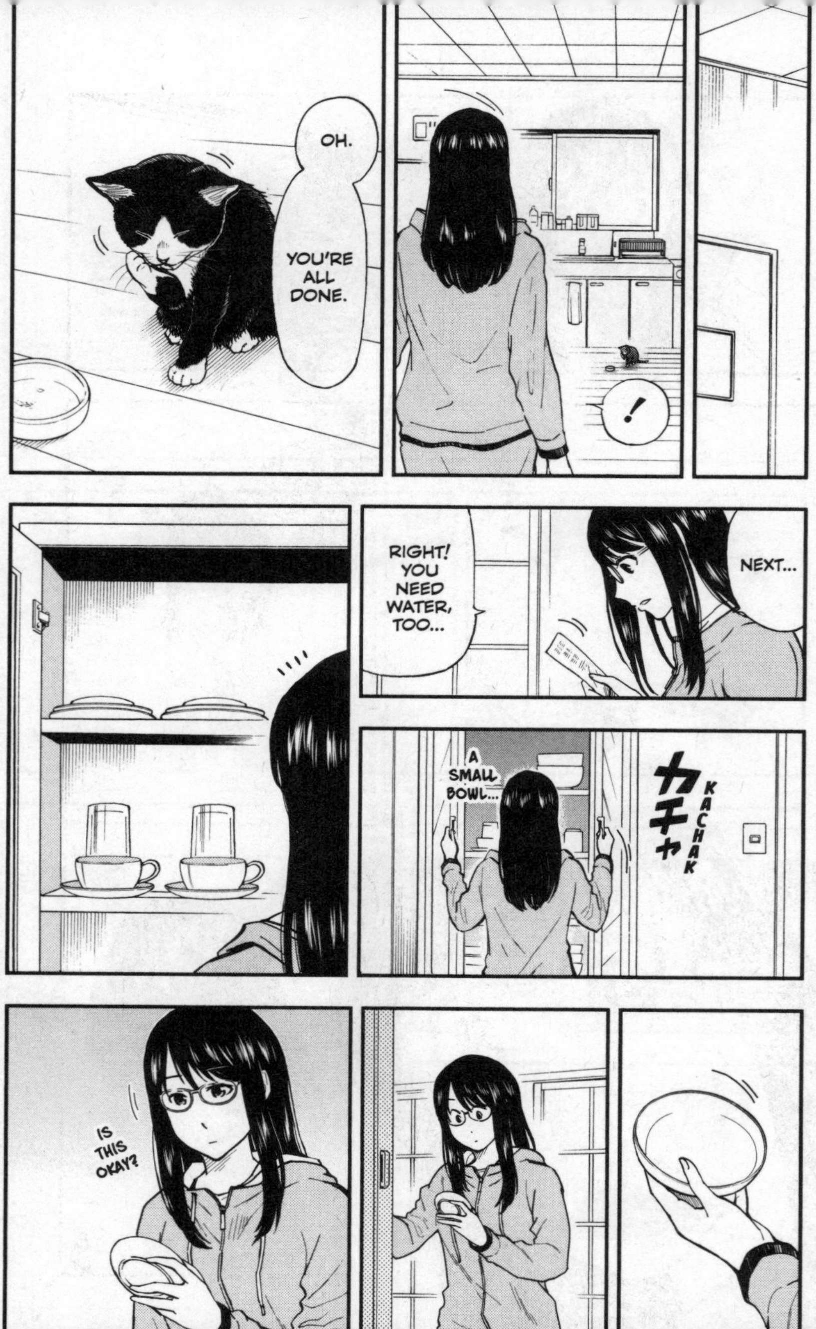
!
OH.
YOU'RE ALL DONE.
NEXT...
RIGHT! YOU NEED WATER, TOO...
カチャ
KACHAK
A SMALL BOWL...
IS THIS OKAY?

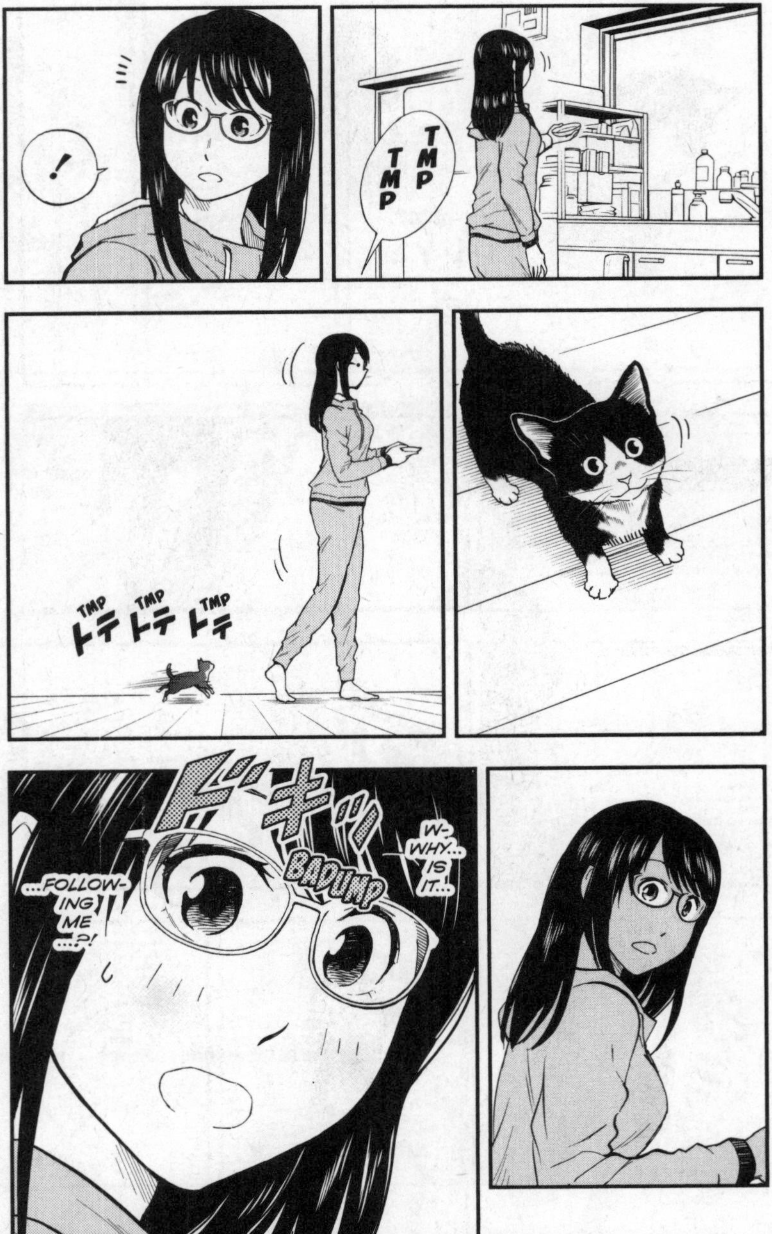
TMP TMP
!
TMP トテ TMP トテ TMP トテ
ドキッ
BADUMP
W-WHY... IS IT...
...FOLLOWING ME ...?!

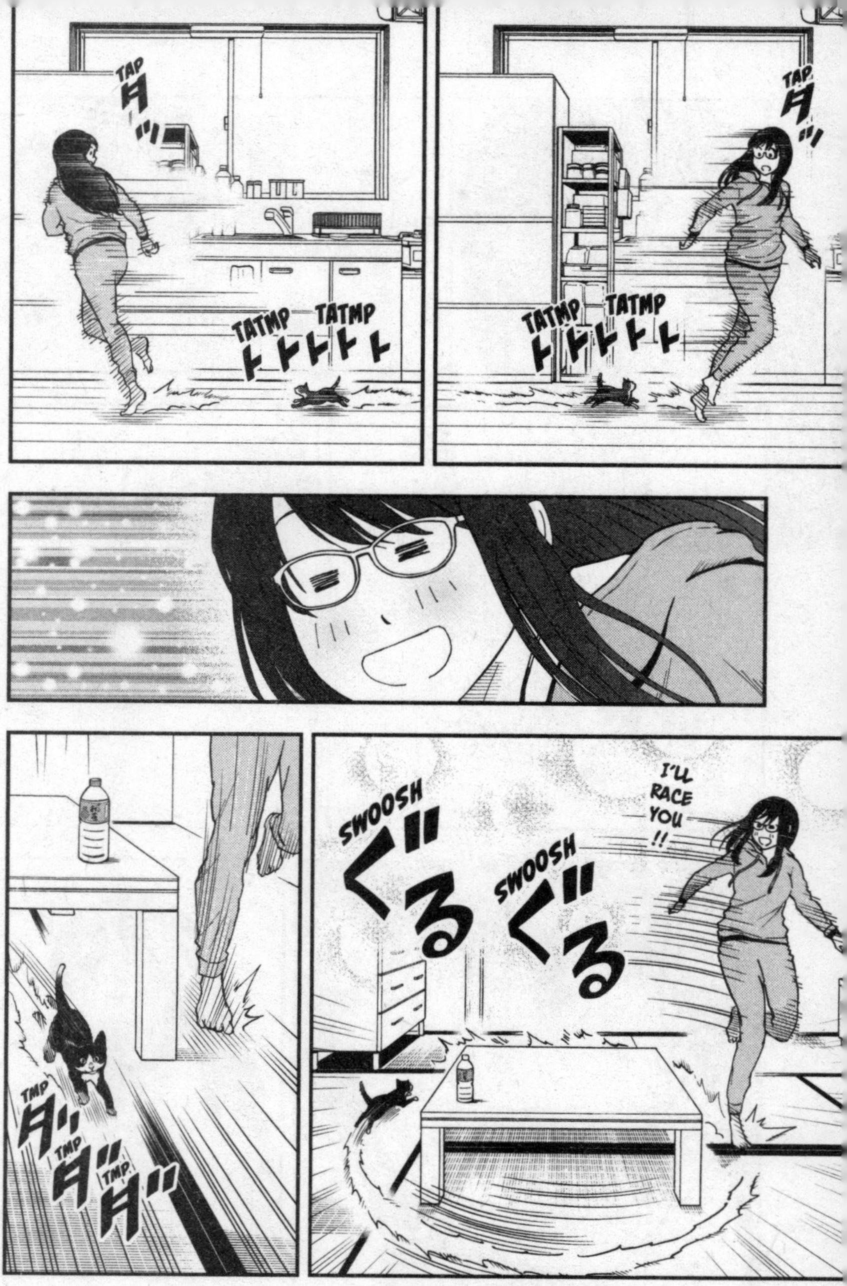
TAP
TATMP TATMP
TAP
TATMP TATMP
I'LL RACE YOU!!
SWOOSH
ぐる
SWOOSH
ぐる
TMP
TMP
TMP

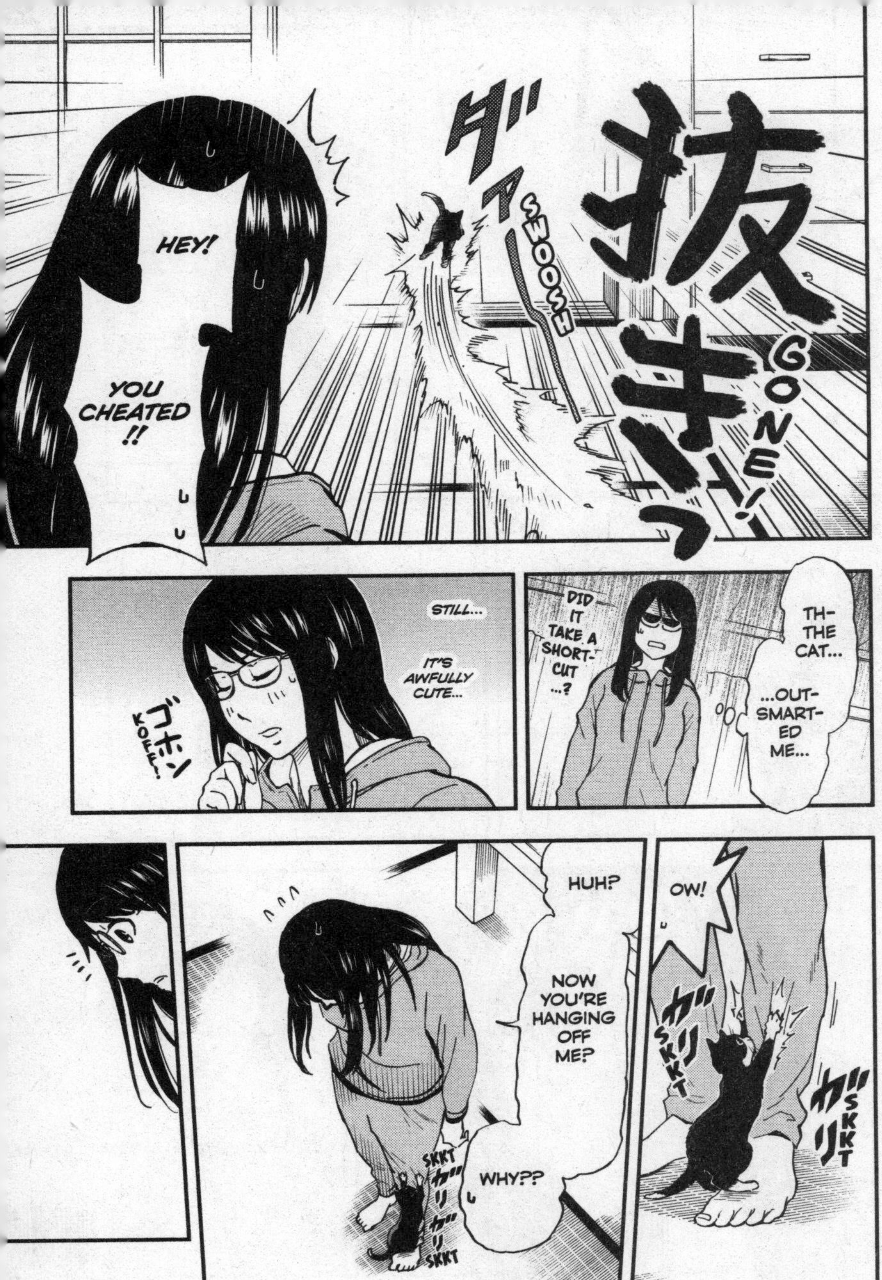
抜きっ
GONE!
ダァ
SWOOSH
HEY!
YOU CHEATED!!
TH- THE CAT...
...OUT-SMARTED ME...
DID IT TAKE A SHORT-CUT ...?
STILL...
IT'S AWFULLY CUTE...
ゴホン
KOFF!
OW!
ガリ
SKKT
ガリ
SKKT
HUH?
NOW YOU'RE HANGING OFF ME?
WHY??
SKKT
ガリガリガリ
SKKT

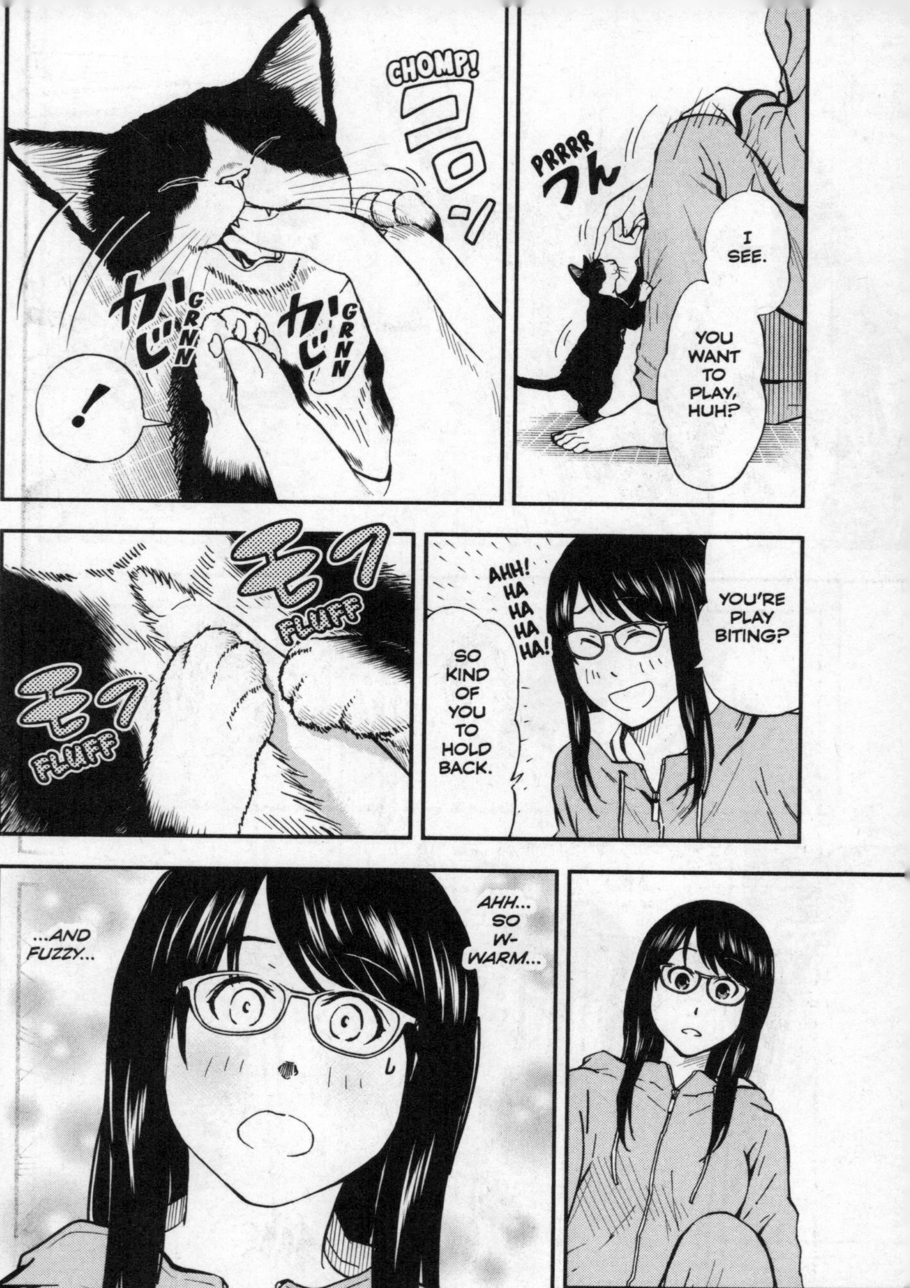
PRRRR
I SEE.
YOU WANT TO PLAY, HUH?
CHOMP!
GRNN
GRNN
!
YOU'RE PLAY BITING?
AHH! HA HA HA HA!
SO KIND OF YOU TO HOLD BACK.
FLUFF
FLUFF
AHH... SO W-WARM...
...AND FUZZY...

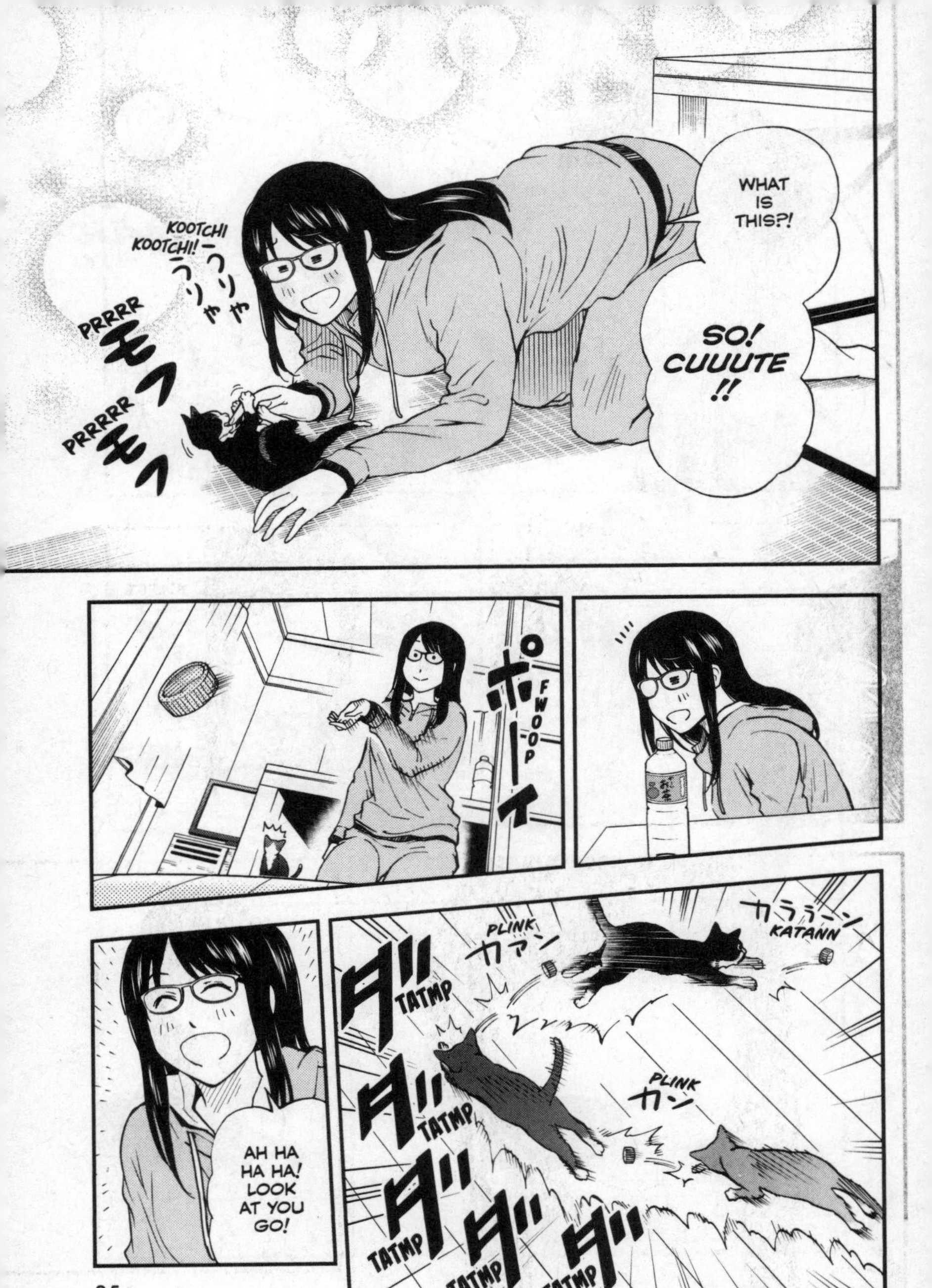
WHAT IS THIS?!
SO! CUUUTE!!
KOOTCHI KOOTCHI!
PRRRR モフ
PRRRRR モフ
!!
ポーイ FWOOOP
カラララーン KATANN
PLINK カァン
ダッ TATMP
ダッ TATMP
PLINK カン
ダッ TATMP
ダッ TATMP
ダッ TATMP
AH HA HA HA! LOOK AT YOU GO!

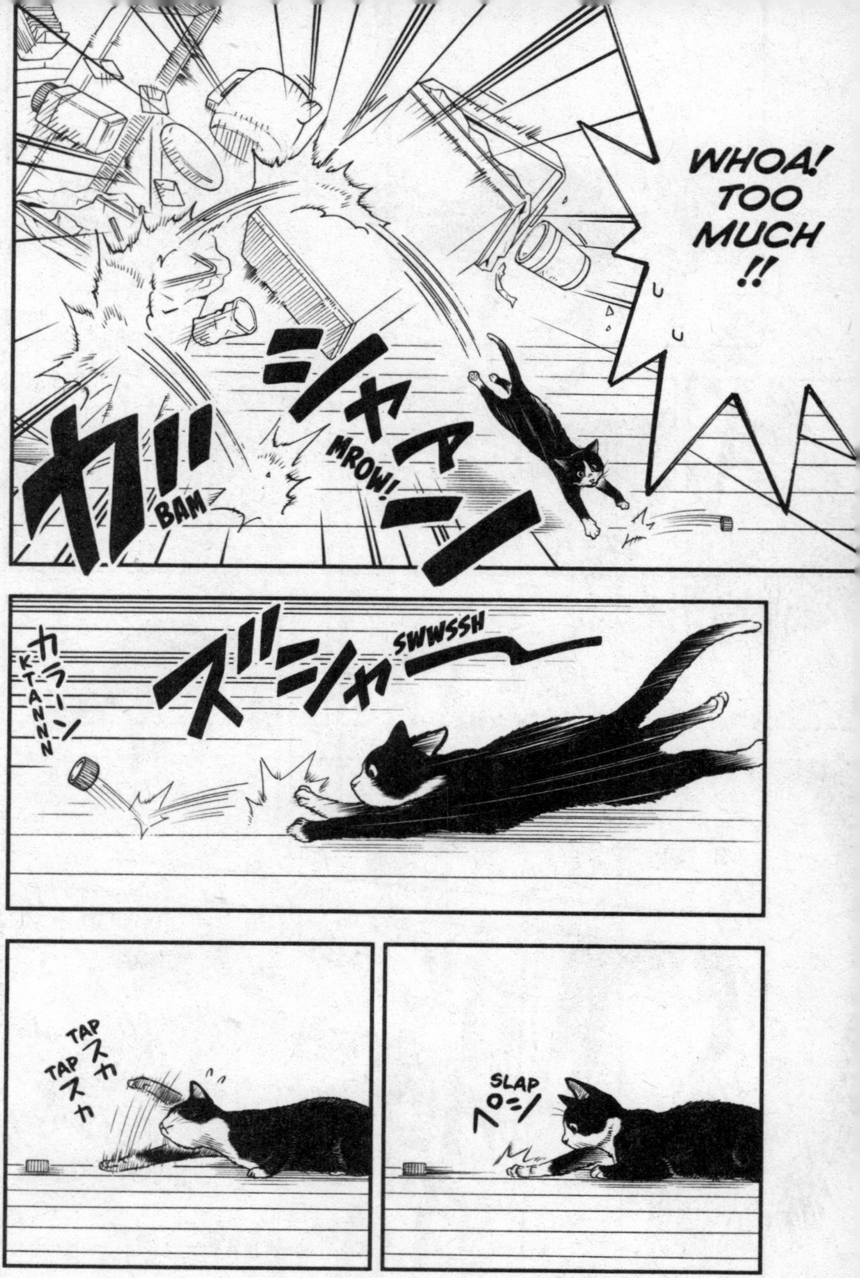
WHOA! TOO MUCH!!
ガシャーン
BAM
MROW!
ズシャー
SWWSSH
カラーン
KTANNN
SLAP
TAP
スカ
TAP
スカ

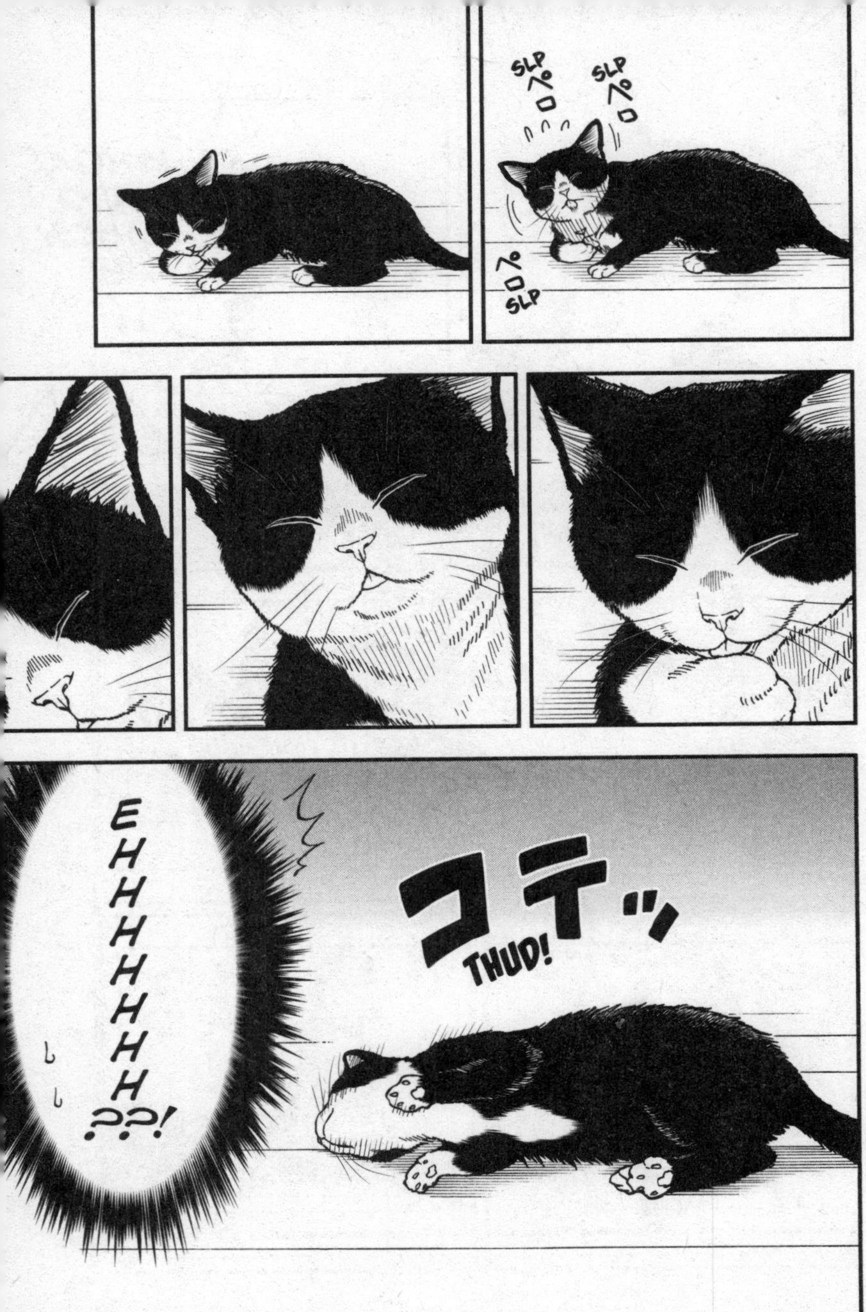
SLP
ペロ
SLP
ペロ
ペロ
SLP
コテッ
THUD!
EHHHHHHHHH??!

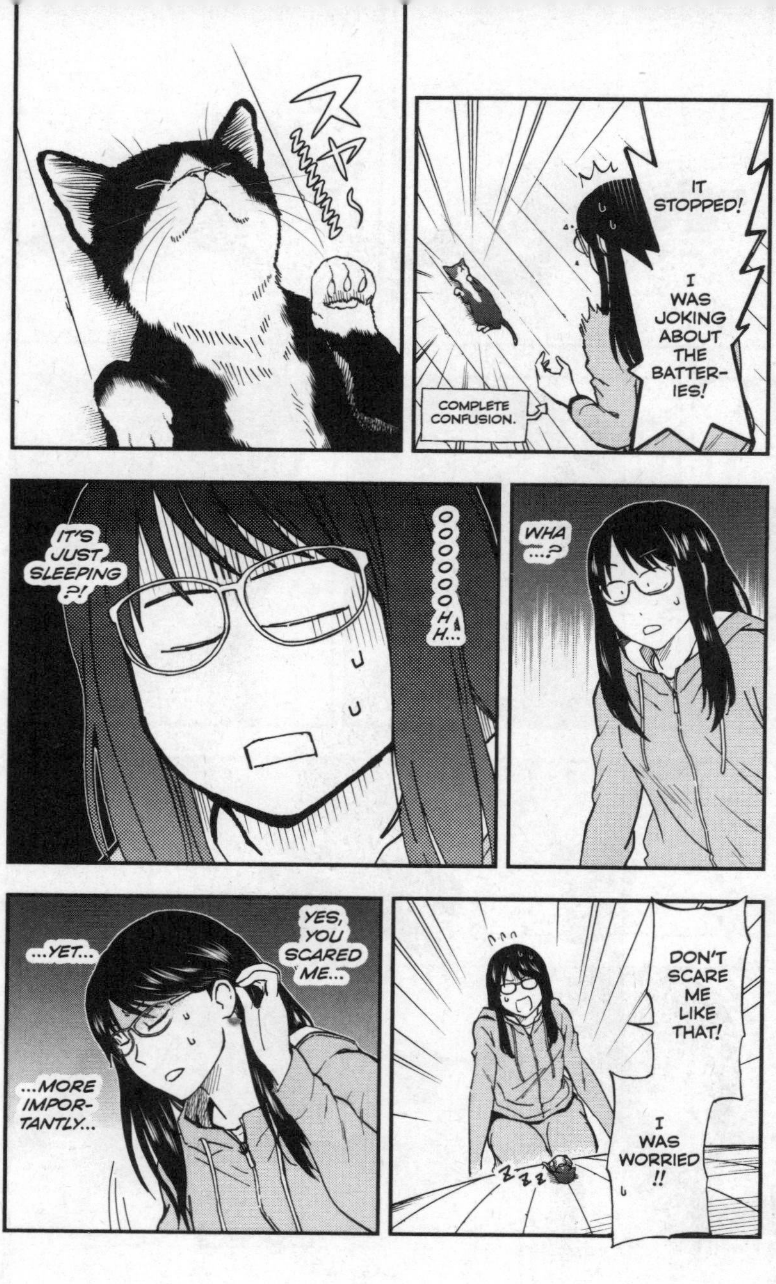
IT STOPPED!
I WAS JOKING ABOUT THE BATTER-IES!
COMPLETE CONFUSION.
スヤ
WHA...?
OOOOOOHH...
IT'S JUST SLEEPING?!
DON'T SCARE ME LIKE THAT!
I WAS WORRIED!!
ZZZ
YES, YOU SCARED ME...
...YET...
...MORE IMPOR-TANTLY...

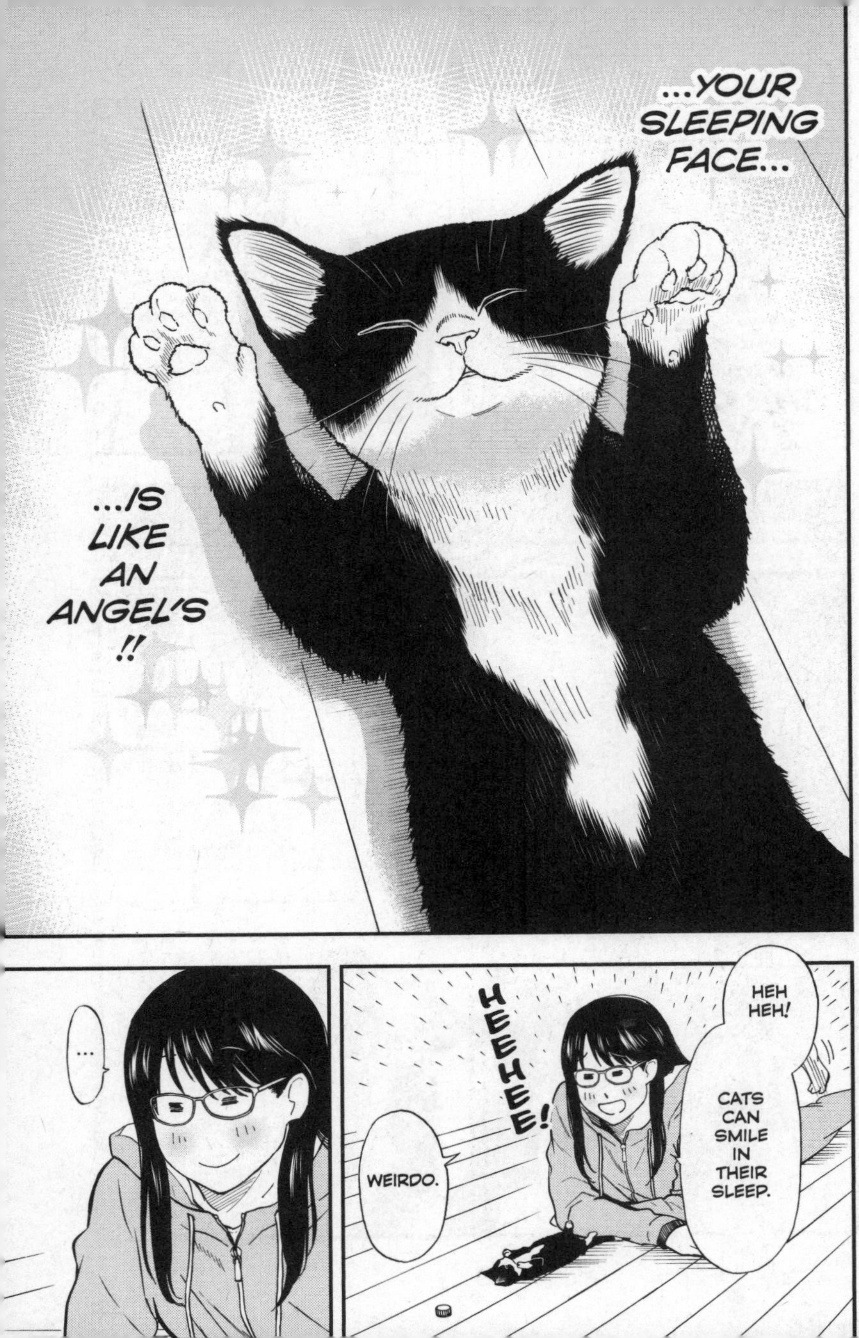
...YOUR SLEEPING FACE...
...IS LIKE AN ANGEL'S!!
HEH HEH!
CATS CAN SMILE IN THEIR SLEEP.
HEEHEE!
WEIRDO.
...

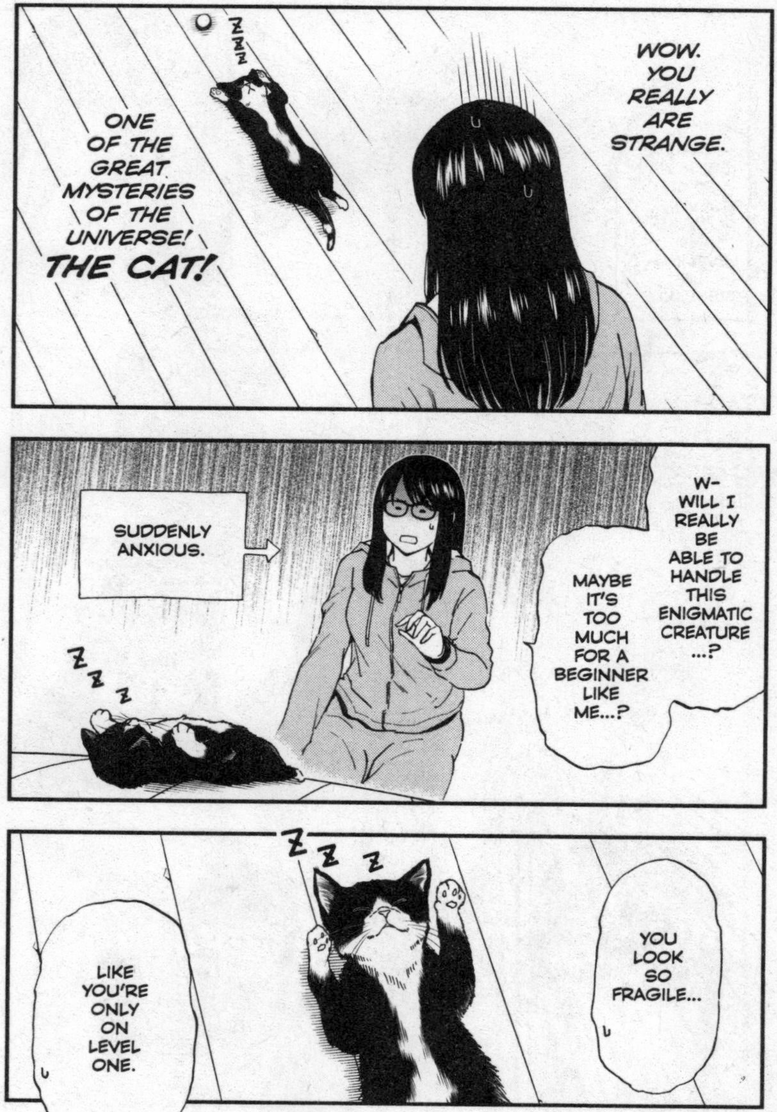
WOW. YOU REALLY ARE STRANGE.
Z Z Z
ONE OF THE GREAT MYSTERIES OF THE UNIVERSE! THE CAT!
W- WILL I REALLY BE ABLE TO HANDLE THIS ENIGMATIC CREATURE ...?
MAYBE IT'S TOO MUCH FOR A BEGINNER LIKE ME...?
SUDDENLY ANXIOUS.
Z Z Z
YOU LOOK SO FRAGILE...
Z Z Z
LIKE YOU'RE ONLY ON LEVEL ONE.

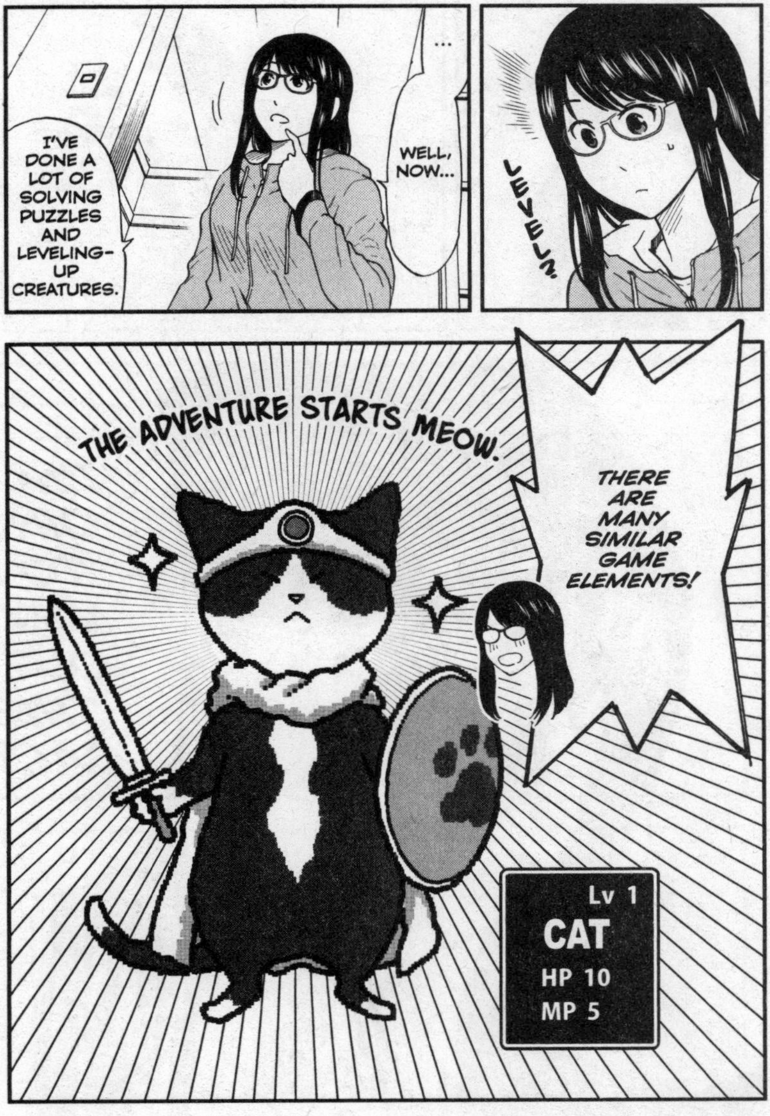
LEVEL?
...
WELL, NOW...
I'VE DONE A LOT OF SOLVING PUZZLES AND LEVELING-UP CREATURES.
THERE ARE MANY SIMILAR GAME ELEMENTS!
THE ADVENTURE STARTS MEOW.
Lv 1
CAT
HP 10
MP 5

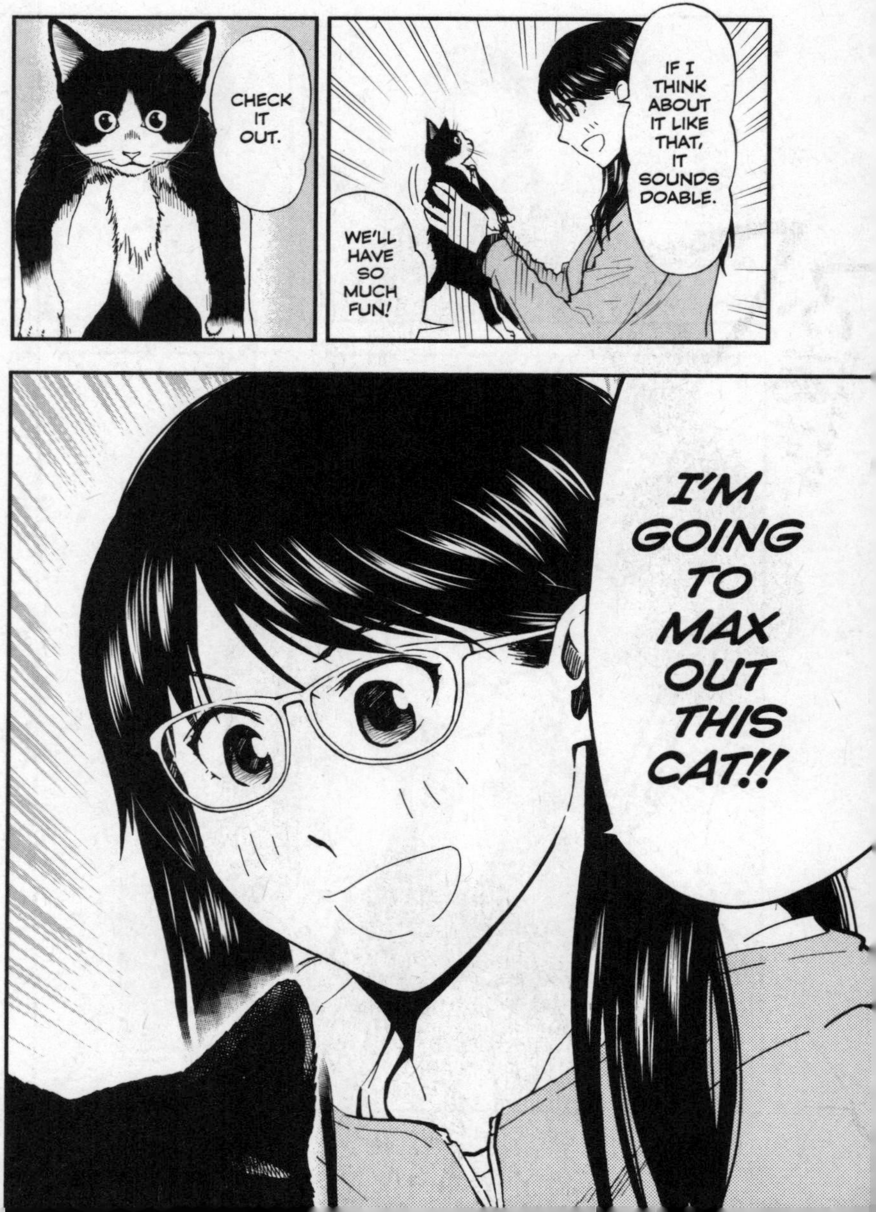
IF I THINK ABOUT IT LIKE THAT, IT SOUNDS DOABLE.
WE'LL HAVE SO MUCH FUN!
CHECK IT OUT.
I'M GOING TO MAX OUT THIS CAT!!

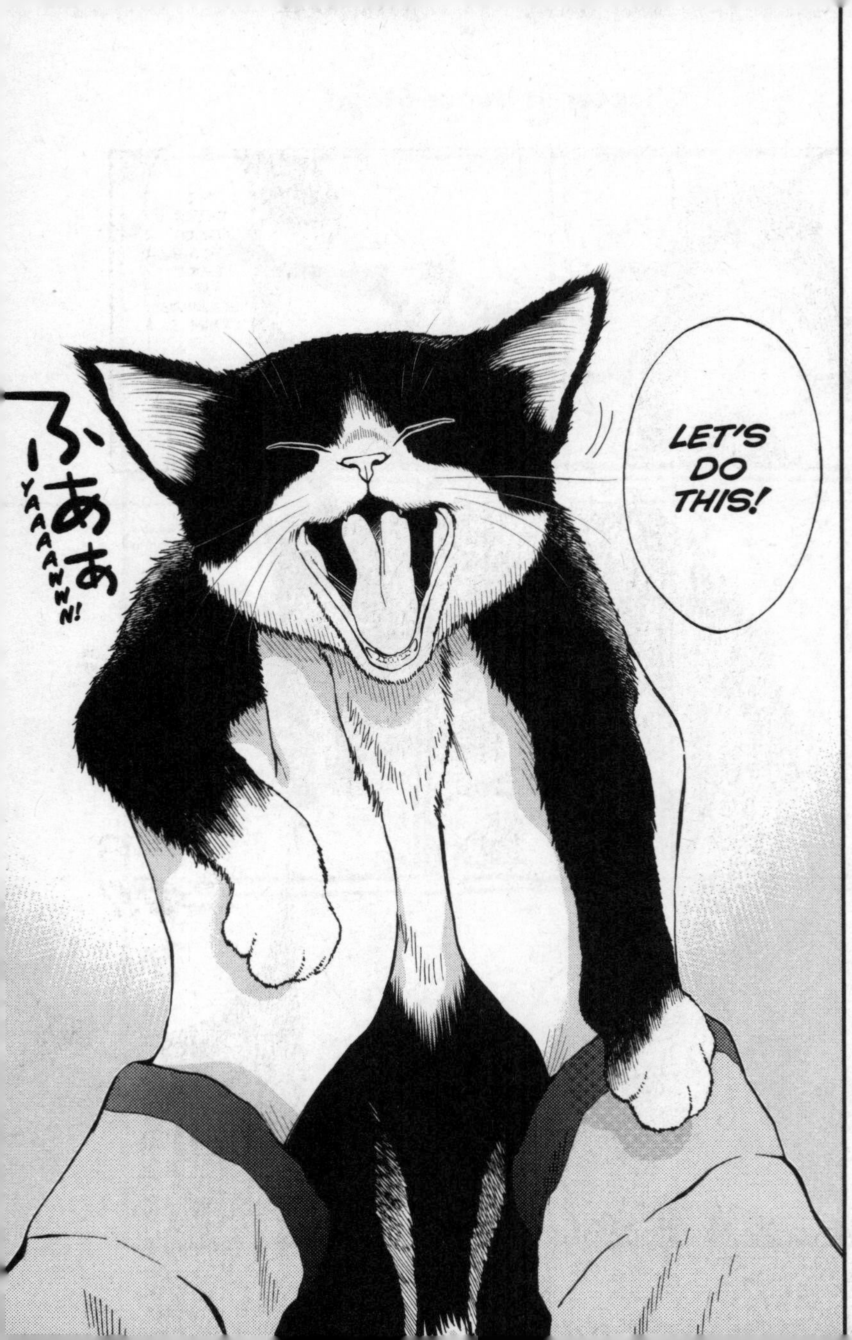
LET'S DO THIS!
ふあぁ
YAAAAAWWN!

Chapter 1: Bonus Stage

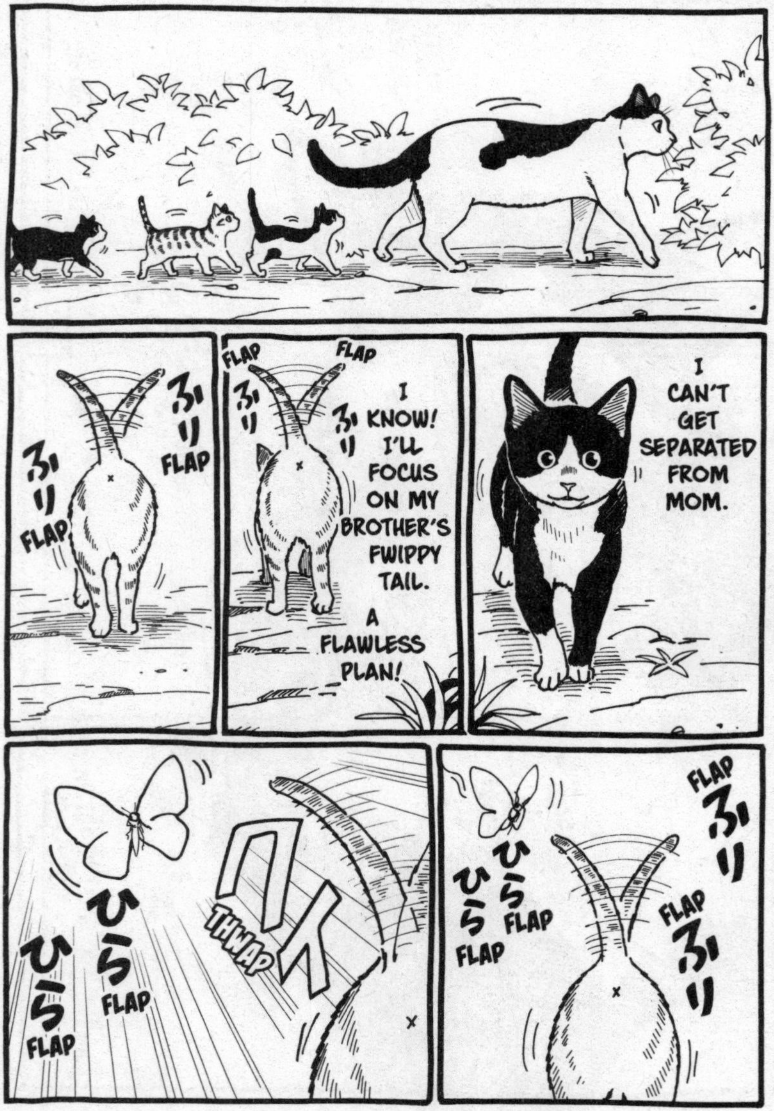
I CAN'T GET SEPARATED FROM MOM.
FLAP
FLAP
ふり
ふり
I KNOW! I'LL FOCUS ON MY BROTHER'S FWIPPY TAIL.
A FLAWLESS PLAN!
ふり
FLAP
ふり
FLAP
FLAP
ふり
FLAP
ふり
ひら
FLAP
ひら
FLAP
ひら
FLAP
ひら
FLAP
THWAP

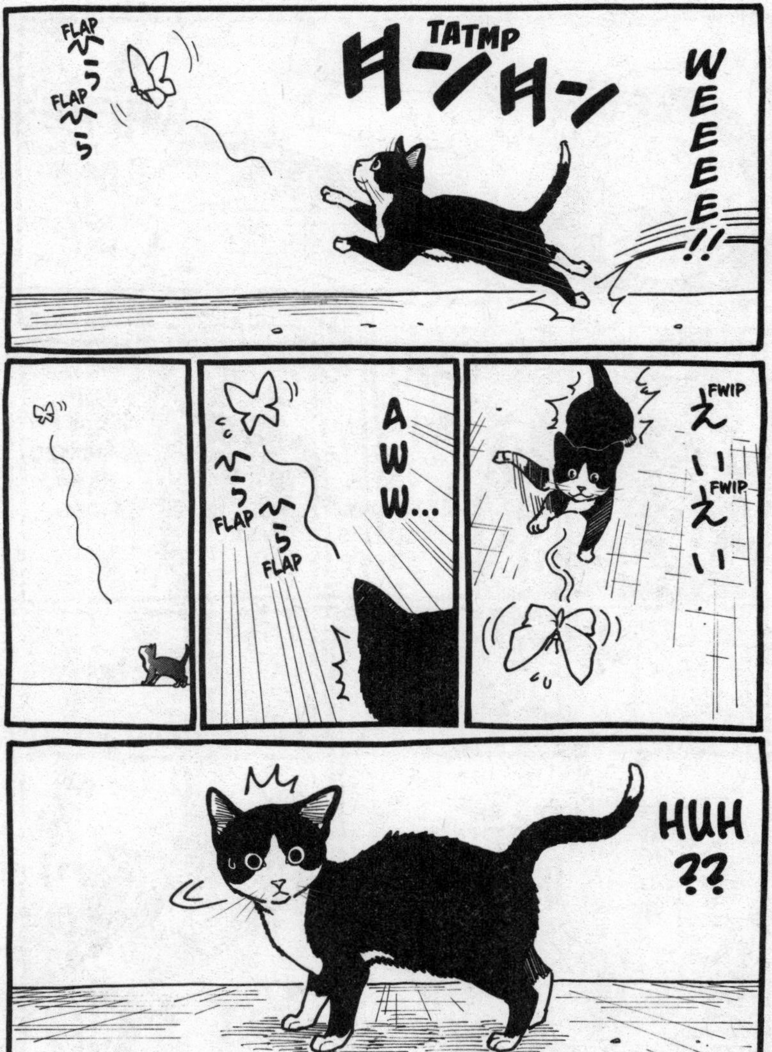
WEEEEE!!
TATMP
FLAP ひら
FLAP ひら
FWIP えい
FWIP えい
AWW...
FLAP ひら
FLAP ひら
HUH ??

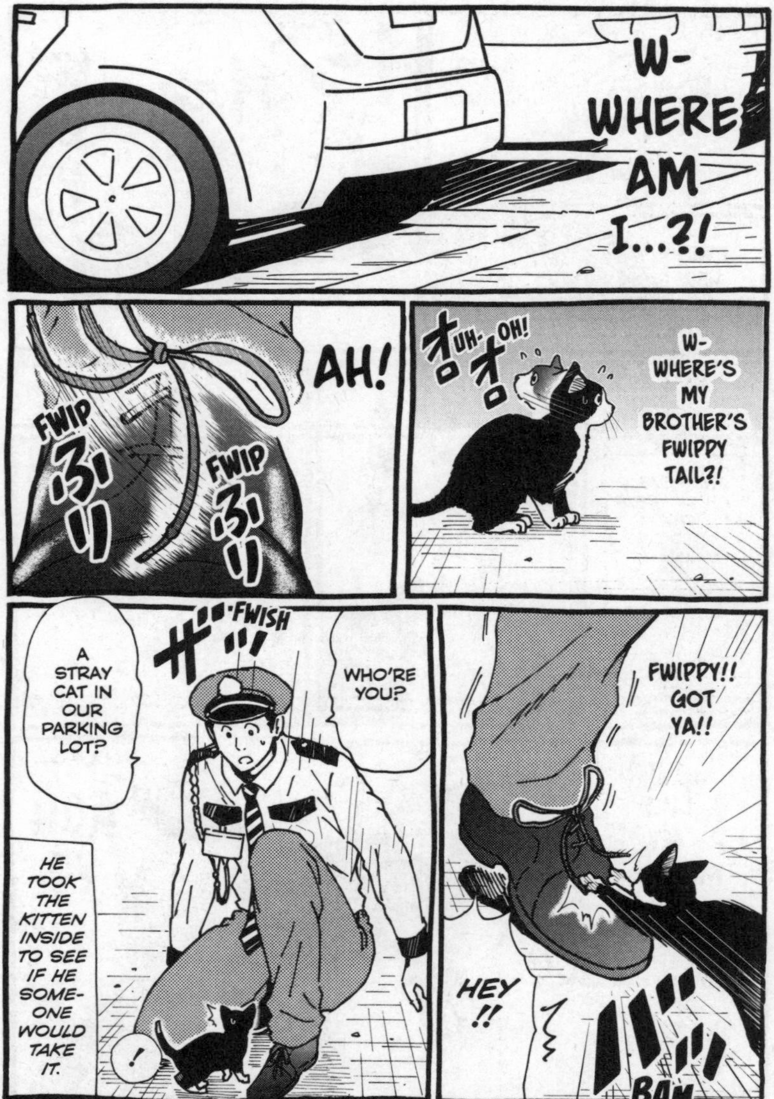

W- WHERE AM I...?!
UH-OH!
W- WHERE'S MY BROTHER'S FWIPPY TAIL?!
AH!
FWIP
FWIP
FWIPPY!! GOT YA!!
HEY !!
BAM
FWISH
WHO'RE YOU?
A STRAY CAT IN OUR PARKING LOT?
HE TOOK THE KITTEN INSIDE TO SEE IF HE SOME-ONE WOULD TAKE IT.
!

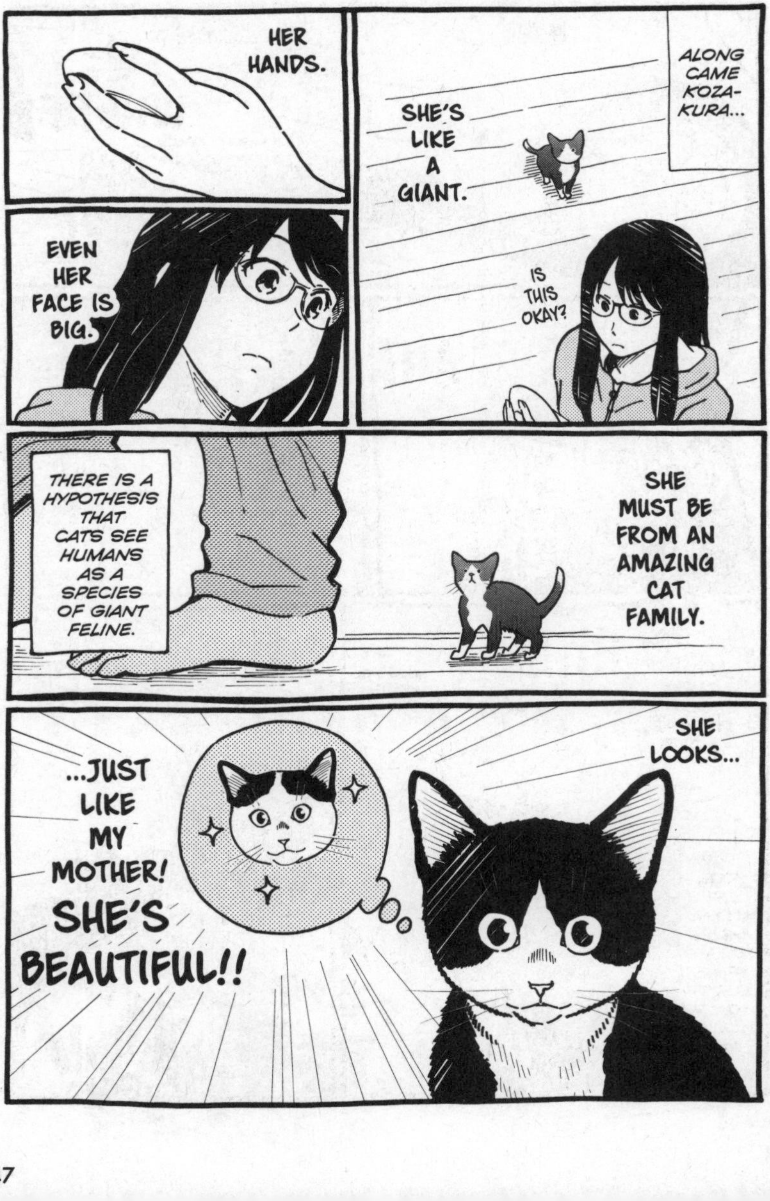
ALONG CAME KOZA-KURA...
SHE'S LIKE A GIANT.
IS THIS OKAY?
HER HANDS.
EVEN HER FACE IS BIG.
SHE MUST BE FROM AN AMAZING CAT FAMILY.
THERE IS A HYPOTHESIS THAT CATS SEE HUMANS AS A SPECIES OF GIANT FELINE.
SHE LOOKS...
...JUST LIKE MY MOTHER!
SHE'S BEAUTIFUL!!

SNIFF!
スン
SNIFF!
スン

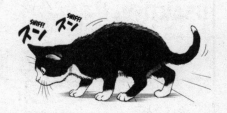

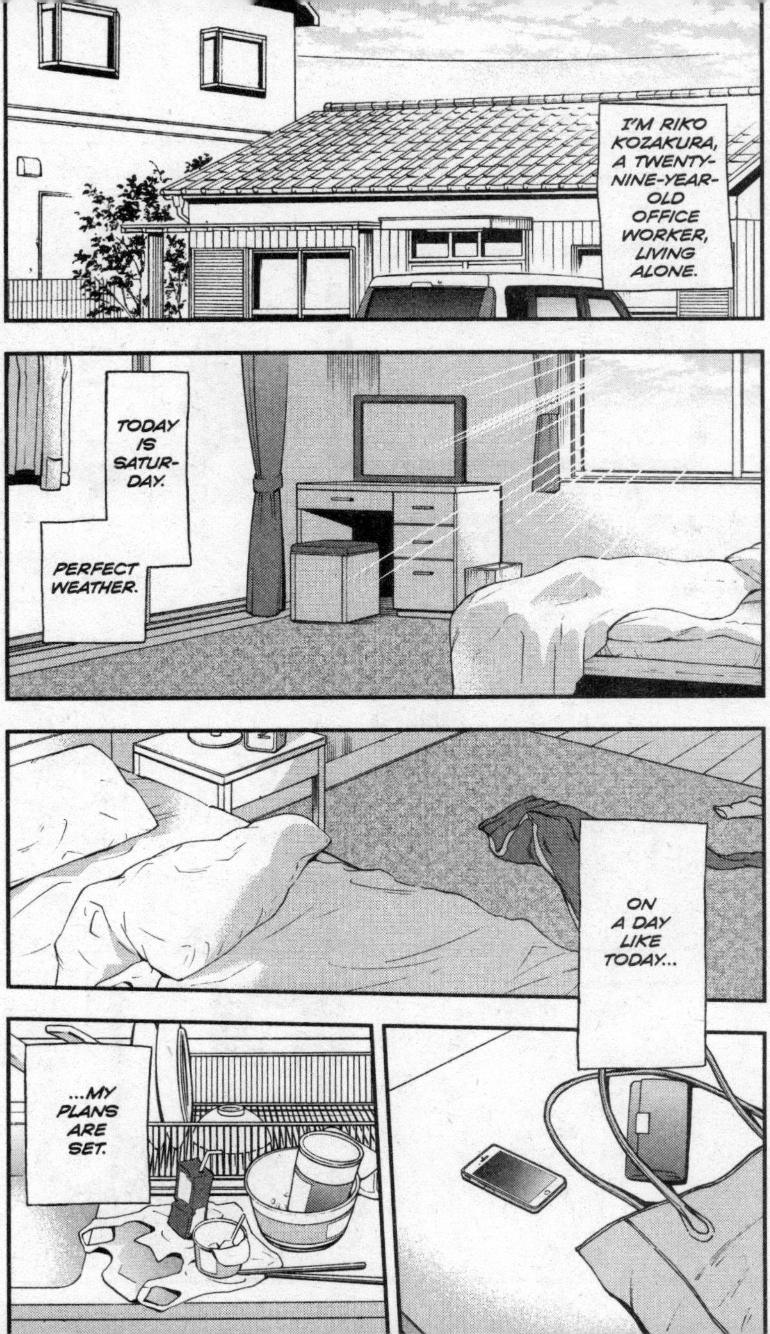
I'M RIKO KOZAKURA, A TWENTY-NINE-YEAR-OLD OFFICE WORKER, LIVING ALONE.
TODAY IS SATURDAY.
PERFECT WEATHER.
ON A DAY LIKE TODAY...
...MY PLANS ARE SET.

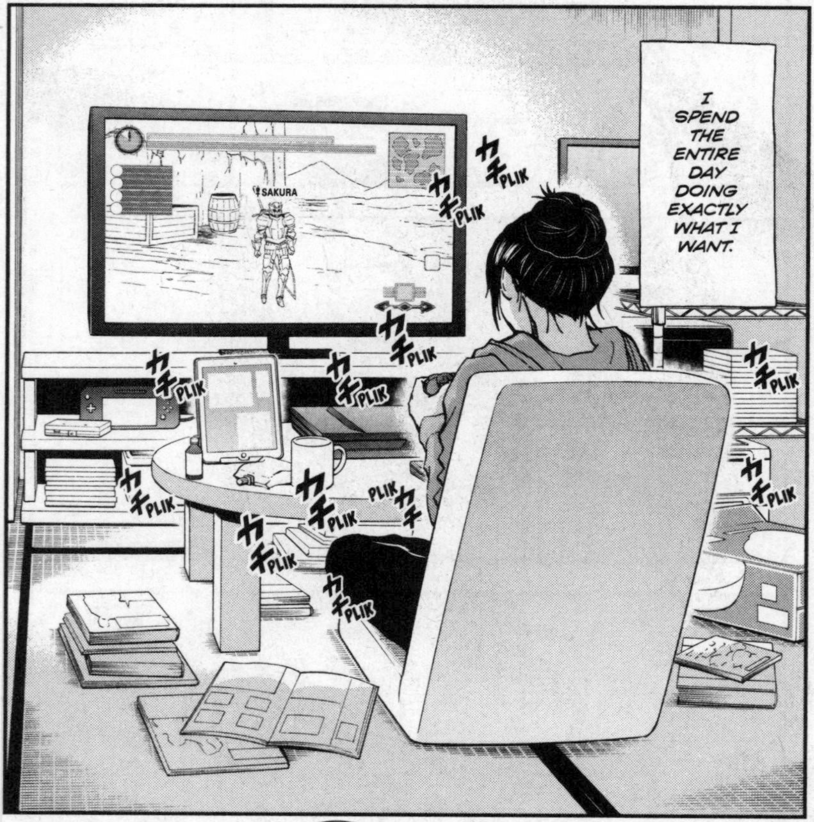

I SPEND THE ENTIRE DAY DOING EXACTLY WHAT I WANT.
SAKURA
カチ PLIK
カチ PLIK
カチ PLIK
カチ PLIK
カチ PLIK
カチ PLIK
カチ PLIK
カチ PLIK
PLIK カチ
カチ PLIK
カチ PLIK
カチ PLIK

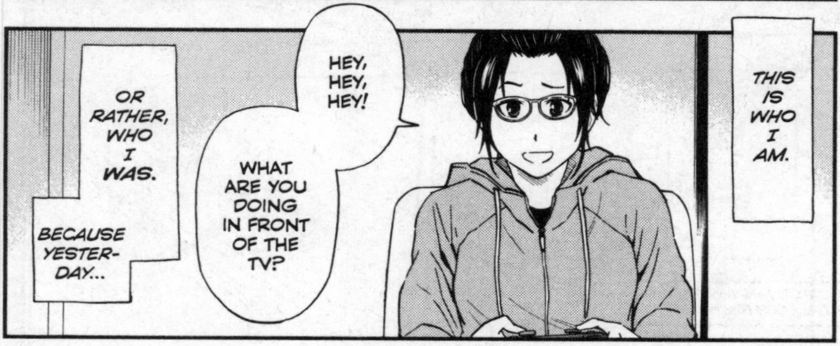

THIS IS WHO I AM.
HEY, HEY, HEY!
WHAT ARE YOU DOING IN FRONT OF THE TV?
OR RATHER, WHO I WAS.
BECAUSE YESTER-DAY...

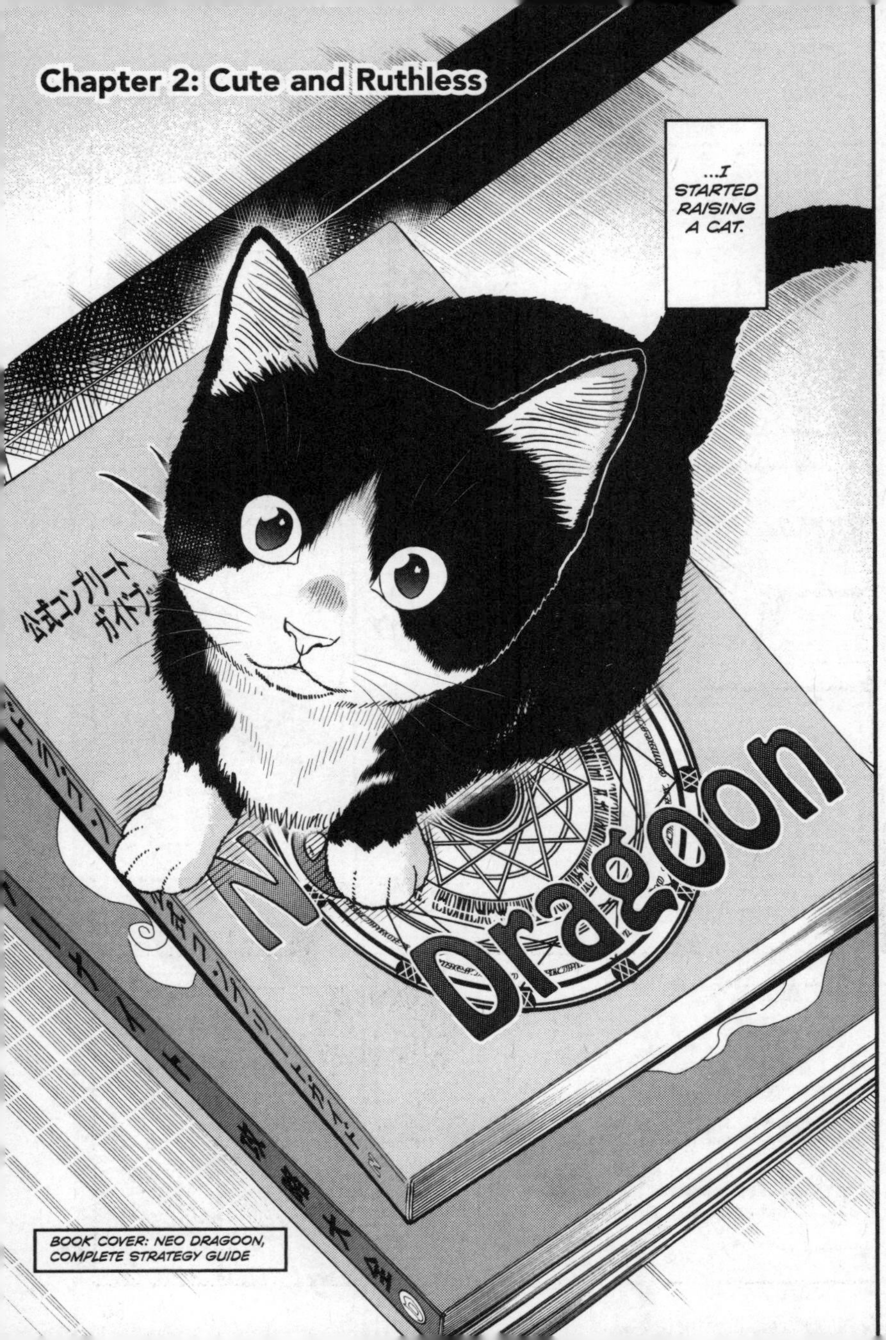
Chapter 2: Cute and Ruthless
...I STARTED RAISING A CAT.
公式コンプリートガイド
Dragoon
BOOK COVER: NEO DRAGOON, COMPLETE STRATEGY GUIDE

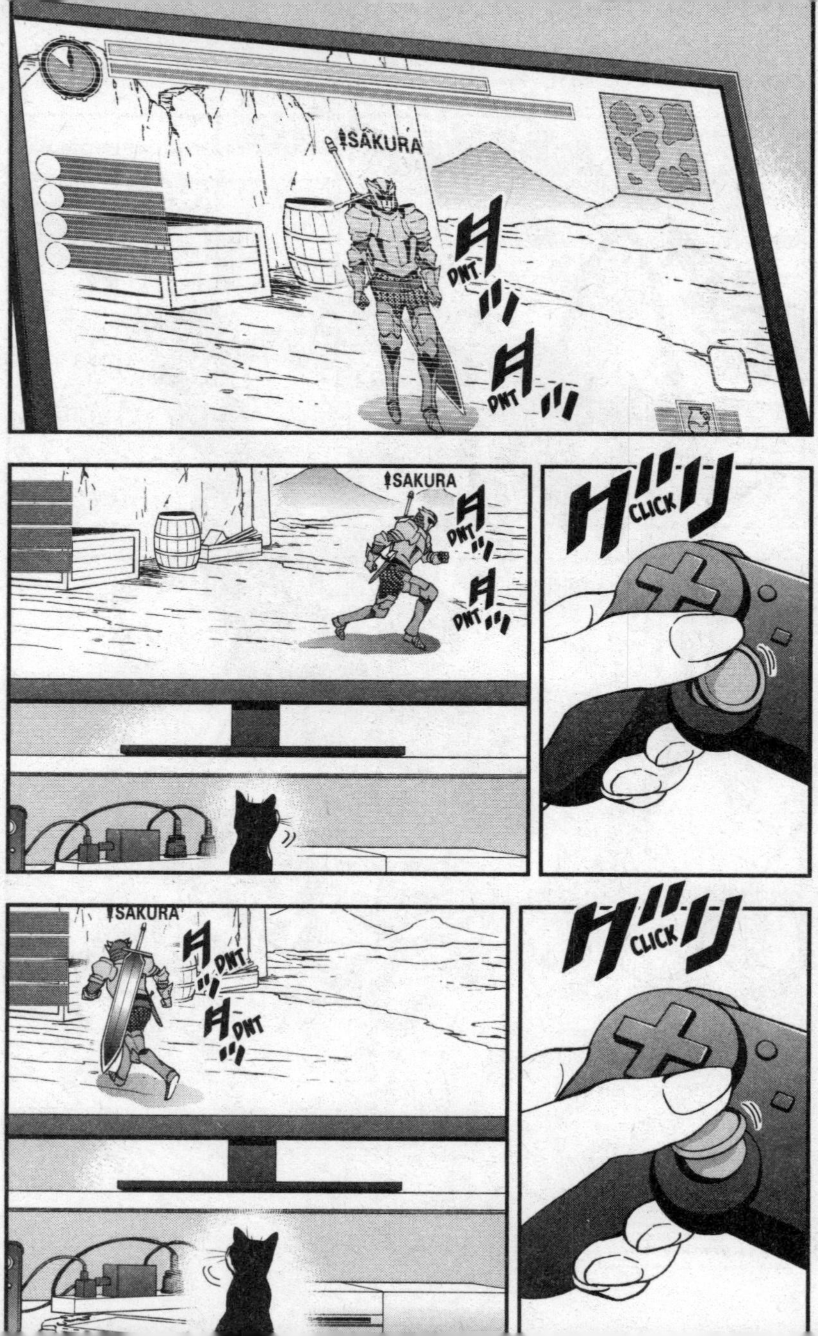
SAKURA
DNT
DNT
CLICK
SAKURA
DNT
DNT
CLICK
SAKURA
DNT
DNT

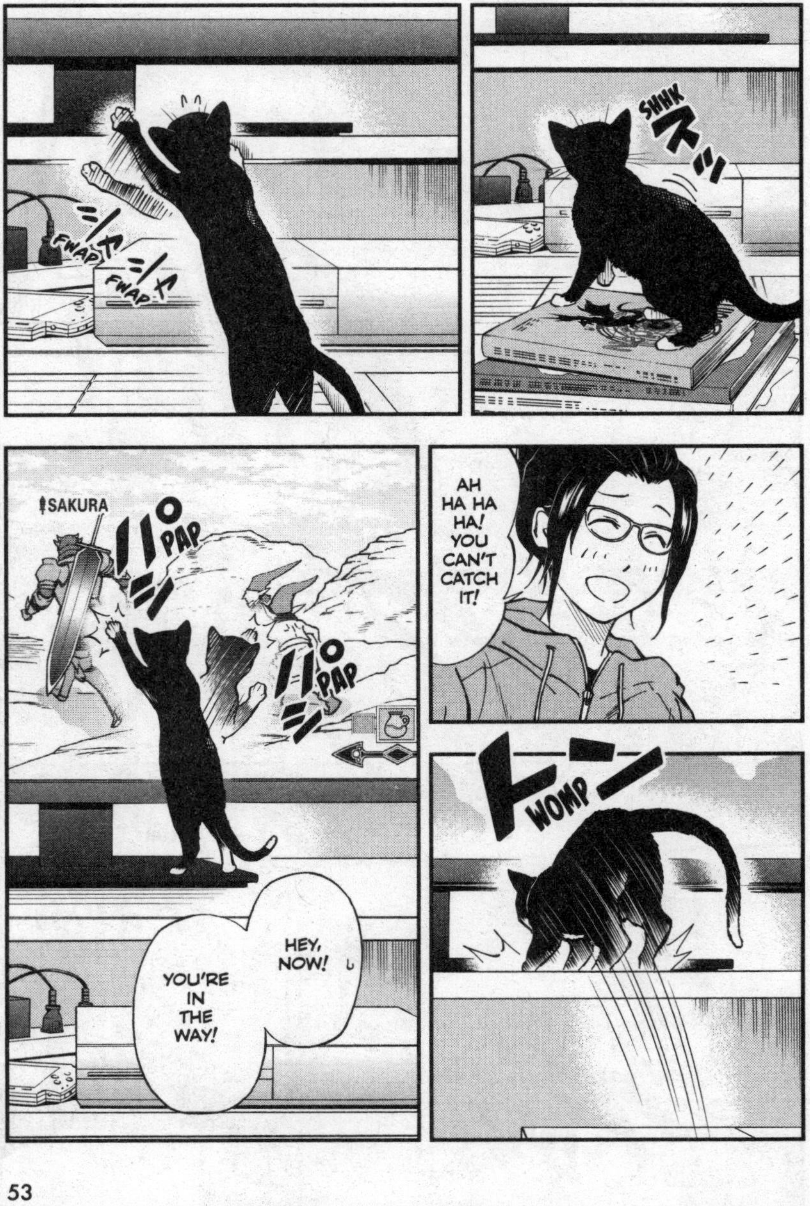
SHHK
FWAP
FWAP
AH HA HA HA! YOU CAN'T CATCH IT!
WOMP
SAKURA
PAP
PAP
HEY, NOW!
YOU'RE IN THE WAY!

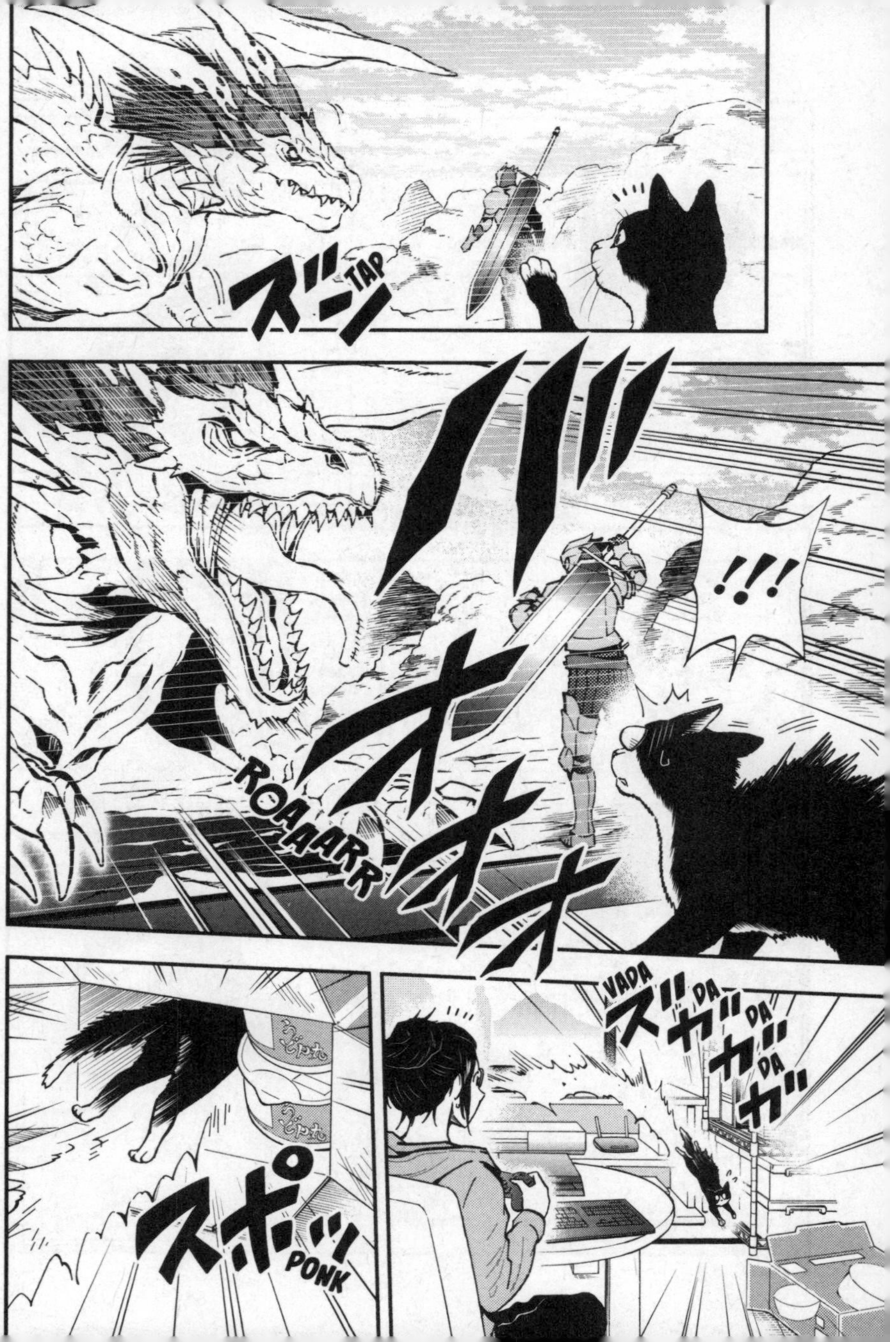
ズン
TAP
!!!
バオオ
ROAAAARR
ズガガガ
VADA DA DA DA
スポッ
PONK

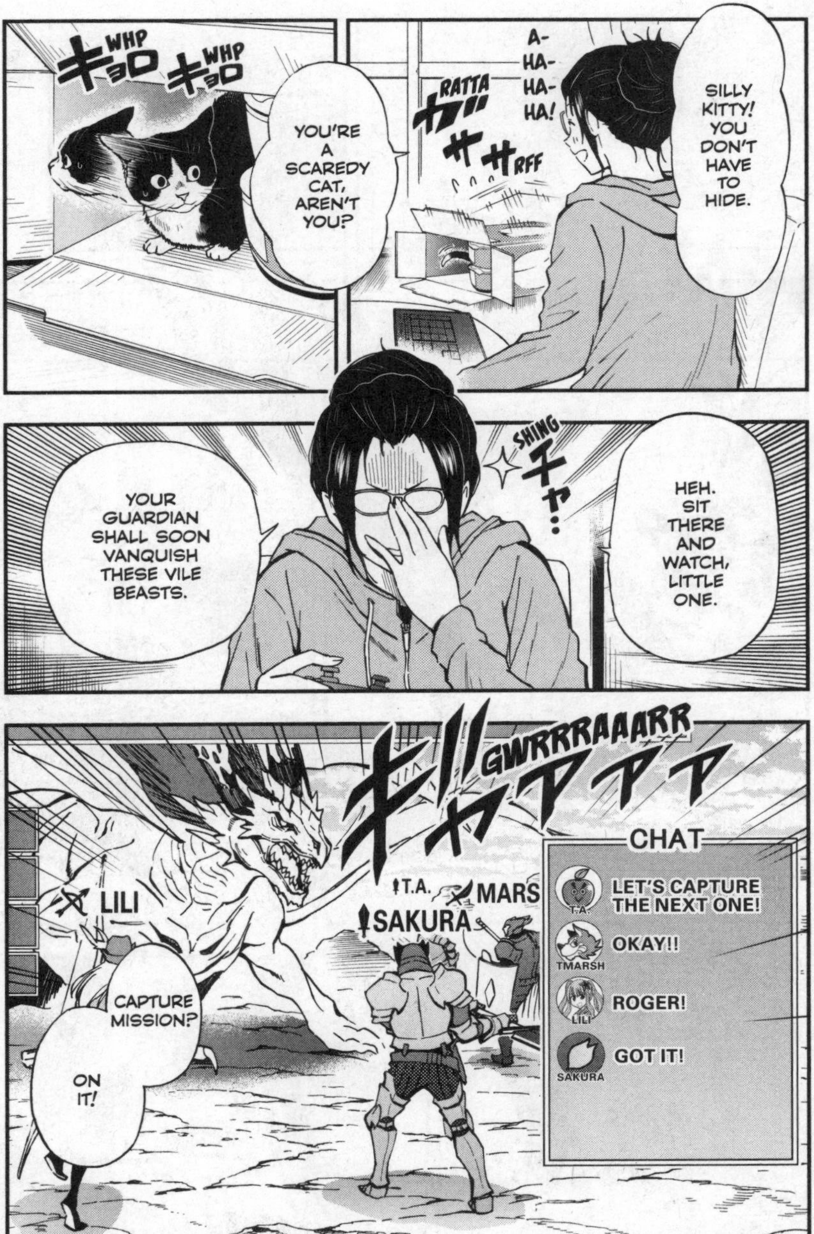

SILLY KITTY! YOU DON'T HAVE TO HIDE.
A-HA-HA-HA!
RATTA
RFF
YOU'RE A SCAREDY CAT, AREN'T YOU?
WHP
WHP
HEH. SIT THERE AND WATCH, LITTLE ONE.
SHING
YOUR GUARDIAN SHALL SOON VANQUISH THESE VILE BEASTS.
GWRRRAAARR
CHAT
T.A.
LET'S CAPTURE THE NEXT ONE!
TMARSH
OKAY!!
LILI
ROGER!
SAKURA
GOT IT!
T.A.
MARS
SAKURA
LILI
CAPTURE MISSION?
ON IT!

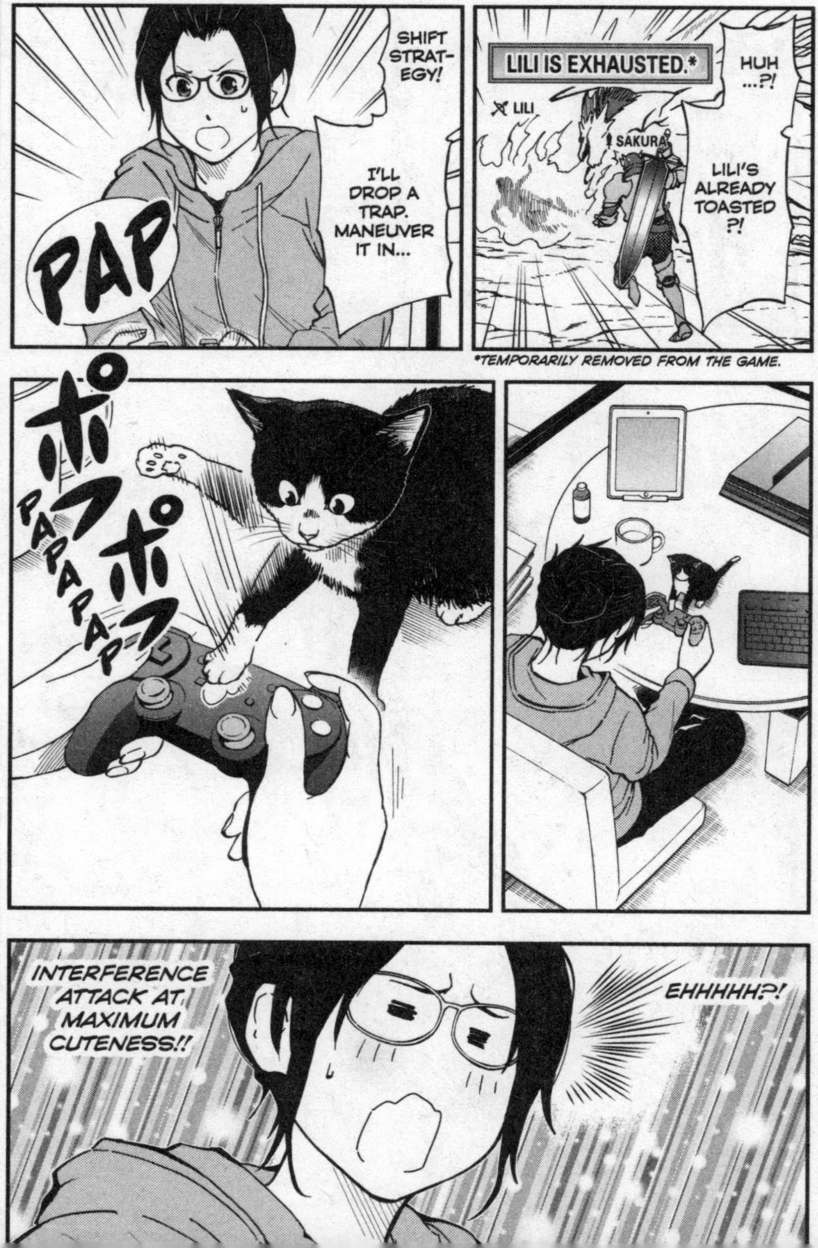
LILI IS EXHAUSTED.*
LILI
SAKURA
HUH ...?!
LILI'S ALREADY TOASTED?!
SHIFT STRAT-EGY!
I'LL DROP A TRAP. MANEUVER IT IN...
PAP
PAPAPAPAP
EHHHHH?!
INTERFERENCE ATTACK AT MAXIMUM CUTENESS!!

*TEMPORARILY REMOVED FROM THE GAME.

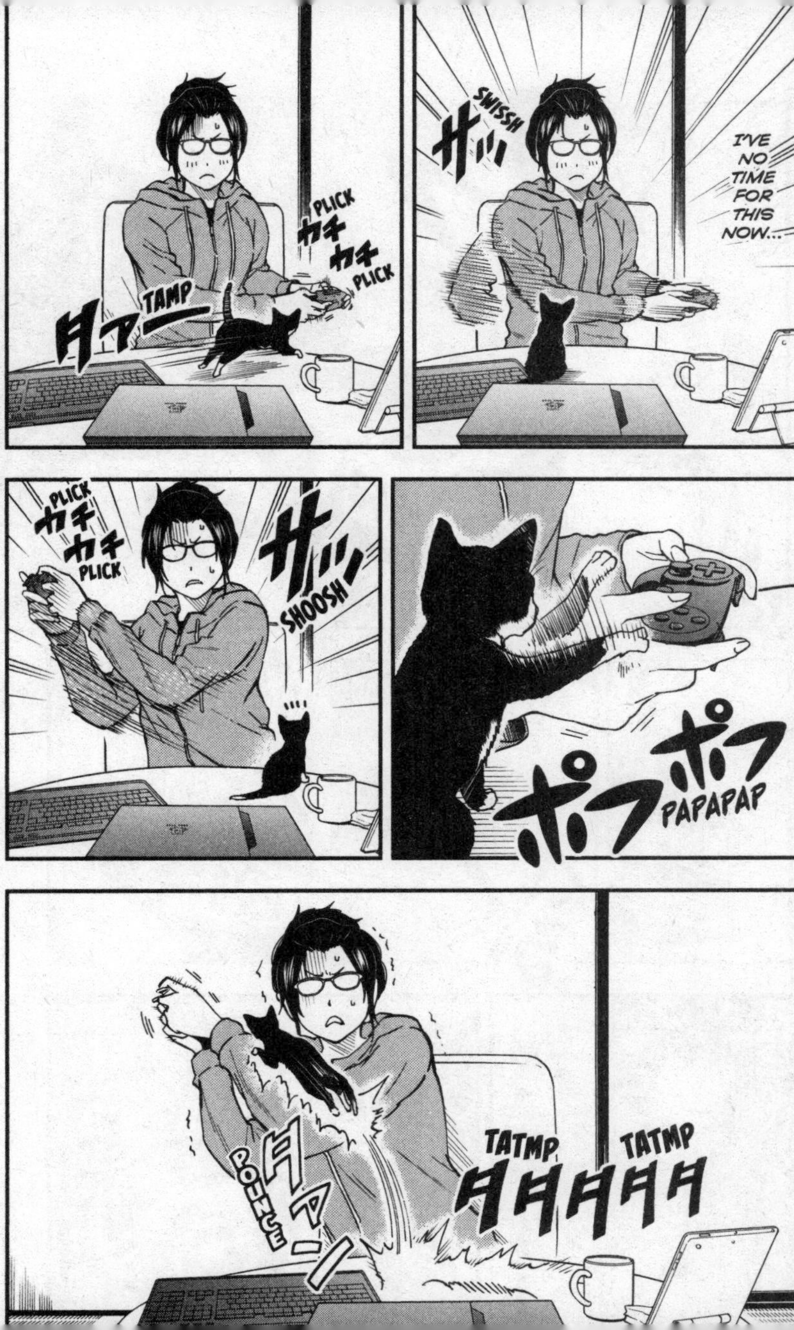
SWISSH
サッ
I'VE NO TIME FOR THIS NOW...
PLICK
カチ
カチ
PLICK
TAMP
タァー
ポフポフ
PAPAPAP
PLICK
カチ
カチ
PLICK
サッ
SHOOSH
POUNCE
タァー
TATMP TATMP
タタタタタタ

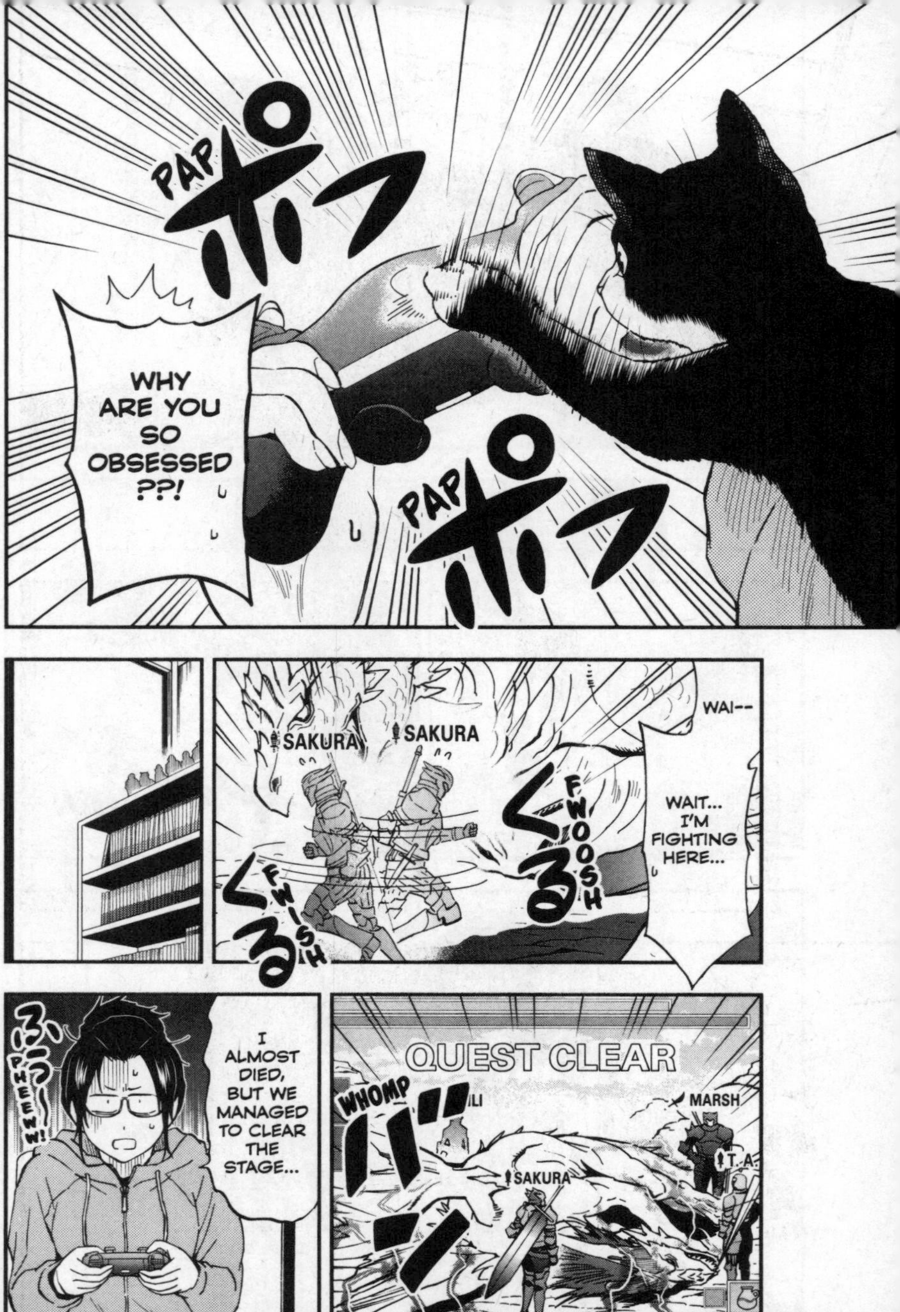
PAP
ポフ
WHY ARE YOU SO OBSESSED ??!
PAP
ポフ
WAI--
WAIT... I'M FIGHTING HERE...
SAKURA
SAKURA
FWOOSH
FWISH
QUEST CLEAR
MARSH
T.A.
SAKURA
LI
WHOMP
I ALMOST DIED, BUT WE MANAGED TO CLEAR THE STAGE...
PHEEWW!

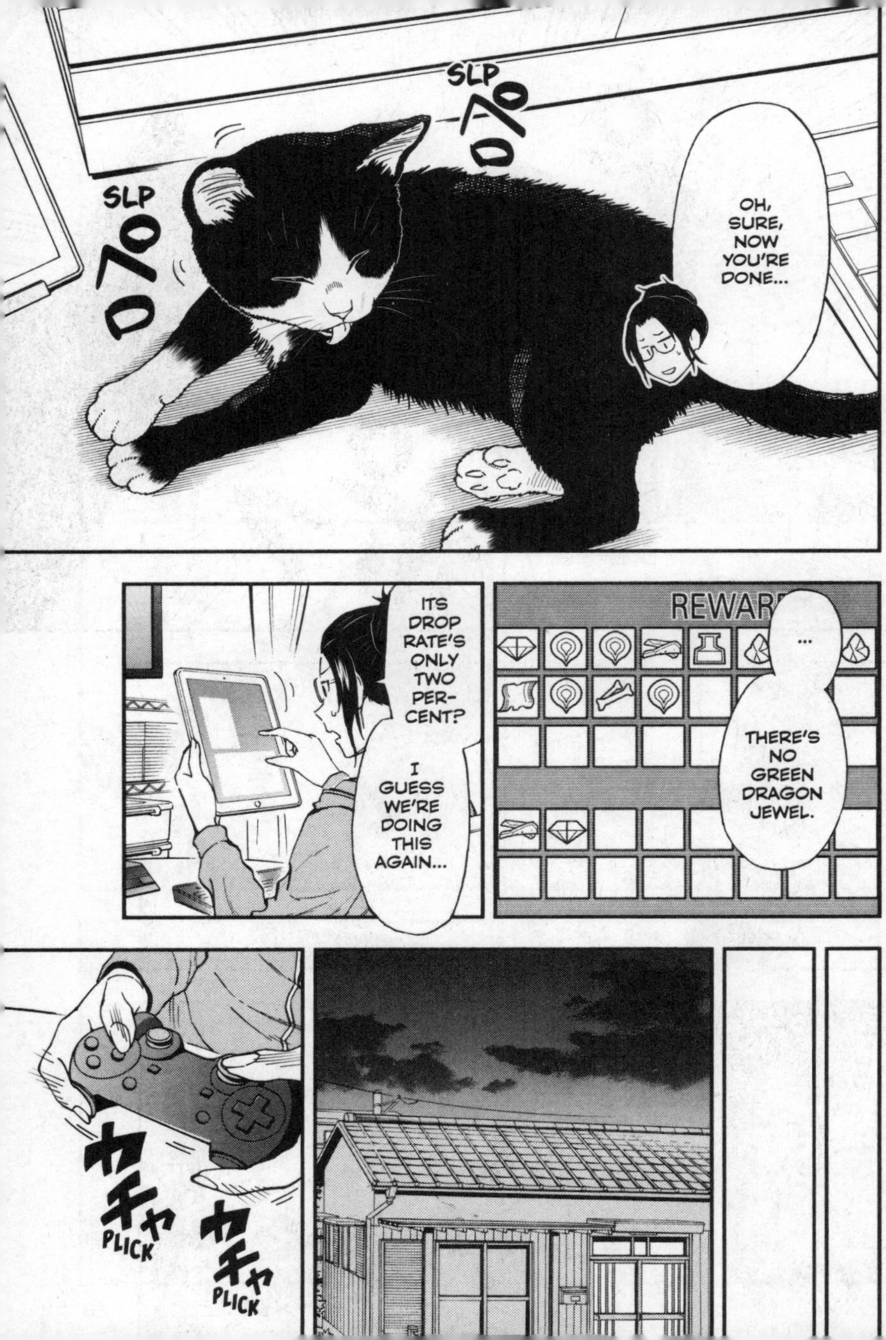
SLP
OH, SURE, NOW YOU'RE DONE...
SLP
REWAR
...
THERE'S NO GREEN DRAGON JEWEL.
ITS DROP RATE'S ONLY TWO PER-CENT?
I GUESS WE'RE DOING THIS AGAIN...
カチャ
PLICK
カチャ
PLICK

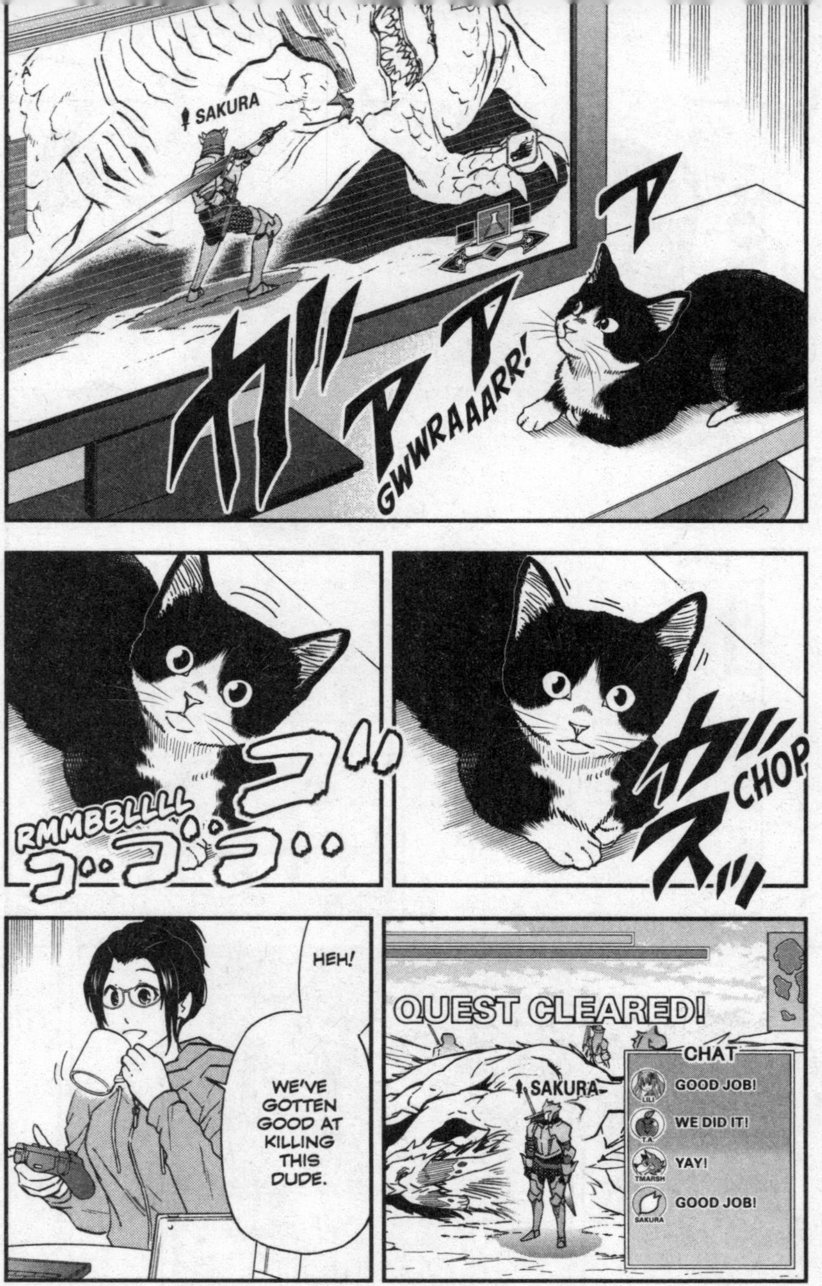
SAKURA
GWWRAAARR!
CHOP
RMMBBLLLL
QUEST CLEARED!
SAKURA
CHAT
LILI
GOOD JOB!
T.A.
WE DID IT!
TMARSH
YAY!
SAKURA
GOOD JOB!
HEH!
WE'VE GOTTEN GOOD AT KILLING THIS DUDE.

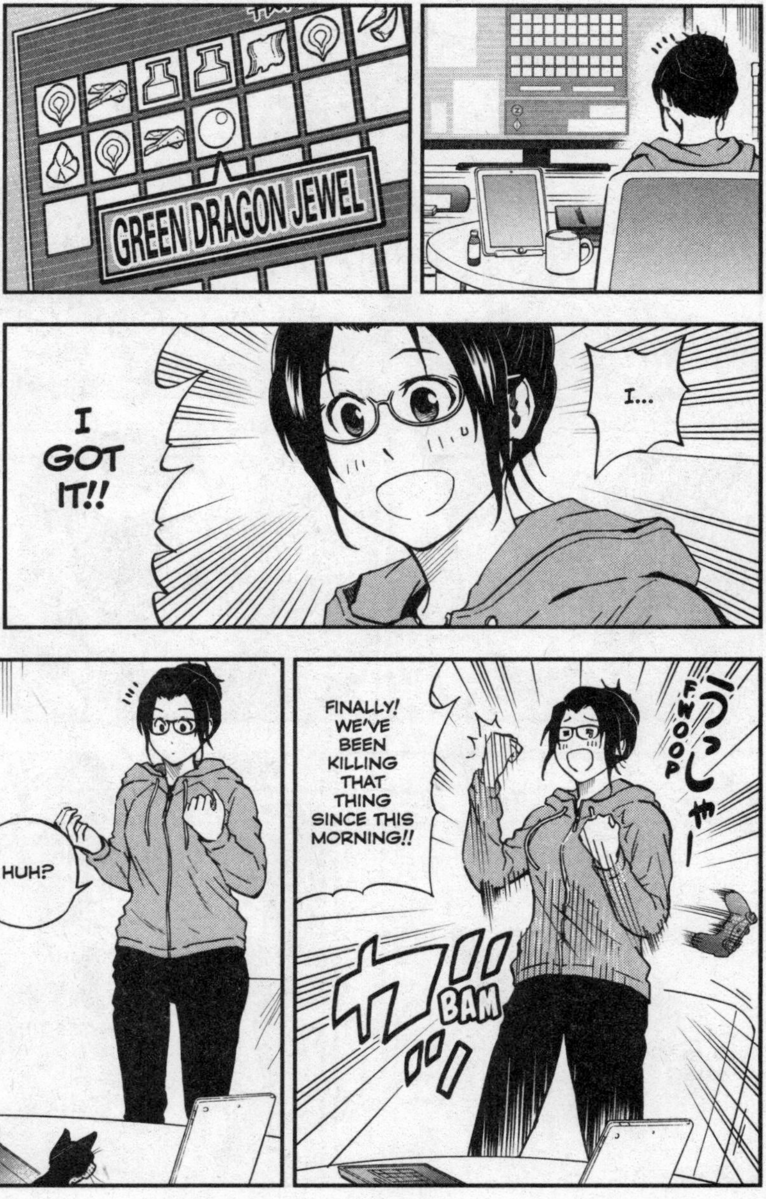
GREEN DRAGON JEWEL
I...
I GOT IT!!
FWOOP
FINALLY! WE'VE BEEN KILLING THAT THING SINCE THIS MORNING!!
BAM
HUH?

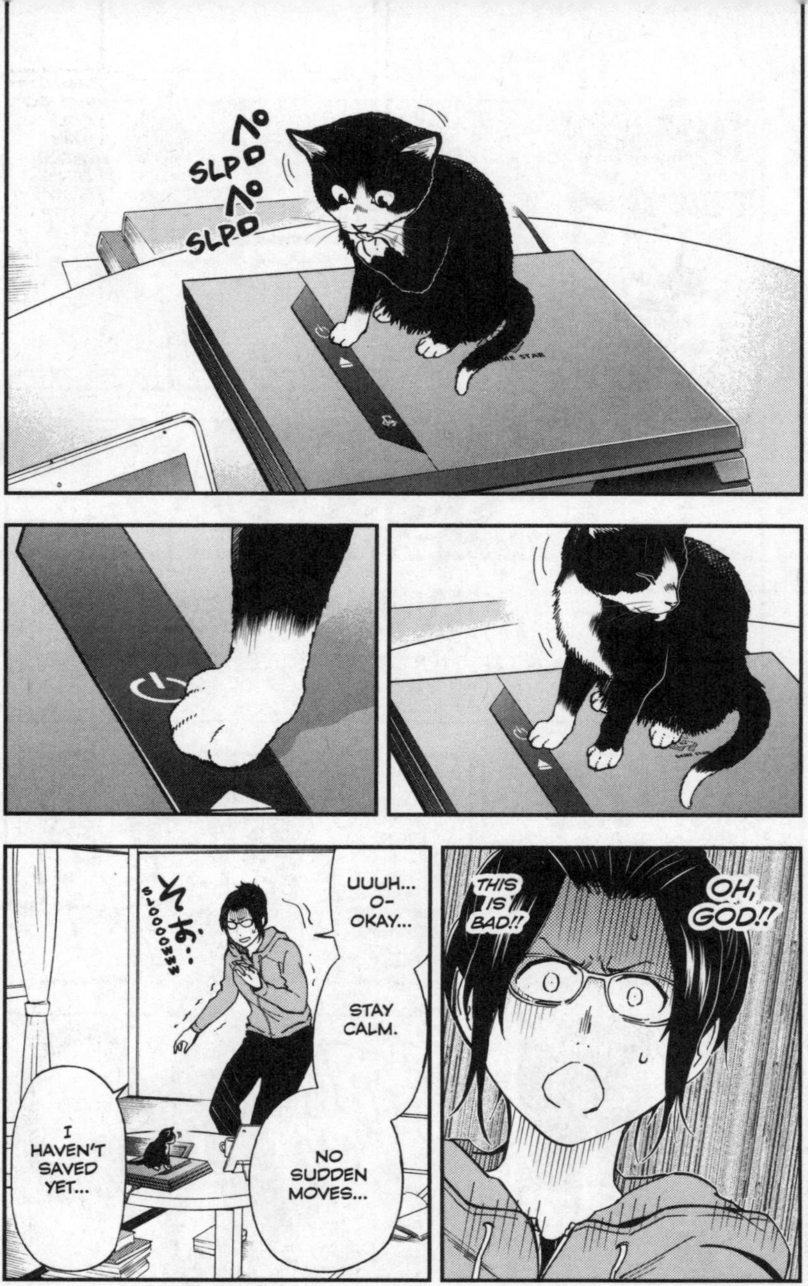

SLP ペロ
SLP ペロ
OH, GOD!!
THIS IS BAD!!
UUUH... O-OKAY...
そぉ... SLOOOOWWW
STAY CALM.
NO SUDDEN MOVES...
I HAVEN'T SAVED YET...

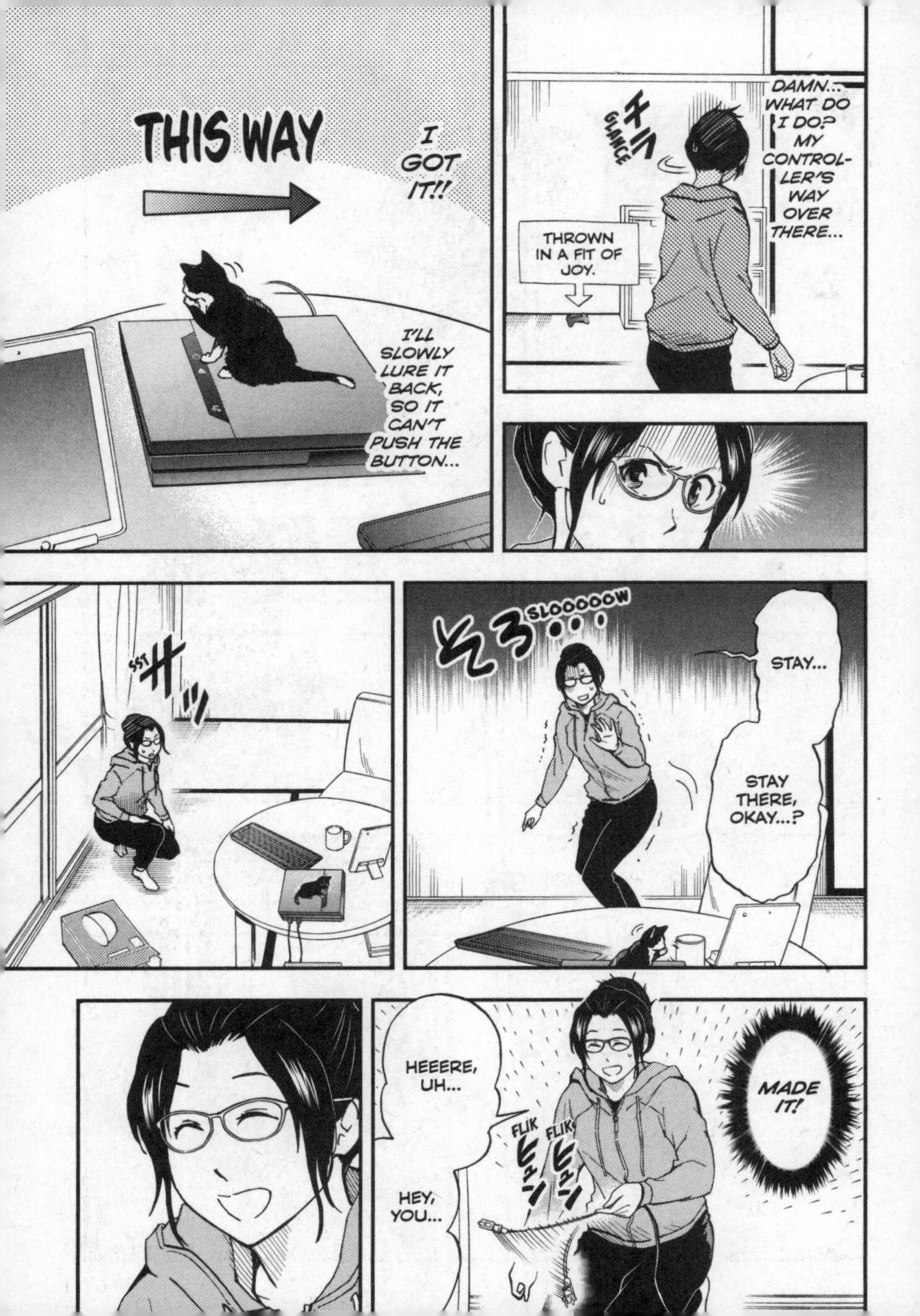

GLANCE
DAMN... WHAT DO I DO? MY CONTROLLER'S WAY OVER THERE...
THROWN IN A FIT OF JOY.
THIS WAY
I GOT IT!!
I'LL SLOWLY LURE IT BACK, SO IT CAN'T PUSH THE BUTTON...
SLOOOOOW
STAY...
STAY THERE, OKAY...?
SST
MADE IT!
HEEERE, UH...
FLIK
FLIK
HEY, YOU...

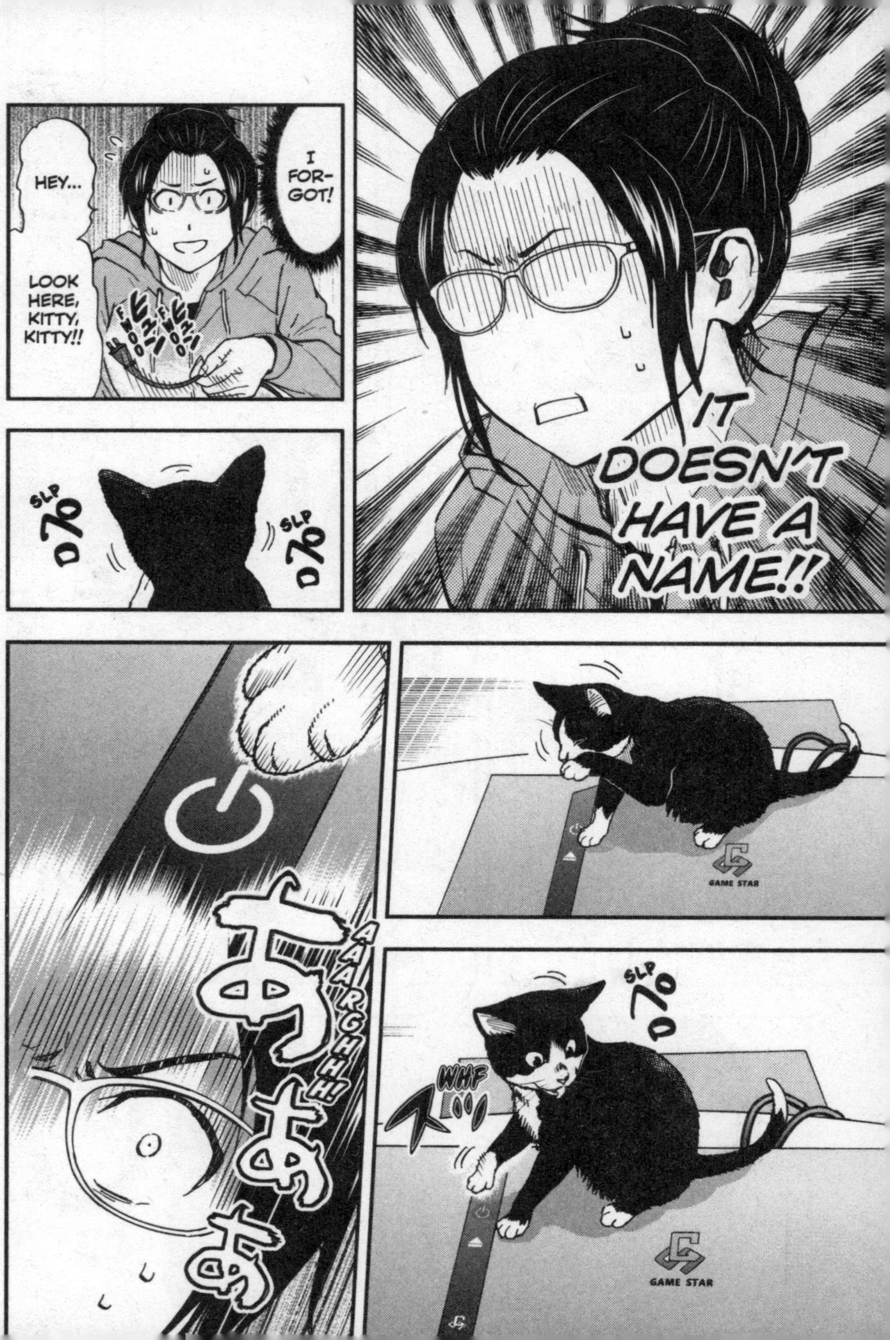
IT DOESN'T HAVE A NAME!!
I FOR-GOT!
HEY...
LOOK HERE, KITTY, KITTY!!
FWOO
FWOO
SLP
SLP
GAME STAR
SLP
WHF
GAME STAR
AAARGHHH!

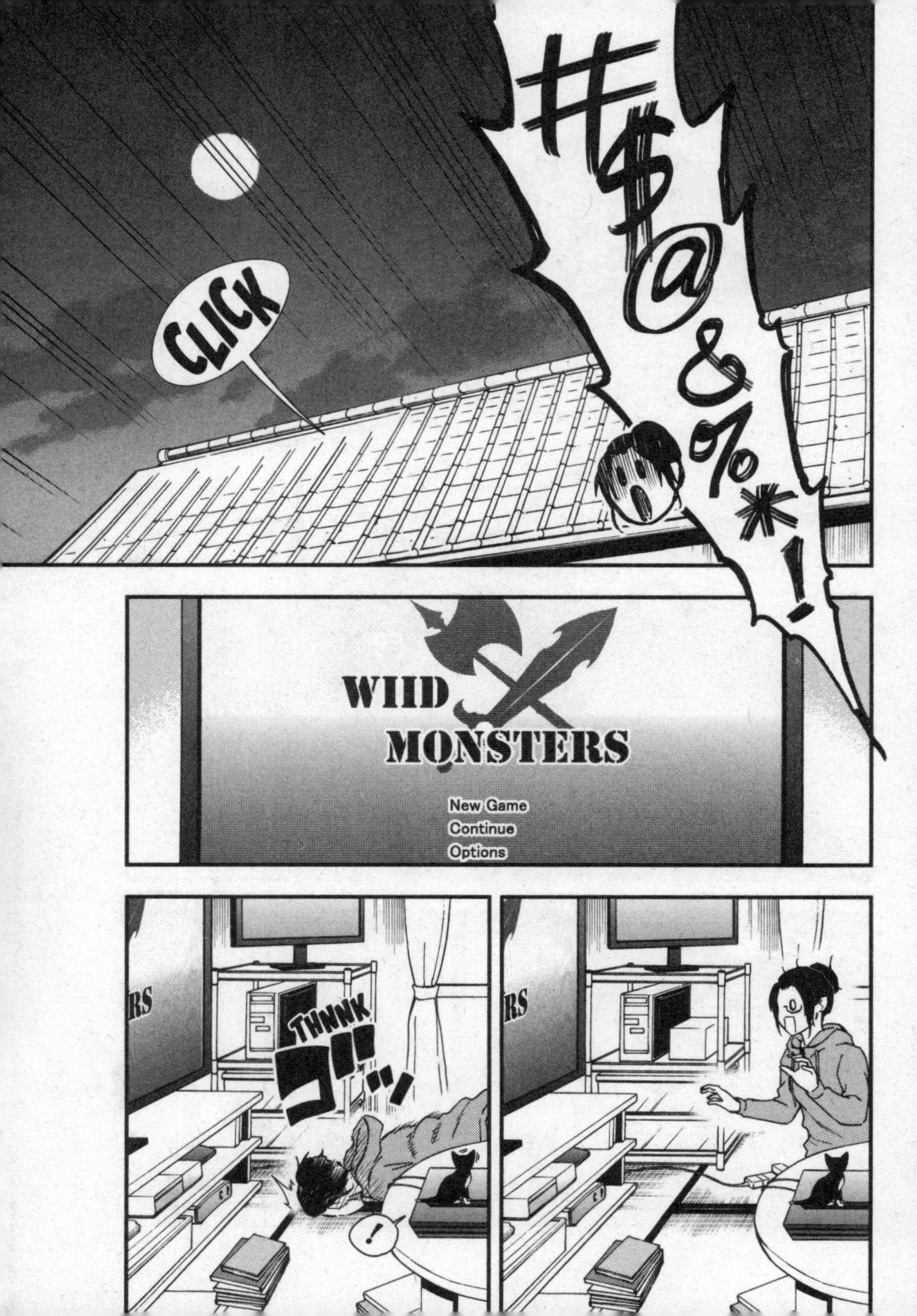
CLICK
#$@&%*!
WIID
MONSTERS
New Game
Continue
Options
THNNK
!

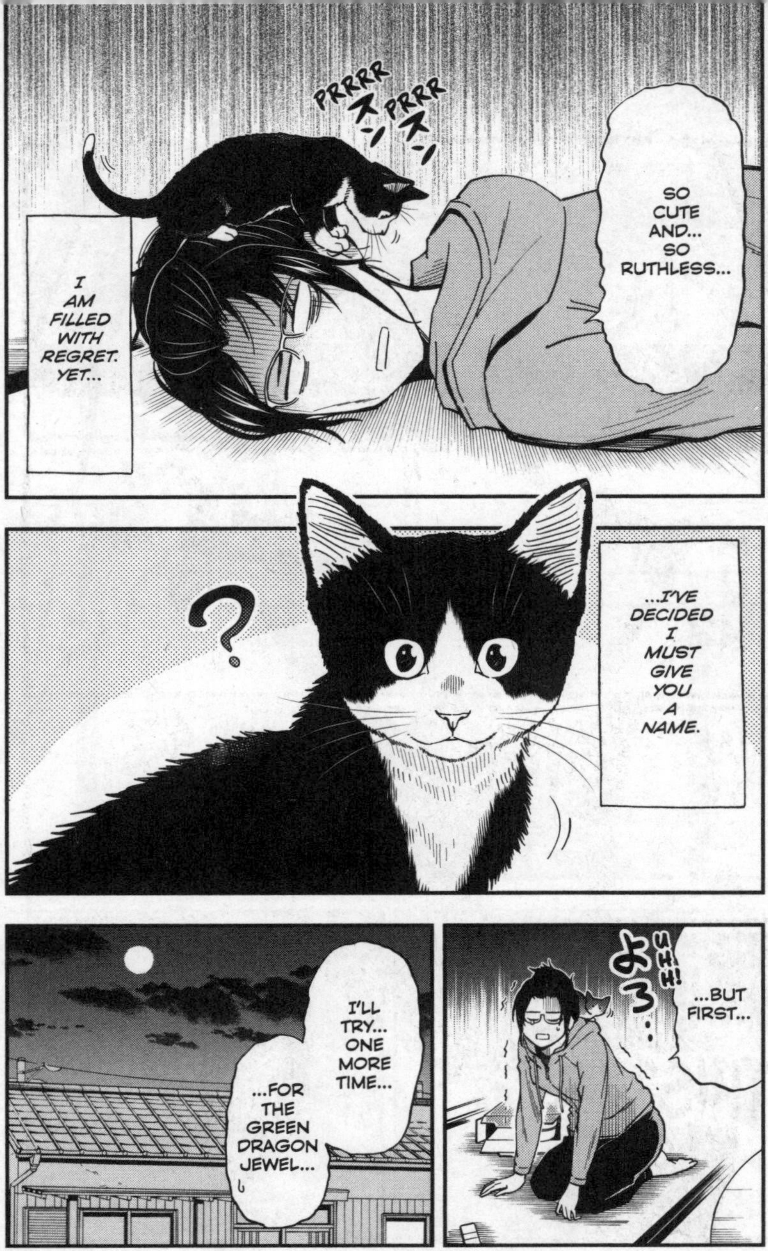
SO CUTE AND... SO RUTHLESS...
PRRRR PRRR
I AM FILLED WITH REGRET. YET...
...I'VE DECIDED I MUST GIVE YOU A NAME.
?
...BUT FIRST...
UHH!
よろ
I'LL TRY... ONE MORE TIME...
...FOR THE GREEN DRAGON JEWEL...

Chapter 2: Bonus Stage

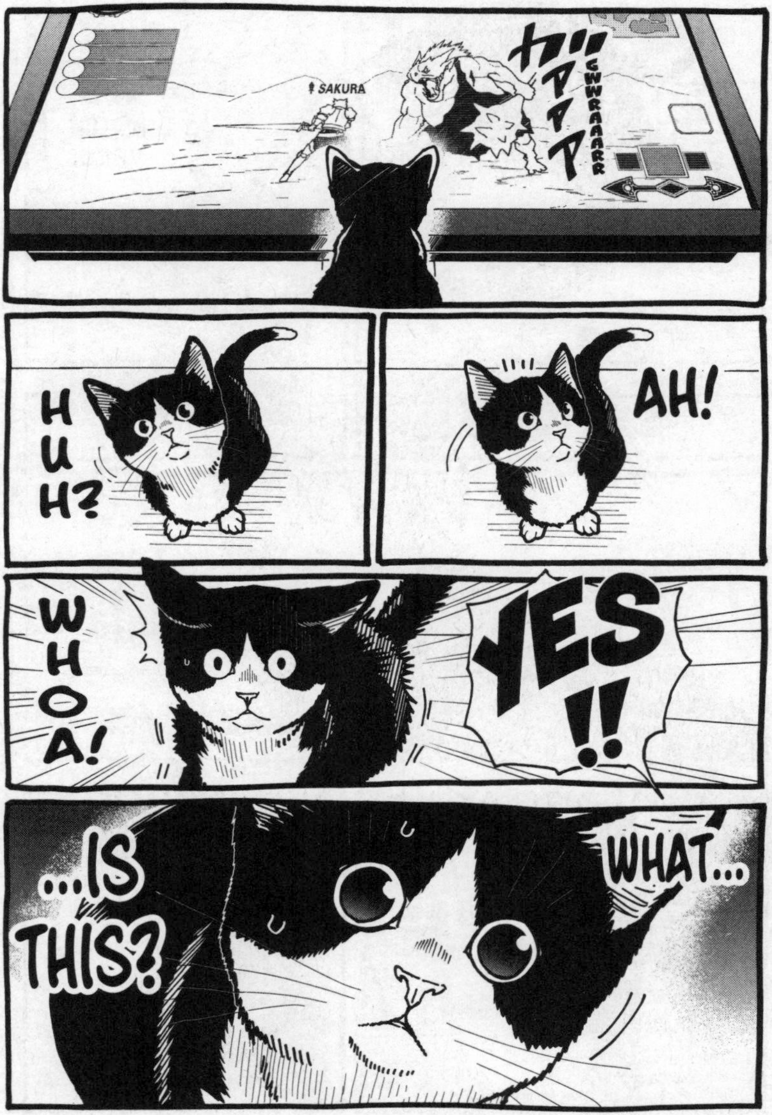

ガァァァ
GWRAAARR
SAKURA
AH!
HUH?
YES!!
WHOA!
WHAT...
...IS THIS?

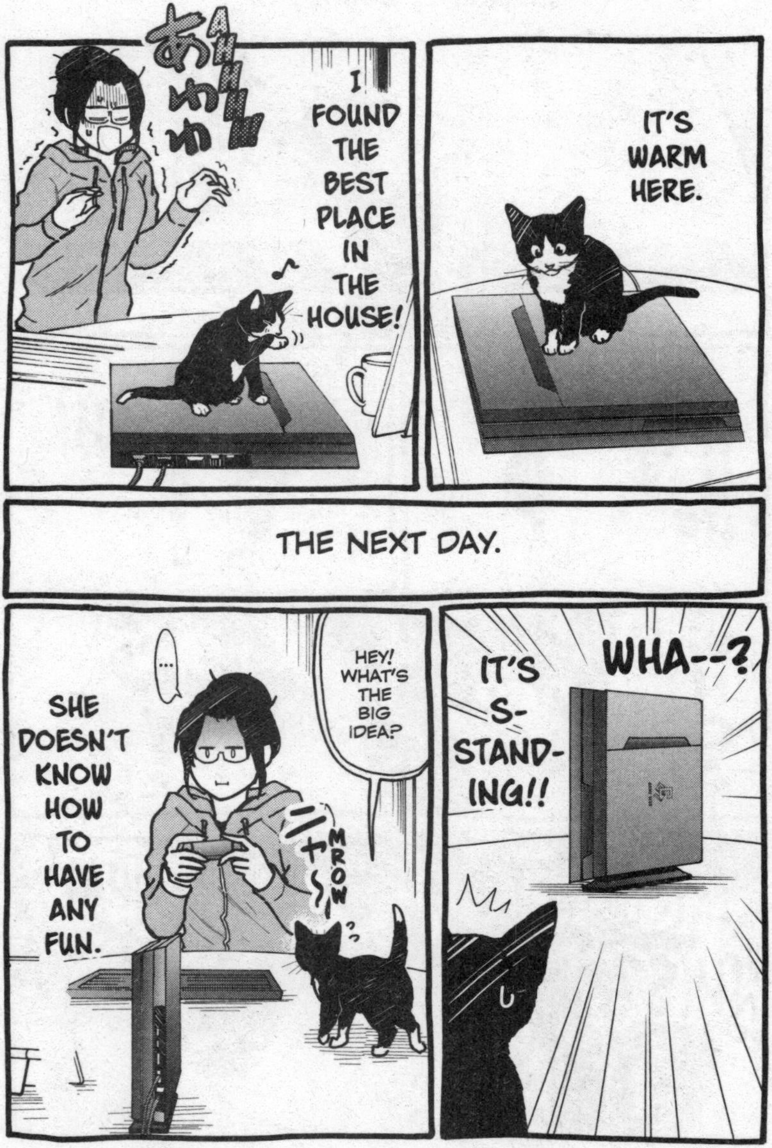
IT'S WARM HERE.
あわわわ
AHHH
I FOUND THE BEST PLACE IN THE HOUSE!
THE NEXT DAY.
WHA--?
IT'S S-STANDING!!
HEY! WHAT'S THE BIG IDEA?
...
SHE DOESN'T KNOW HOW TO HAVE ANY FUN.
ニャ~
MROW

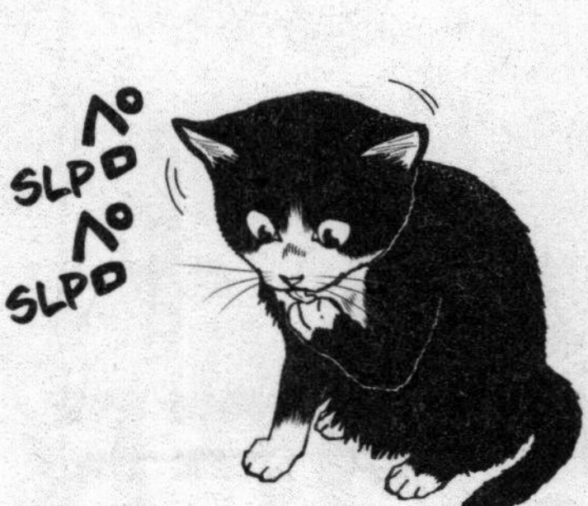
SLPP SLPP

CAT ✚
GAMER

Chapter 3: Male/Female Panic

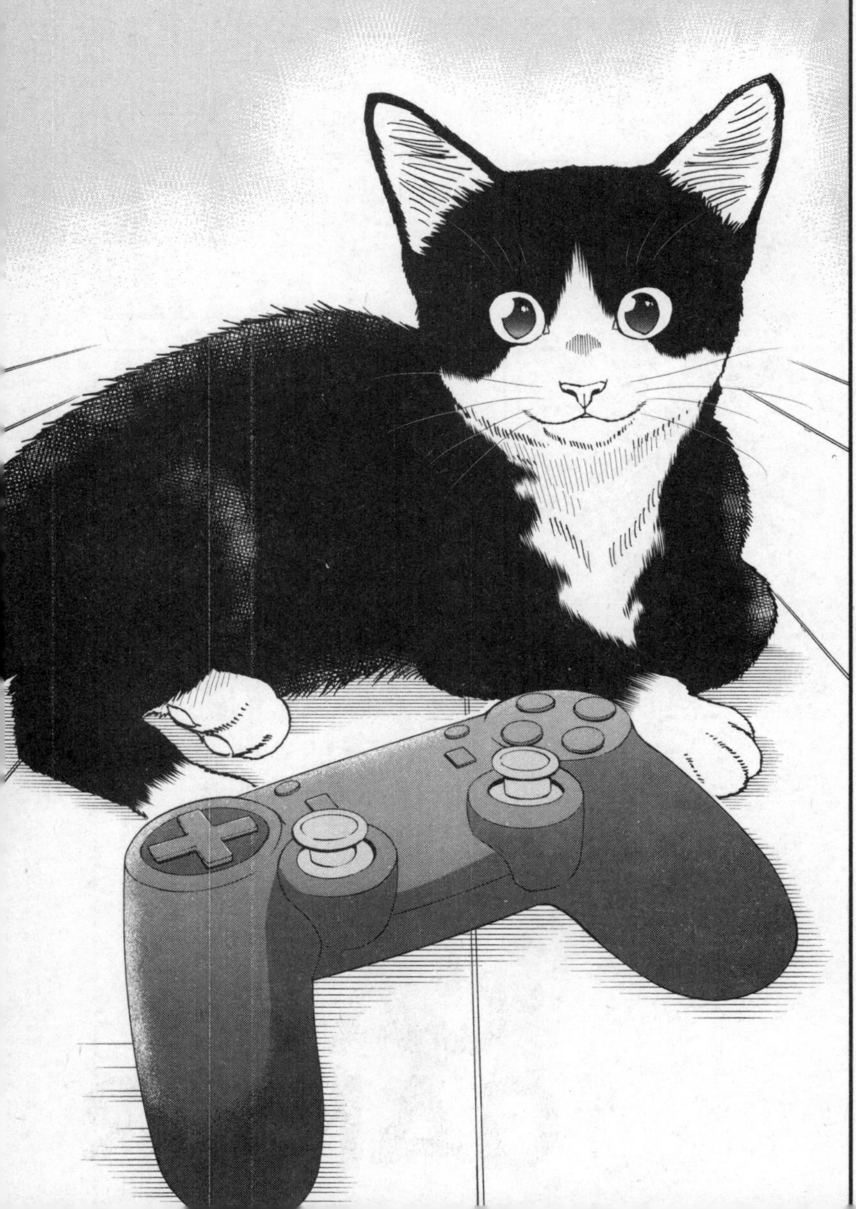

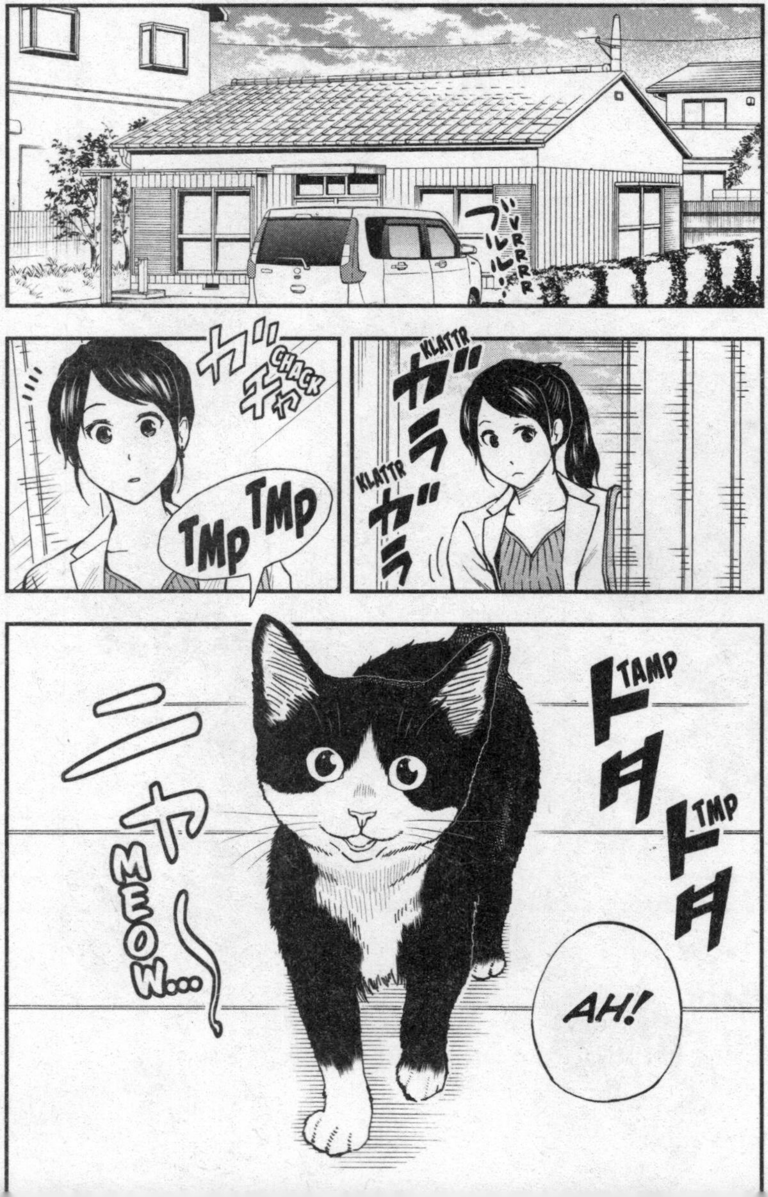
ブルル…
VRRRR
ガラガラ
KLATTR KLATTR
ガチャ
CHACK
TMp TMp
トタトタ
TAMP TMP
ニャ～
MEOW…
AH!

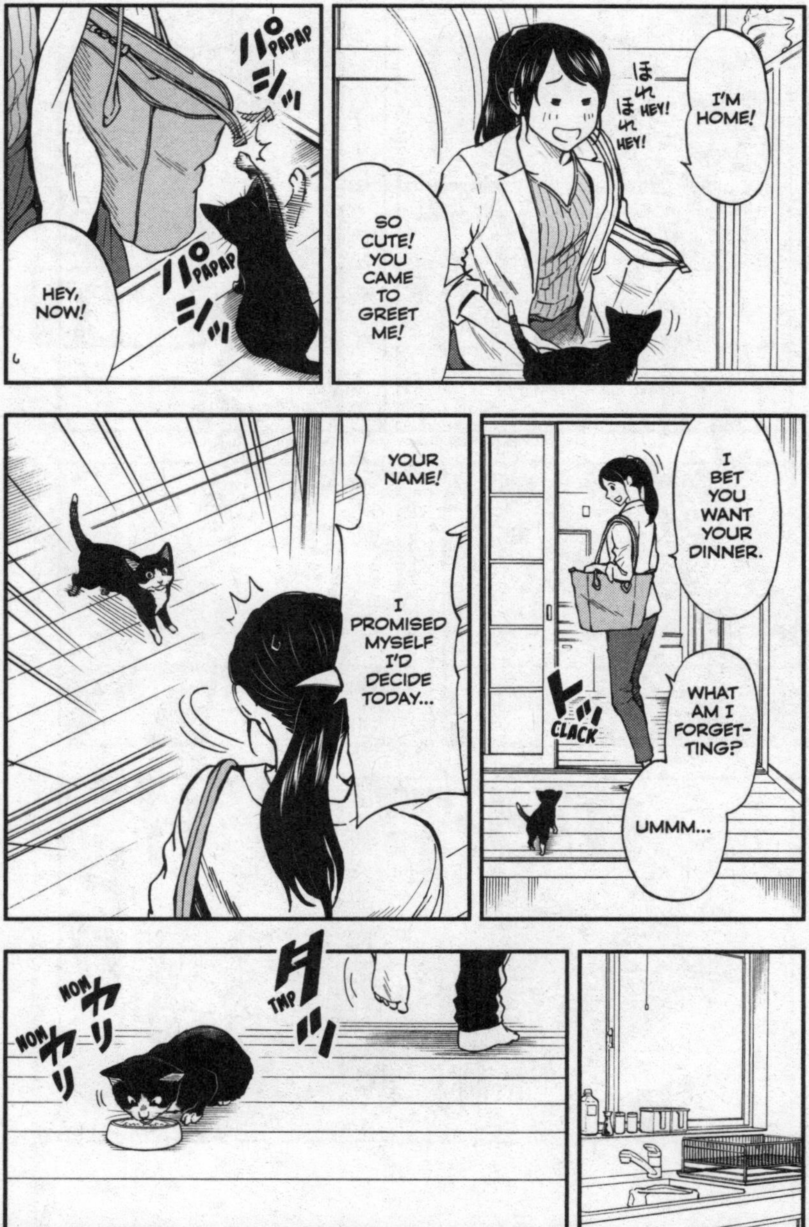
I'M HOME!
ほれ HEY!
ほれ HEY!
SO CUTE! YOU CAME TO GREET ME!
パ PAPAP シッ
パ PAPAP シッ
HEY, NOW!
I BET YOU WANT YOUR DINNER.
ドッ CLACK
WHAT AM I FORGET-TING?
UMMM...
YOUR NAME!
I PROMISED MYSELF I'D DECIDE TODAY...
タッ TMP
カリ NOM
カリ NOM

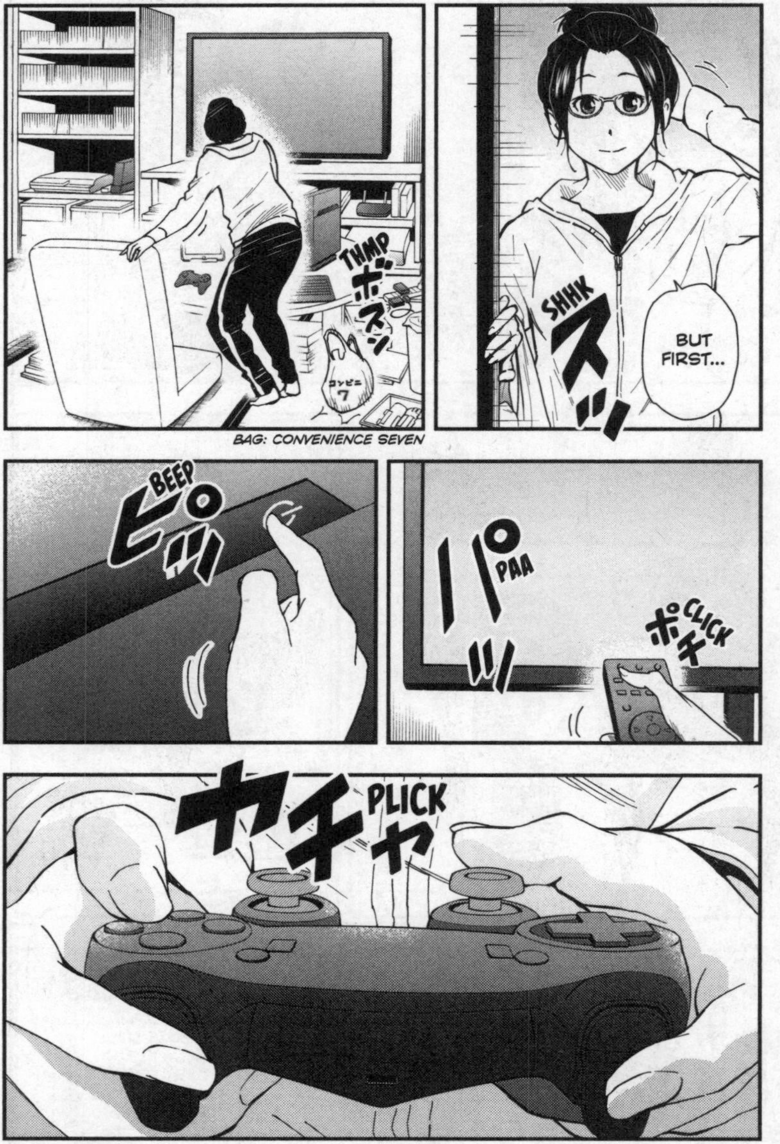
SHHK
スッ
BUT FIRST...
THMP
ボスン
コンビニ
7
BAG: CONVENIENCE SEVEN
パッ
PAA
ポチ
CLICK
BEEP
ピッ
カチャ
PLICK

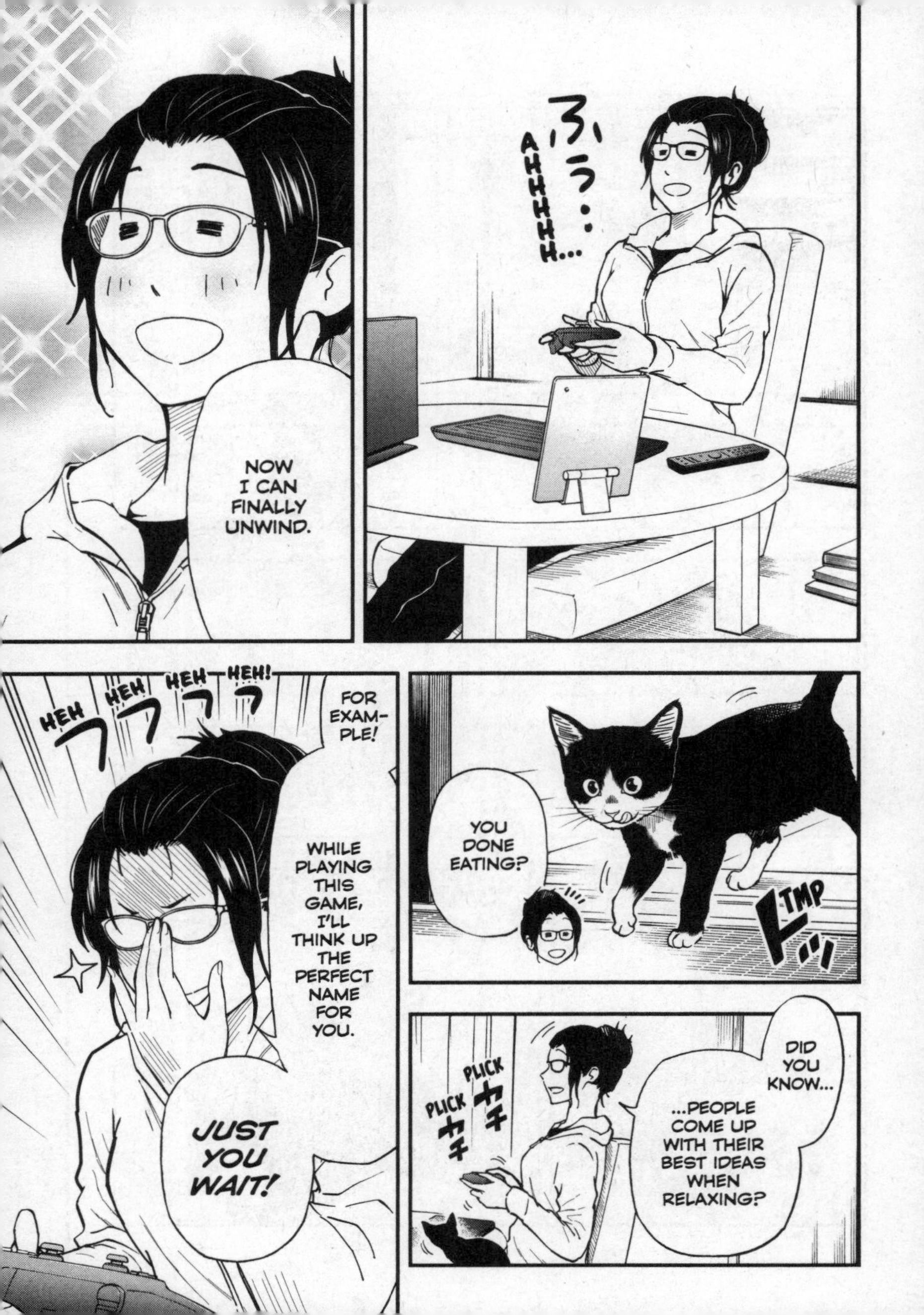

ふう・・
AHHHHHH...
NOW I CAN FINALLY UNWIND.
YOU DONE EATING?
TMP
PLICK
PLICK
DID YOU KNOW...
...PEOPLE COME UP WITH THEIR BEST IDEAS WHEN RELAXING?
FOR EXAMPLE!
HEH HEH HEH-HEH!
WHILE PLAYING THIS GAME, I'LL THINK UP THE PERFECT NAME FOR YOU.
JUST YOU WAIT!

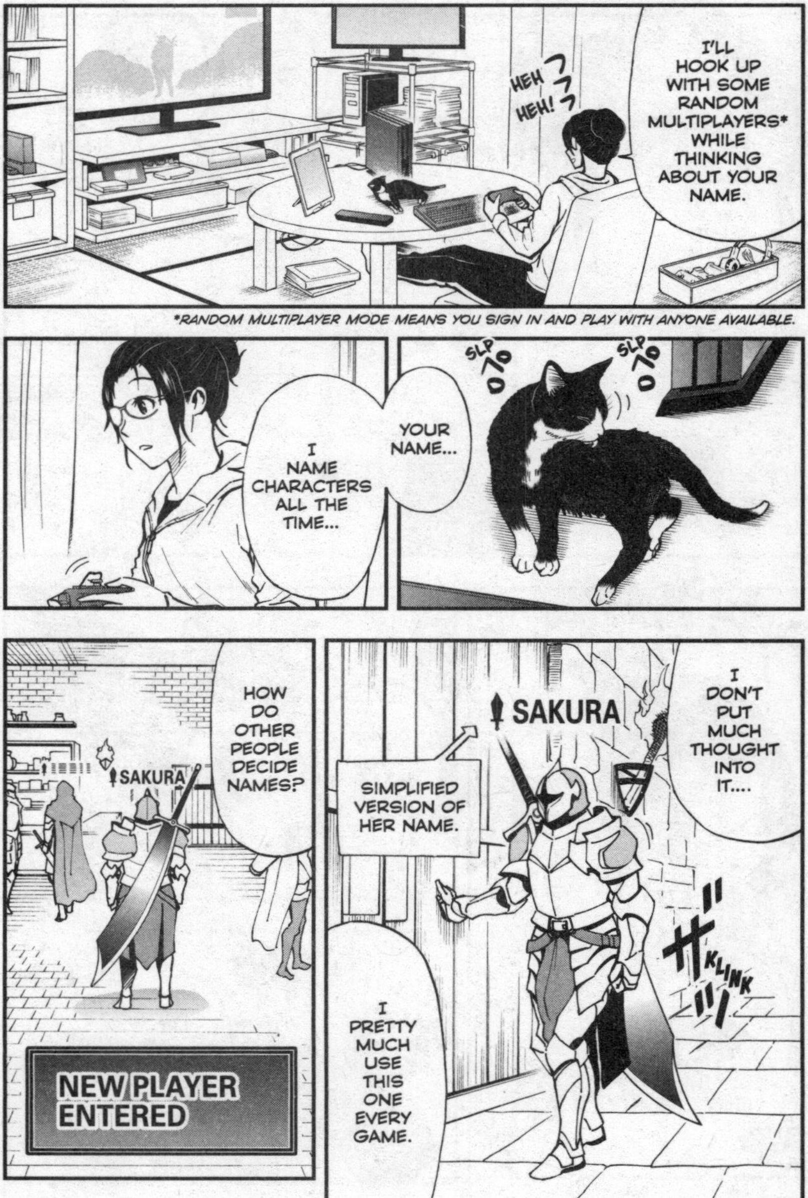
I'LL HOOK UP WITH SOME RANDOM MULTIPLAYERS* WHILE THINKING ABOUT YOUR NAME.
HEH HEH!
*RANDOM MULTIPLAYER MODE MEANS YOU SIGN IN AND PLAY WITH ANYONE AVAILABLE.
SLP SLP
YOUR NAME...
I NAME CHARACTERS ALL THE TIME...
SAKURA
I DON'T PUT MUCH THOUGHT INTO IT....
SIMPLIFIED VERSION OF HER NAME.
KLINK
I PRETTY MUCH USE THIS ONE EVERY GAME.
HOW DO OTHER PEOPLE DECIDE NAMES?
SAKURA
NEW PLAYER ENTERED

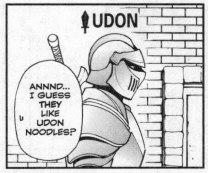

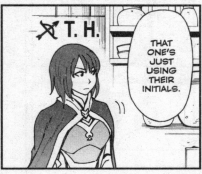

T. H.
THAT ONE'S JUST USING THEIR INITIALS.
UDON
ANNND... I GUESS THEY LIKE UDON NOODLES?
JET-BLACK FALLEN ANGEL
A KID MADE UP THAT NAME...
S-CLASS DUNG BEETLE
WHY WOULD YOU CHOOSE THAT?!
THIS ISN'T HELPING...
WHY'RE EVERYONE'S NAMES SO WEIRD?
THIS IS GOING TO BE YOUR NAME FOR THE REST OF YOUR LIFE! I HAVE TO THINK THIS THROUGH...
SOMETHING AUSPICIOUS...

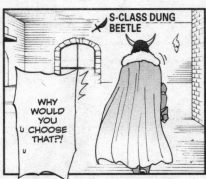

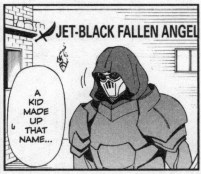

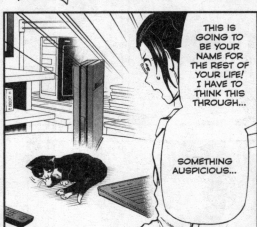

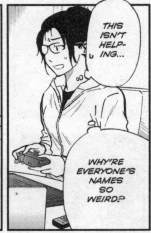

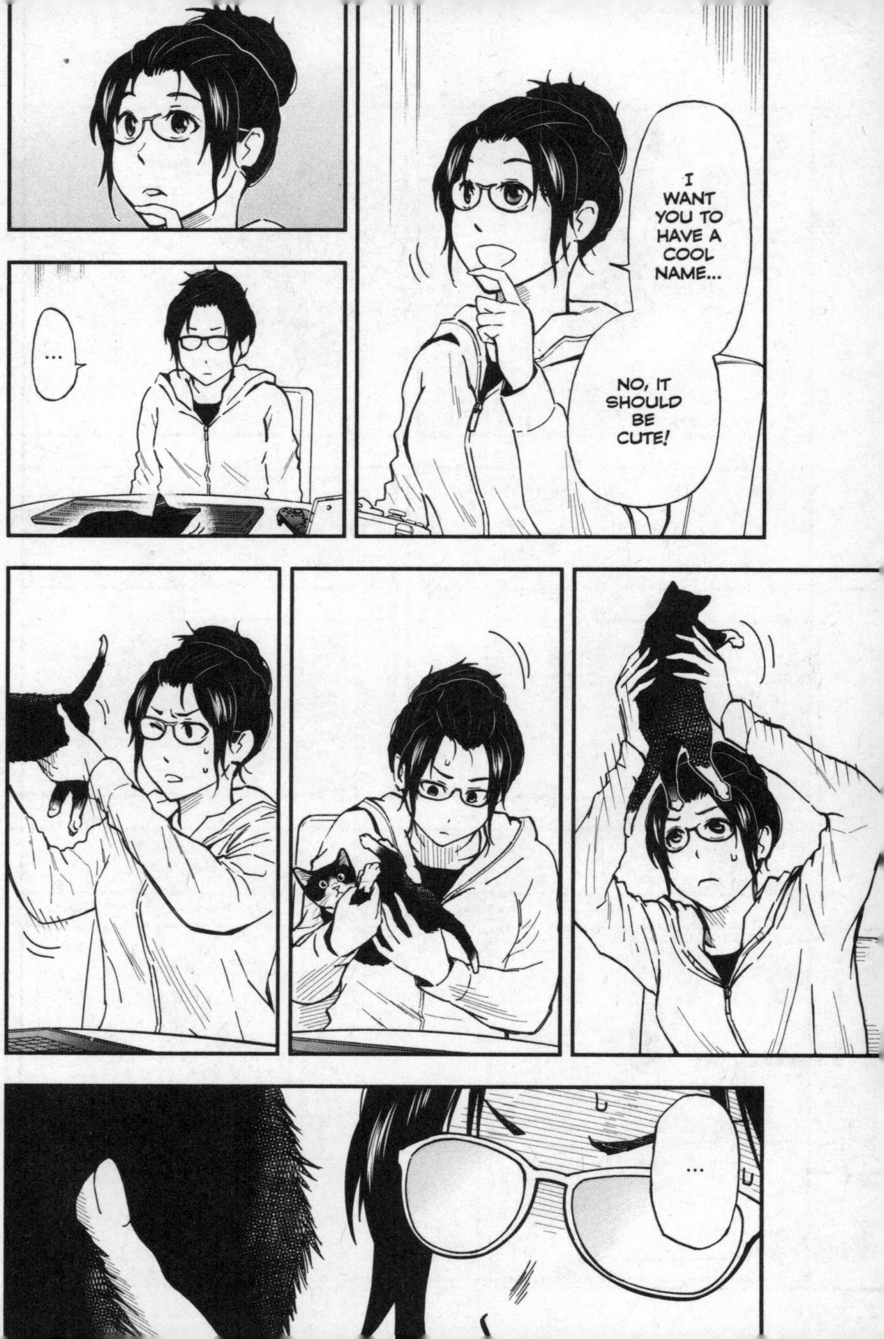
I WANT YOU TO HAVE A COOL NAME...
NO, IT SHOULD BE CUTE!
...
...

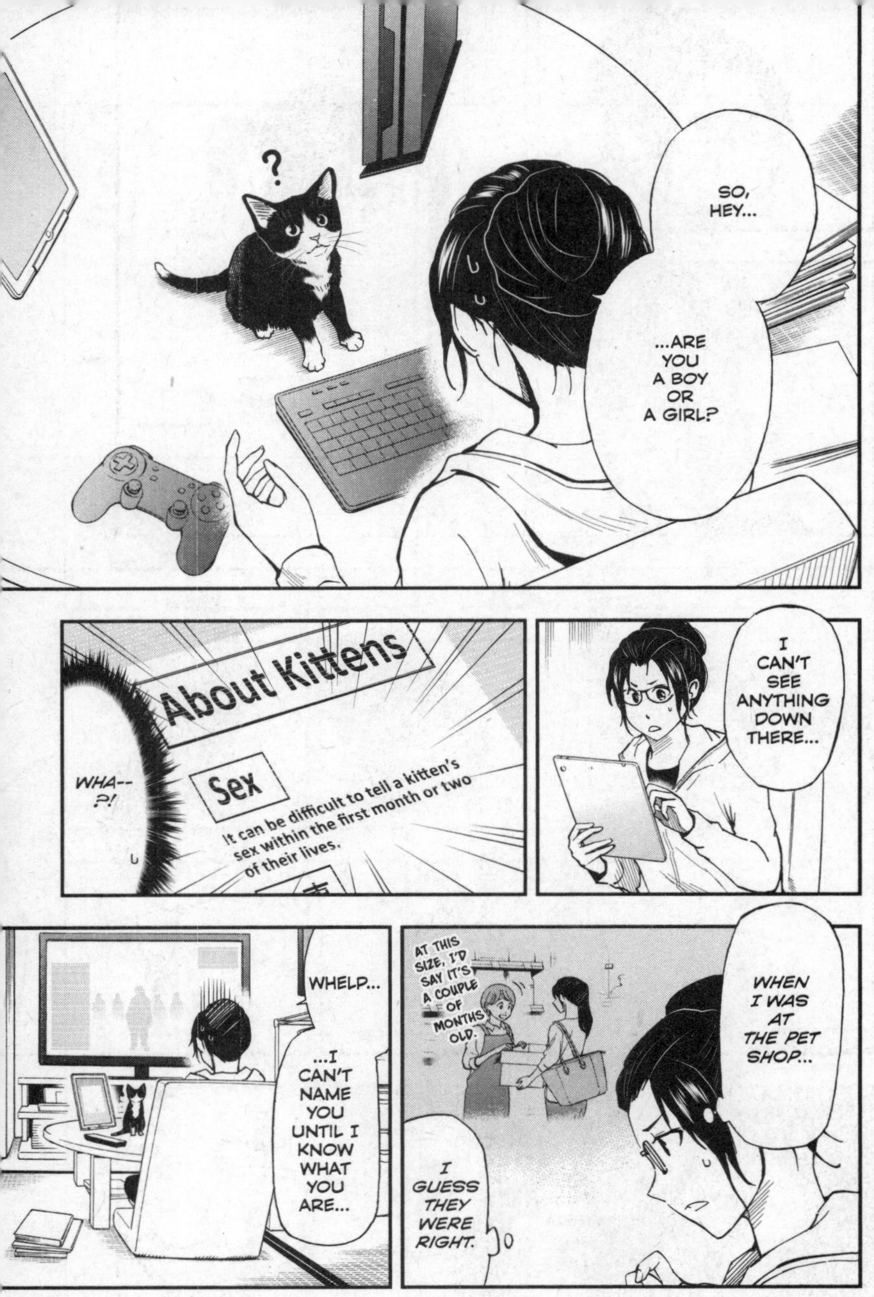
?
SO, HEY...
...ARE YOU A BOY OR A GIRL?
I CAN'T SEE ANYTHING DOWN THERE...
About Kittens
Sex
It can be difficult to tell a kitten's sex within the first month or two of their lives.
WHA-- ?!
WHEN I WAS AT THE PET SHOP...
AT THIS SIZE, I'D SAY IT'S A COUPLE OF MONTHS OLD.
I GUESS THEY WERE RIGHT.
WHELP...
...I CAN'T NAME YOU UNTIL I KNOW WHAT YOU ARE...

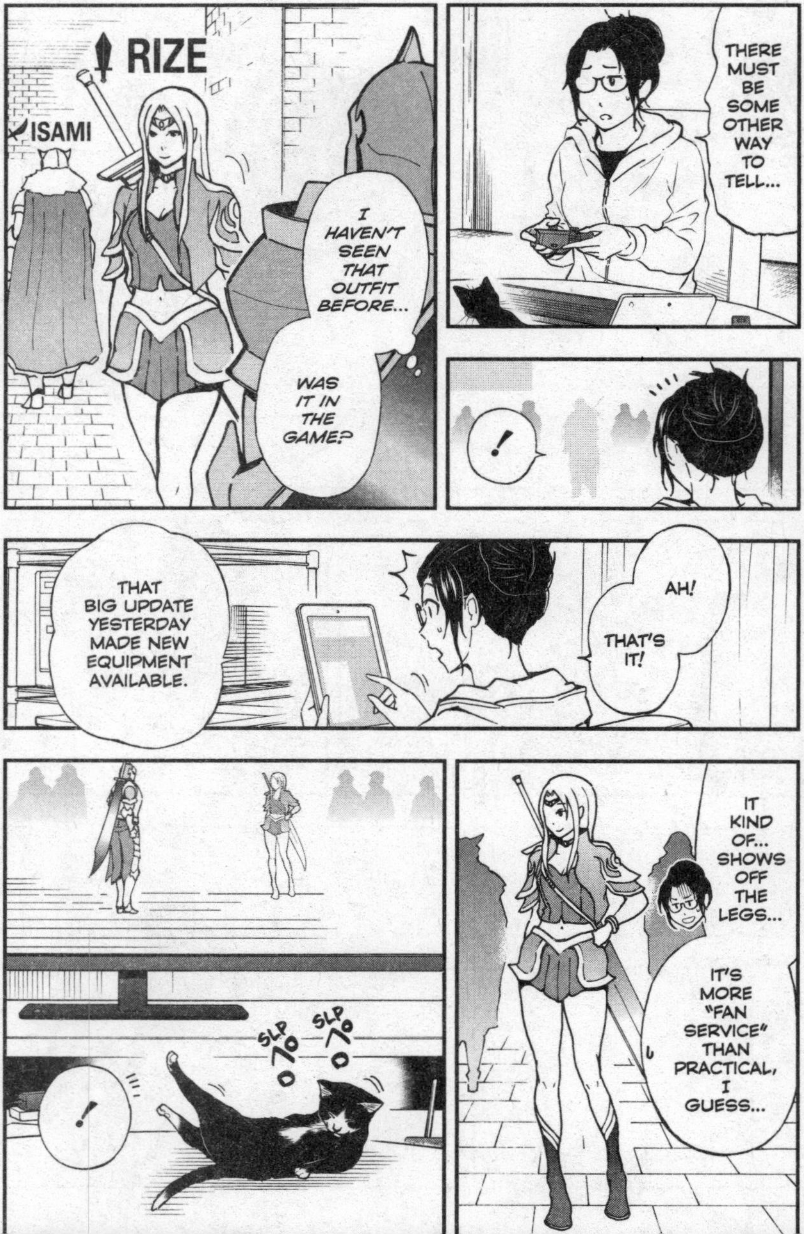
THERE MUST BE SOME OTHER WAY TO TELL...
!
RIZE
ISAMI
I HAVEN'T SEEN THAT OUTFIT BEFORE...
WAS IT IN THE GAME?
AH!
THAT'S IT!
THAT BIG UPDATE YESTERDAY MADE NEW EQUIPMENT AVAILABLE.
IT KIND OF... SHOWS OFF THE LEGS...
IT'S MORE "FAN SERVICE" THAN PRACTICAL, I GUESS...
SLP
SLP
!

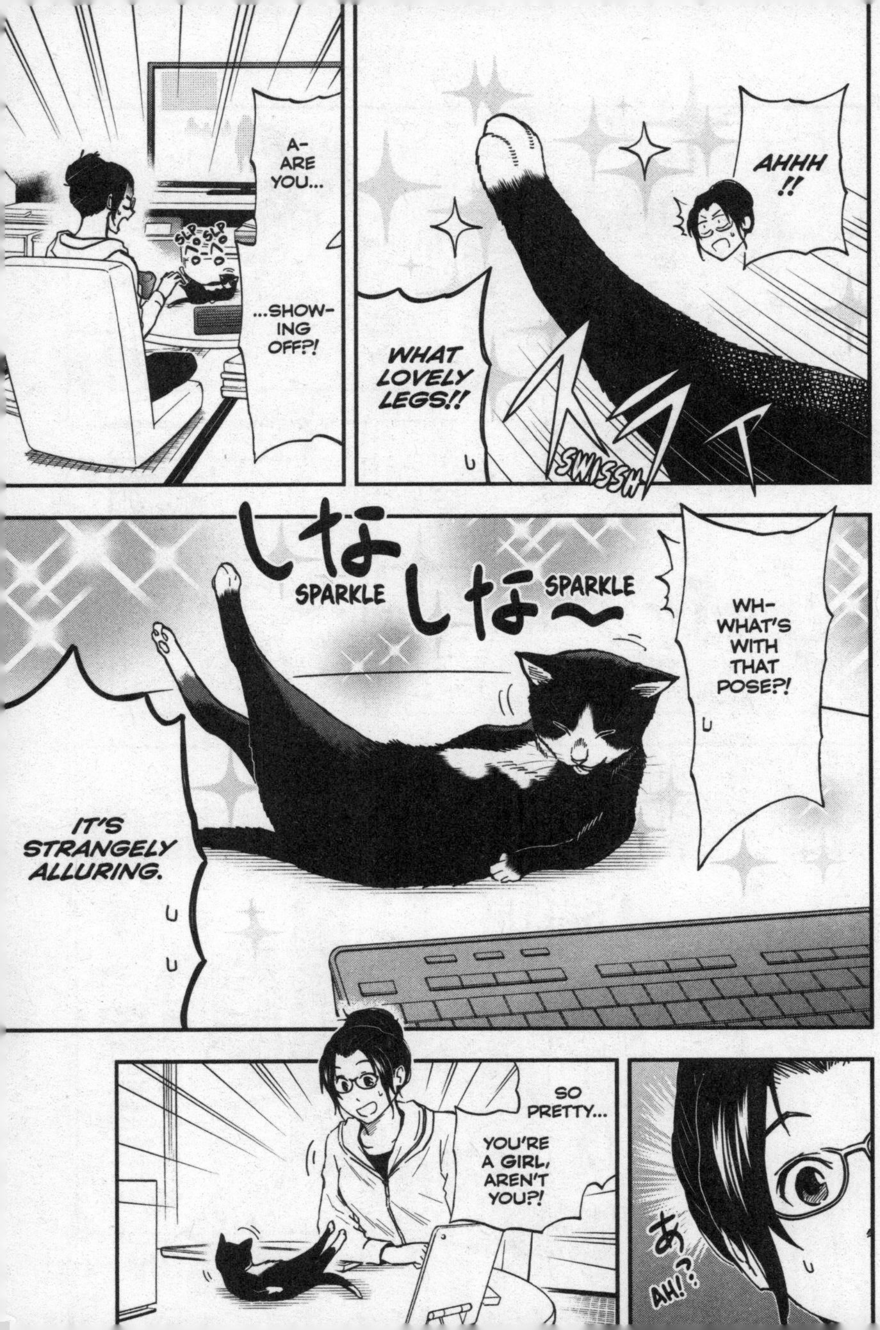
AHHH!!
WHAT LOVELY LEGS!!
SWISSH
A-ARE YOU...
...SHOWING OFF?!
WH-WHAT'S WITH THAT POSE?!
しなしな〜
SPARKLE
SPARKLE
IT'S STRANGELY ALLURING.
あっ
AH!?
SO PRETTY...
YOU'RE A GIRL, AREN'T YOU?!

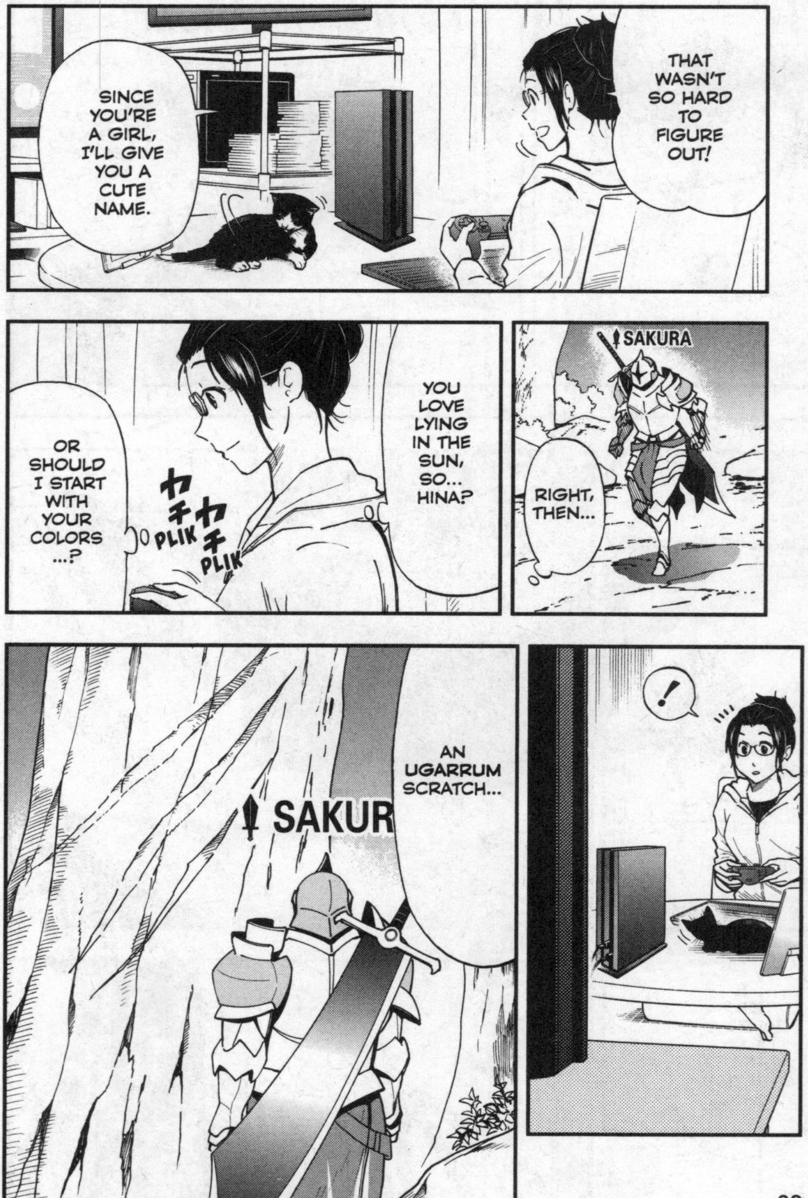
THAT WASN'T SO HARD TO FIGURE OUT!
SINCE YOU'RE A GIRL, I'LL GIVE YOU A CUTE NAME.
SAKURA
RIGHT, THEN...
YOU LOVE LYING IN THE SUN, SO... HINA?
カチ PLIK
カチ PLIK
OR SHOULD I START WITH YOUR COLORS ...?
!
AN UGARRUM SCRATCH...
SAKUR

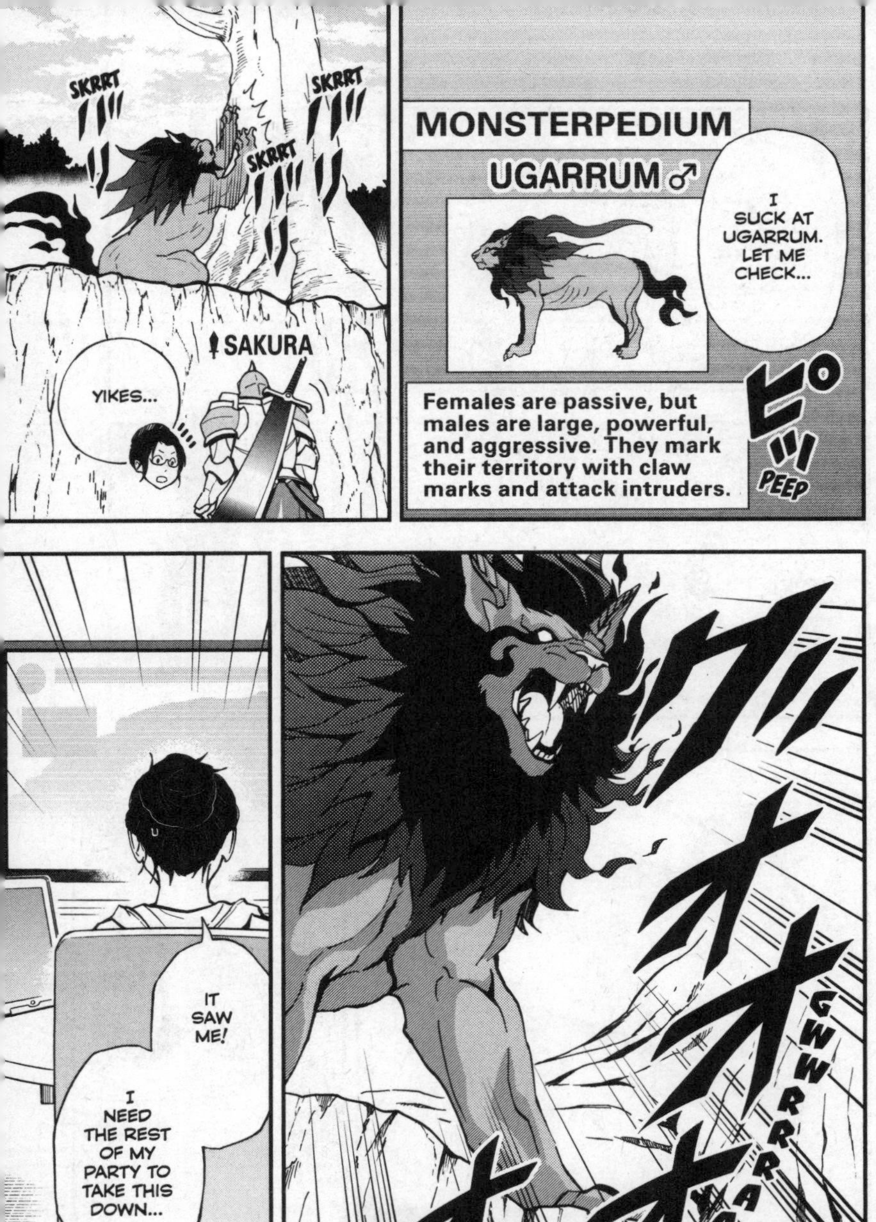
MONSTERPEDIUM
UGARRUM ♂
Females are passive, but males are large, powerful, and aggressive. They mark their territory with claw marks and attack intruders.
I SUCK AT UGARRUM. LET ME CHECK...
PEEP
SKRRT
SKRRT
SKRRT
SAKURA
YIKES...
GWWRRRRA
YARRRR
IT SAW ME!
I NEED THE REST OF MY PARTY TO TAKE THIS DOWN...

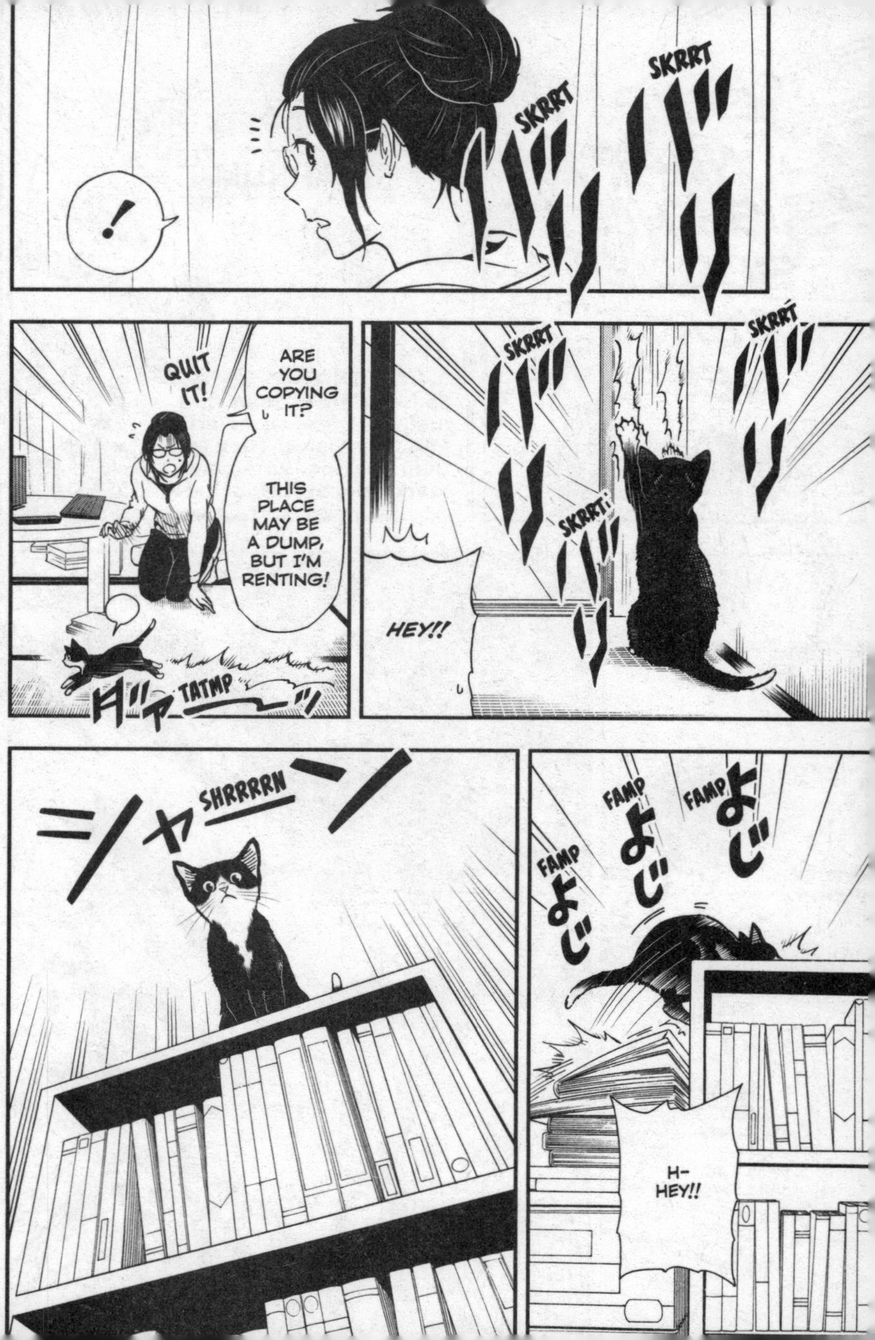
SKRRT
SKRRT
!
SKRRT
SKRRT
SKRRT
HEY!!
QUIT IT!
ARE YOU COPYING IT?
THIS PLACE MAY BE A DUMP, BUT I'M RENTING!
TATMP
FAMP
FAMP
FAMP
H-HEY!!
SHRRRRN

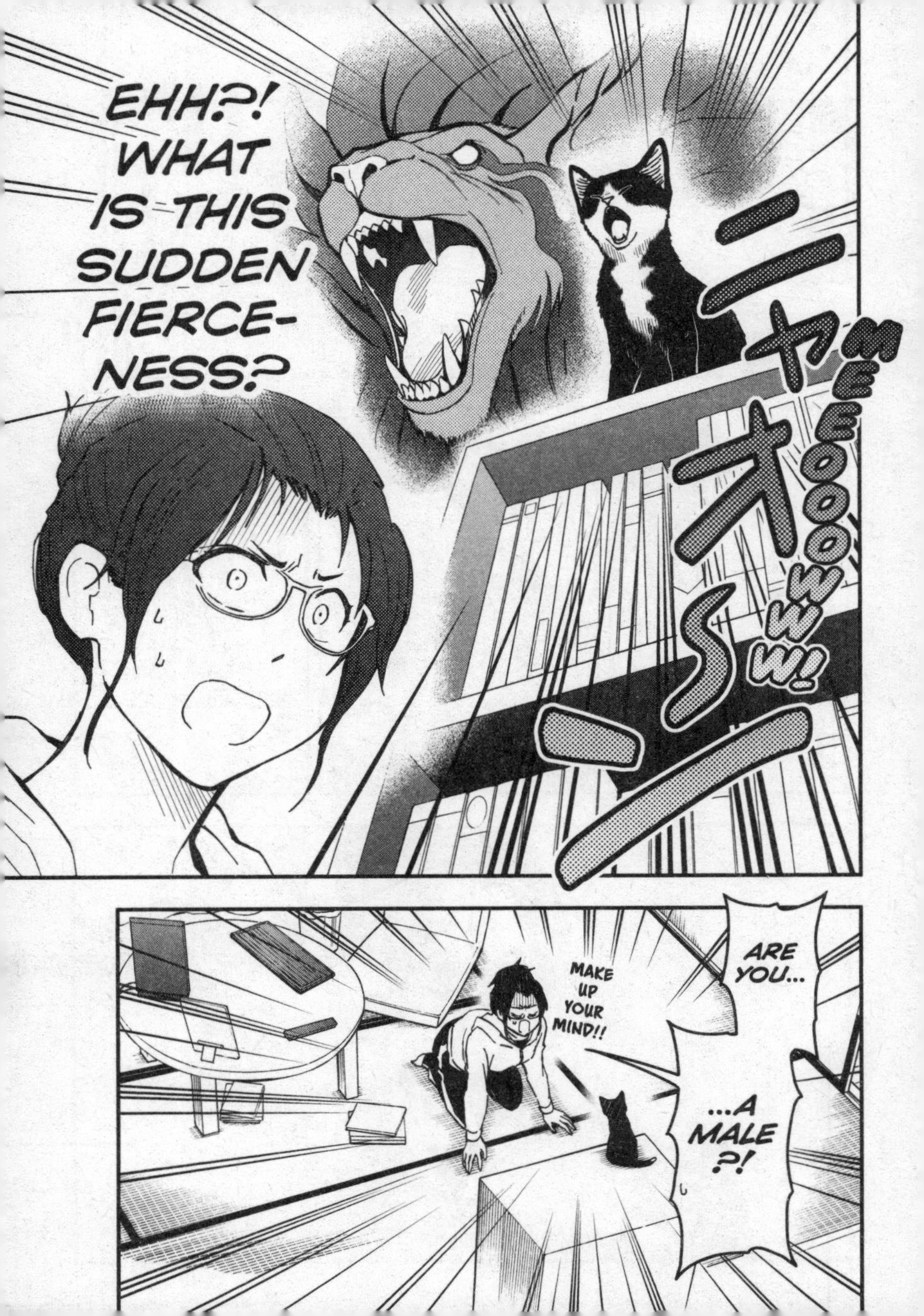

ニャーオーン
MEEOOOWWW!
EHH?! WHAT IS THIS SUDDEN FIERCE-NESS?
ARE YOU...
...A MALE?!
MAKE UP YOUR MIND!!

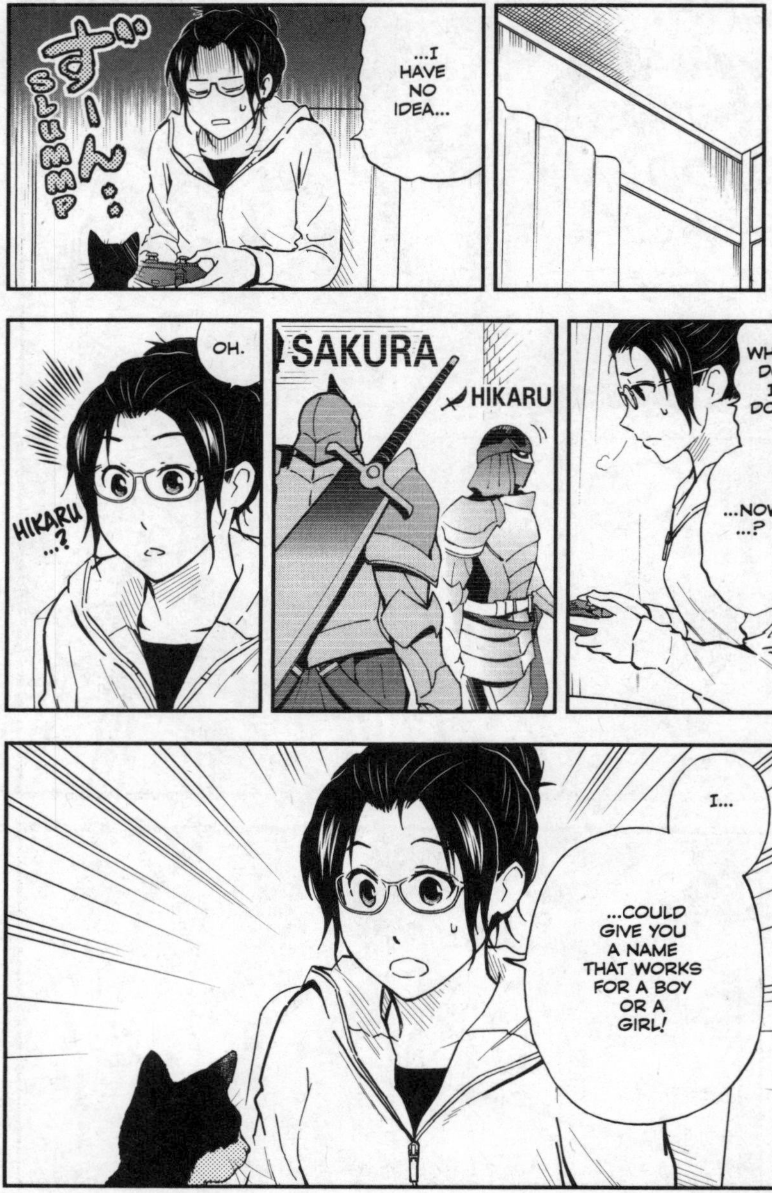
ずーん…
SLUMP
...I HAVE NO IDEA...
WHAT DO I DO...
...NOW ...?
SAKURA
HIKARU
OH.
HIKARU ...?
I...
...COULD GIVE YOU A NAME THAT WORKS FOR A BOY OR A GIRL!

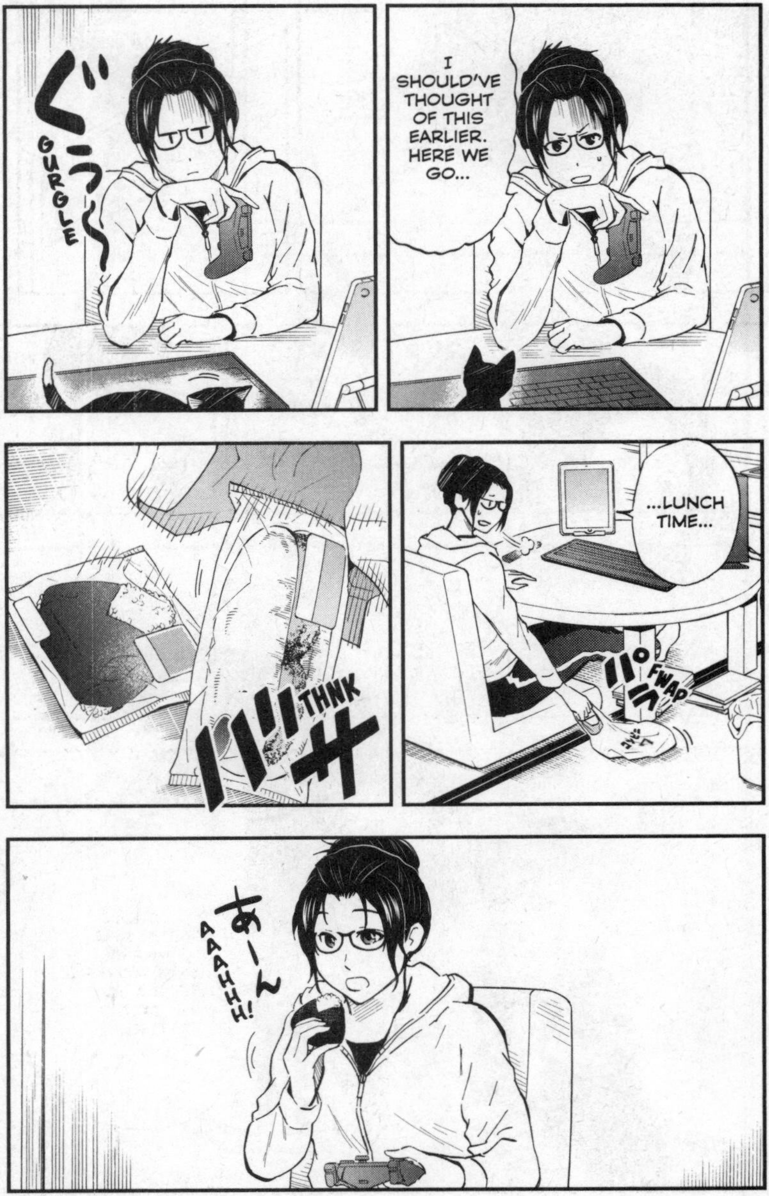
I SHOULD'VE THOUGHT OF THIS EARLIER. HERE WE GO...
GURGLE
...LUNCH TIME...
FWAP
THNK
あ～ん
AAAHHH!

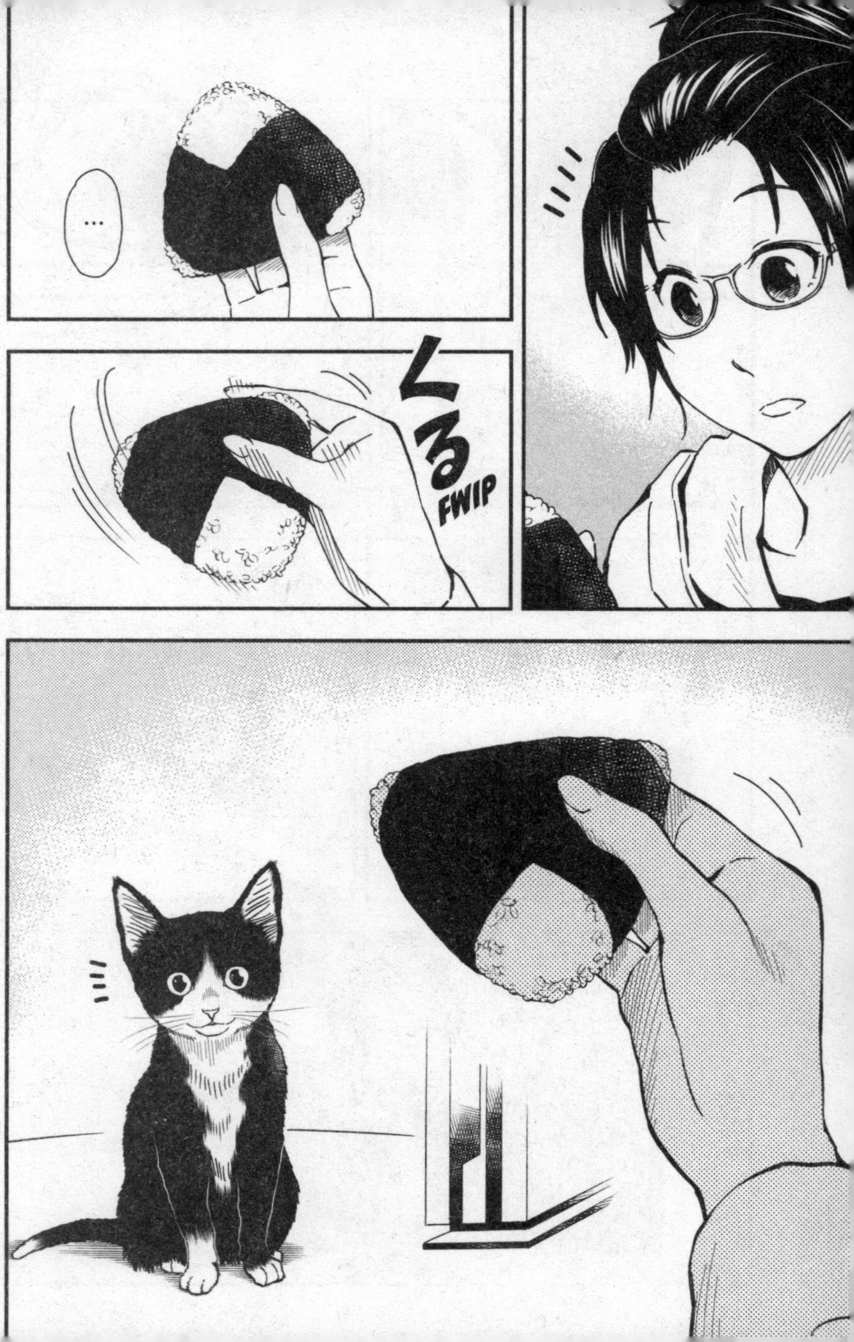
...
くる
FWIP

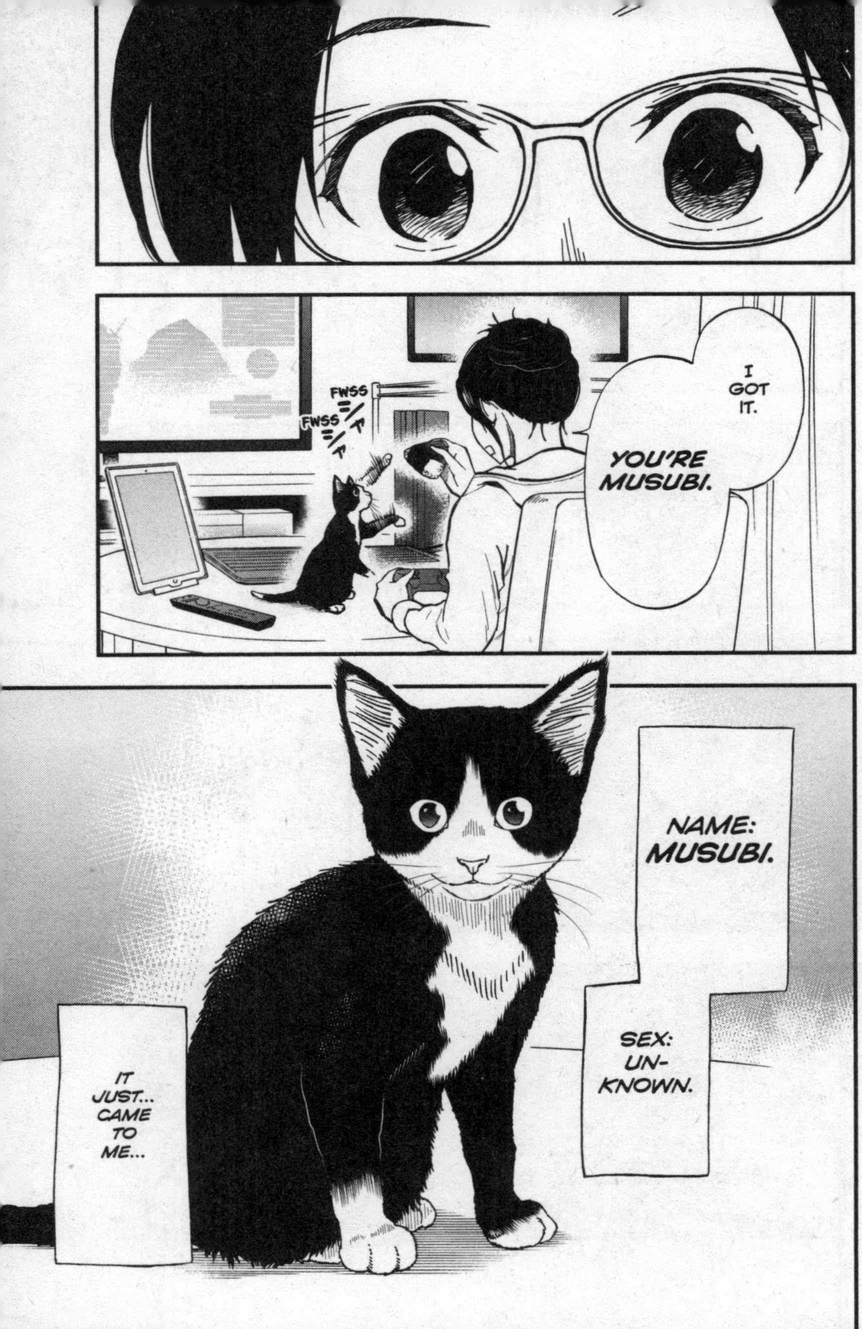
I GOT IT. YOU'RE MUSUBI.
FWSS
FWSS
NAME: MUSUBI.
SEX: UN-KNOWN.
IT JUST... CAME TO ME...

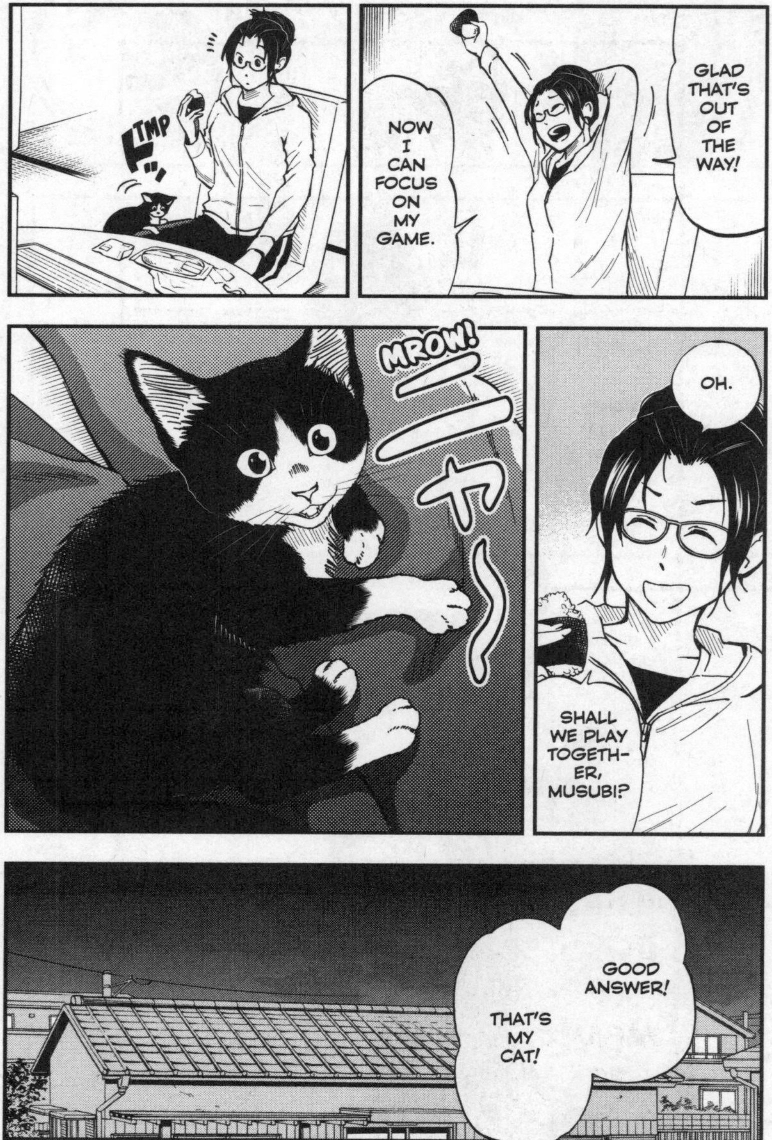
GLAD THAT'S OUT OF THE WAY!
NOW I CAN FOCUS ON MY GAME.
TMP
OH.
SHALL WE PLAY TOGETH-ER, MUSUBI?
MROW!
GOOD ANSWER!
THAT'S MY CAT!

Chapter 3: Bonus Stage

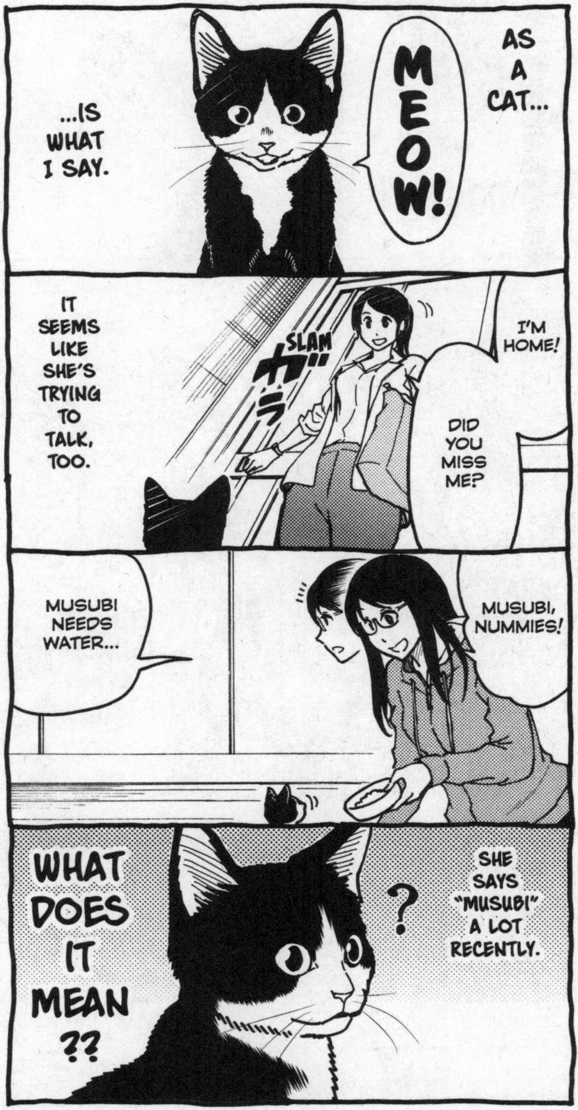
AS A CAT...
MEOW!
...IS WHAT I SAY.
I'M HOME!
DID YOU MISS ME?
SLAM
IT SEEMS LIKE SHE'S TRYING TO TALK, TOO.
MUSUBI, NUMMIES!
MUSUBI NEEDS WATER...
SHE SAYS "MUSUBI" A LOT RECENTLY.
?
WHAT DOES IT MEAN ??

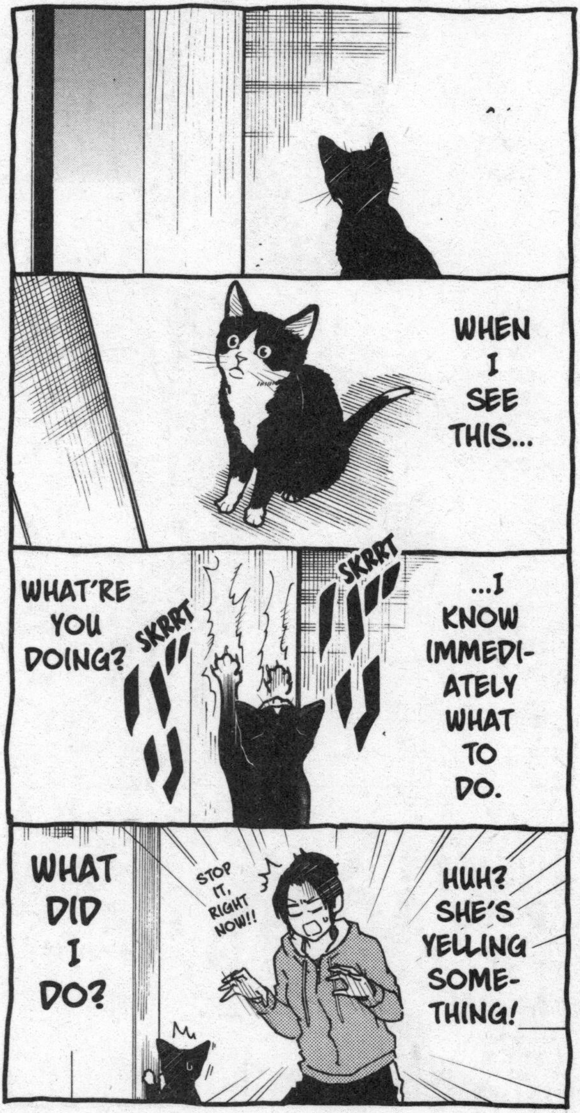
WHEN I SEE THIS...
...I KNOW IMMEDI-ATELY WHAT TO DO.
SKRRT
SKRRT
WHAT'RE YOU DOING?
HUH? SHE'S YELLING SOME-THING!
STOP IT, RIGHT NOW!!
WHAT DID I DO?

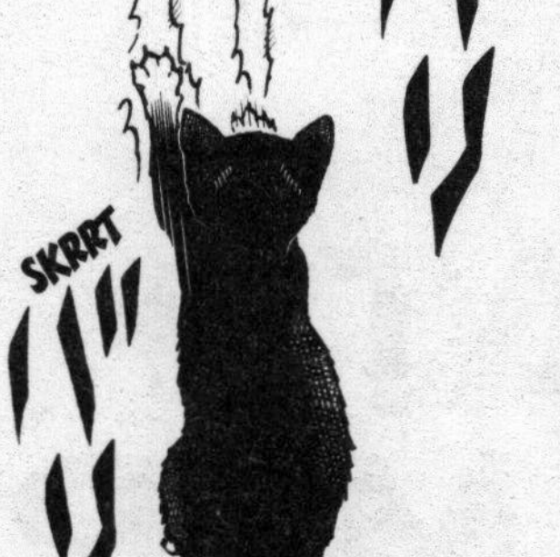
SKRRT
SKRRT

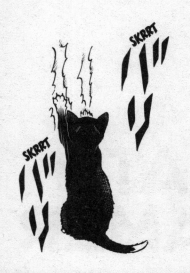

CAT +
GAMER

Chapter 4: Status Effect

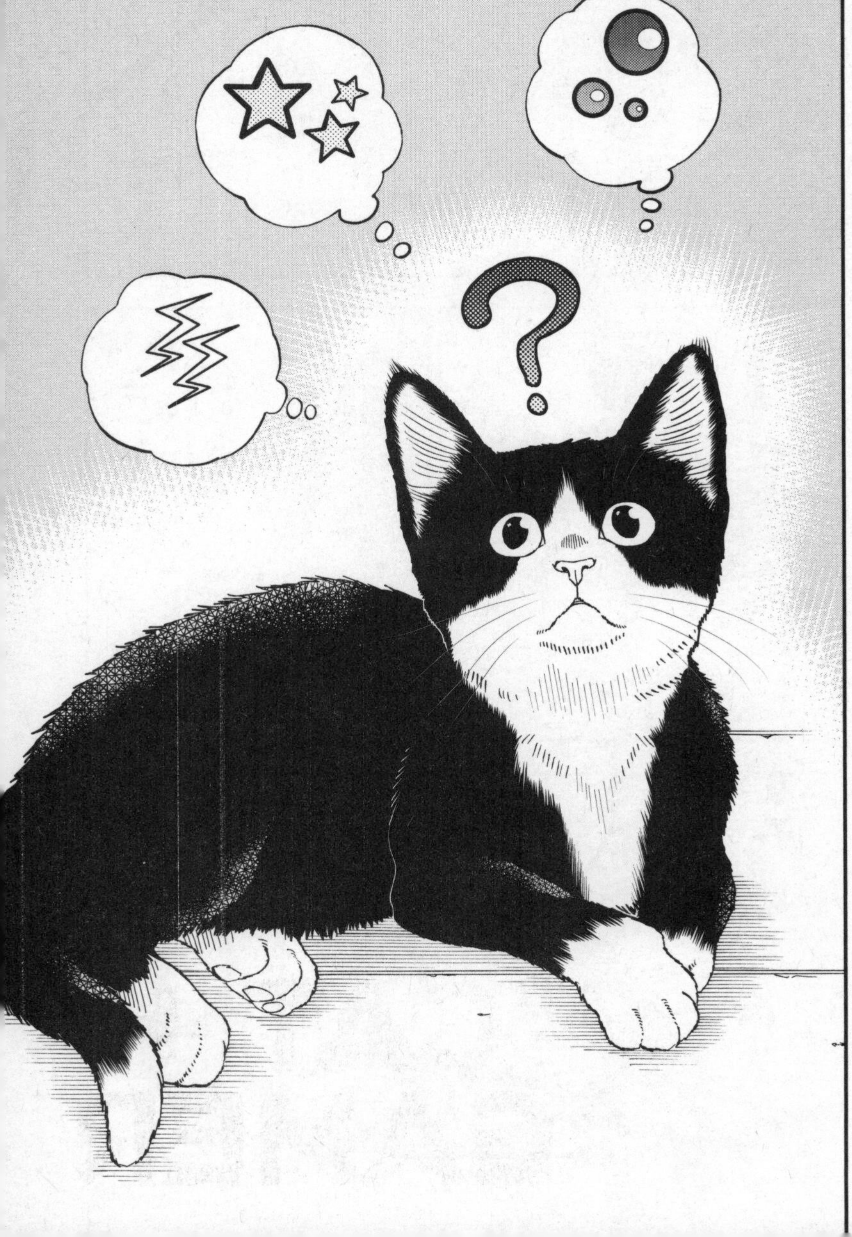

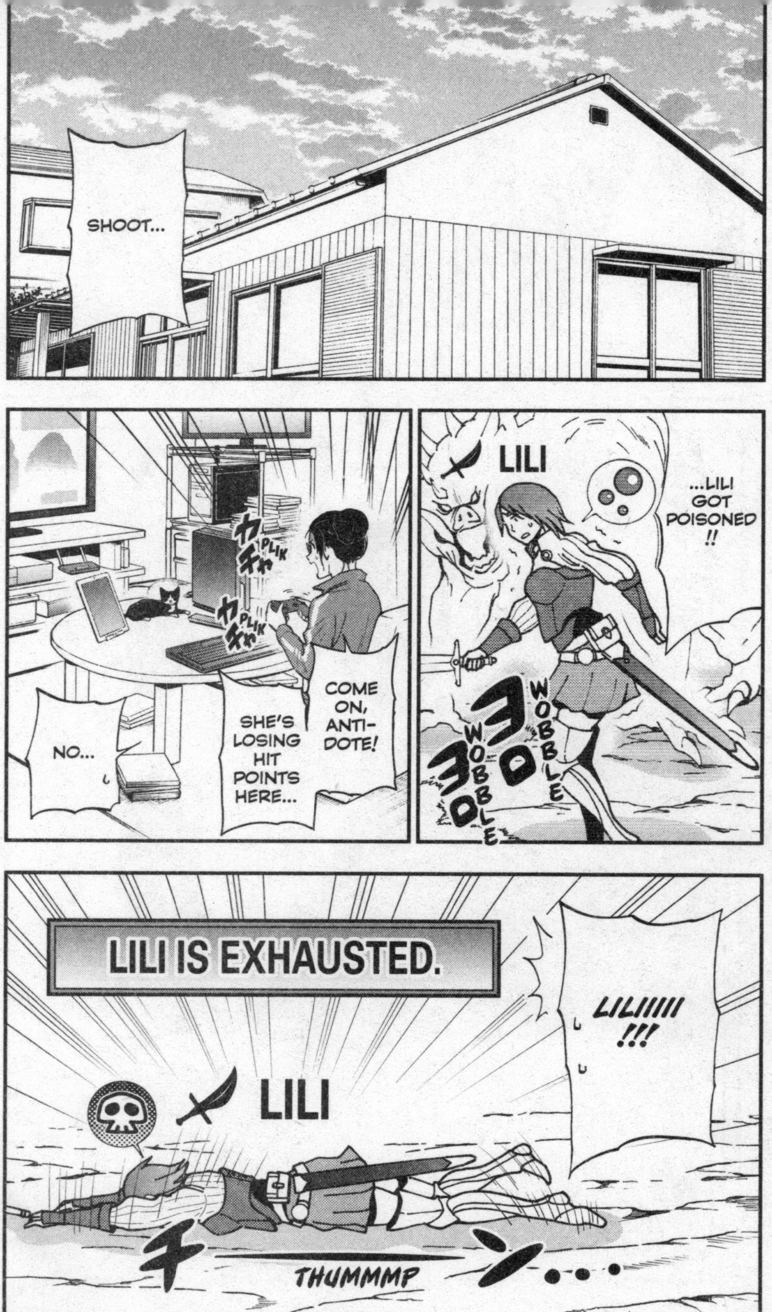
SHOOT...
LILI
...LILI GOT POISONED !!
ヨロ
WOBBLE
ヨロ
WOBBLE
COME ON, ANTI-DOTE!
SHE'S LOSING HIT POINTS HERE...
カチャ
PLIK
カチャ
PLIK
NO...
LILI IS EXHAUSTED.
LILIIIII !!!
LILI
チーン...
THUMMMP

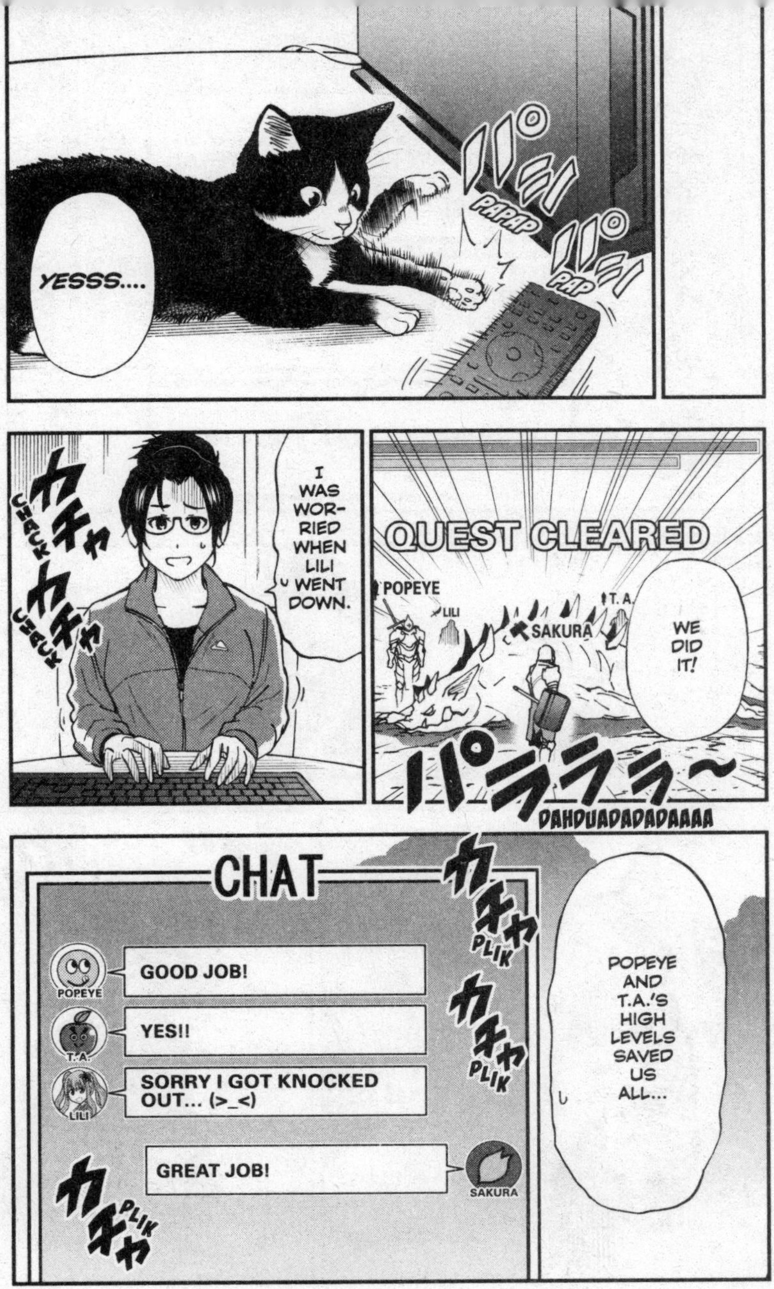
PAPAP
PAP
YESSS....
QUEST CLEARED
POPEYE
LILI
SAKURA
T.A.
WE DID IT!
パラララ~
DAHDUADADADAAAA
I WAS WOR-RIED WHEN LILI WENT DOWN.
カチャ
CHACK
カチャ
CHACK
POPEYE AND T.A.'S HIGH LEVELS SAVED US ALL...
CHAT
カチャ
PLIK
カチャ
PLIK
POPEYE
GOOD JOB!
T.A.
YES!!
LILI
SORRY I GOT KNOCKED OUT... (>_<)
SAKURA
GREAT JOB!
カチャ
PLIK

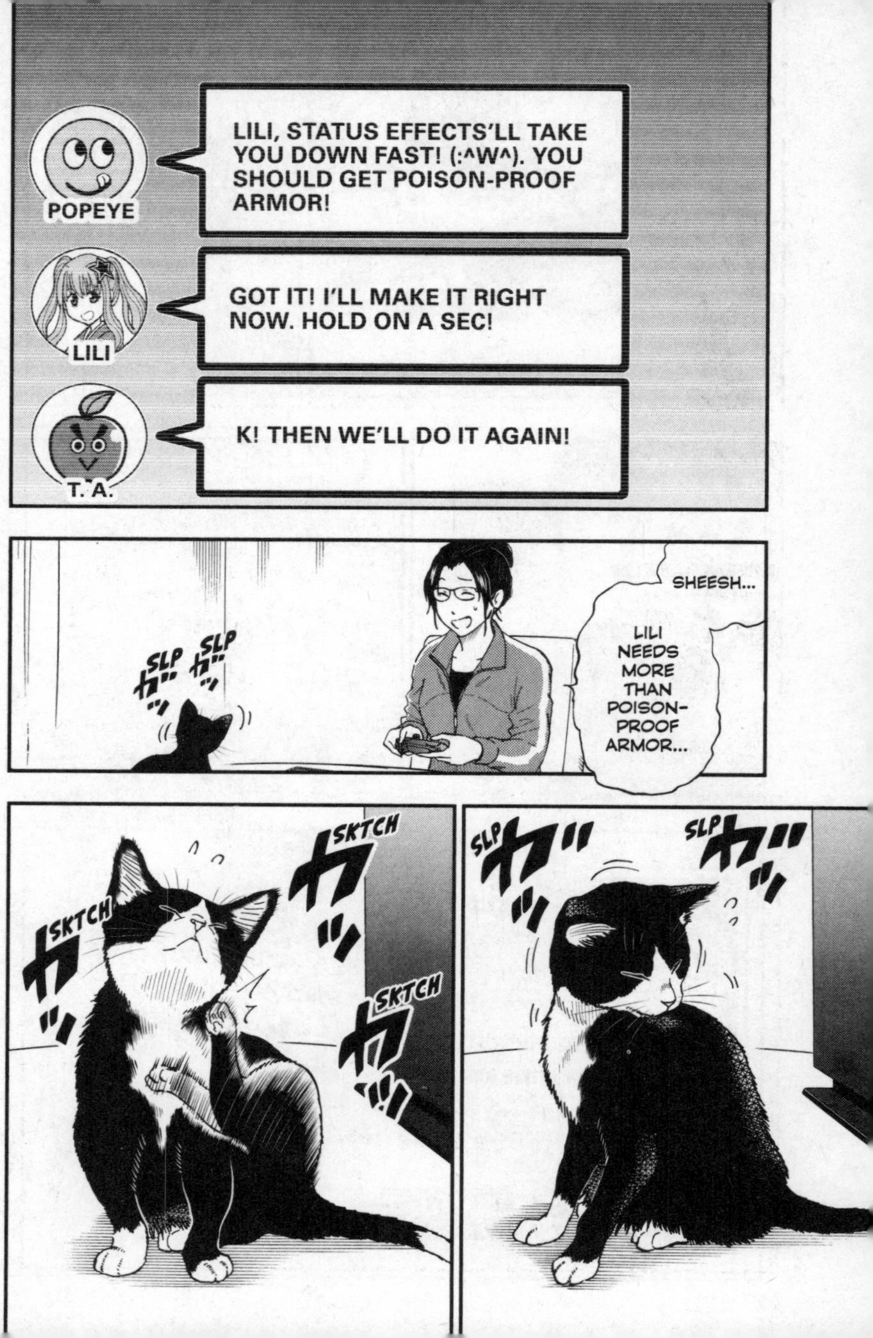
POPEYE
LILI, STATUS EFFECTS'LL TAKE YOU DOWN FAST! (:^W^). YOU SHOULD GET POISON-PROOF ARMOR!
LILI
GOT IT! I'LL MAKE IT RIGHT NOW. HOLD ON A SEC!
T. A.
K! THEN WE'LL DO IT AGAIN!
SHEESH...
LILI NEEDS MORE THAN POISON-PROOF ARMOR...
SLP
SLP
SLP
SLP
SKTCH
SKTCH
SKTCH

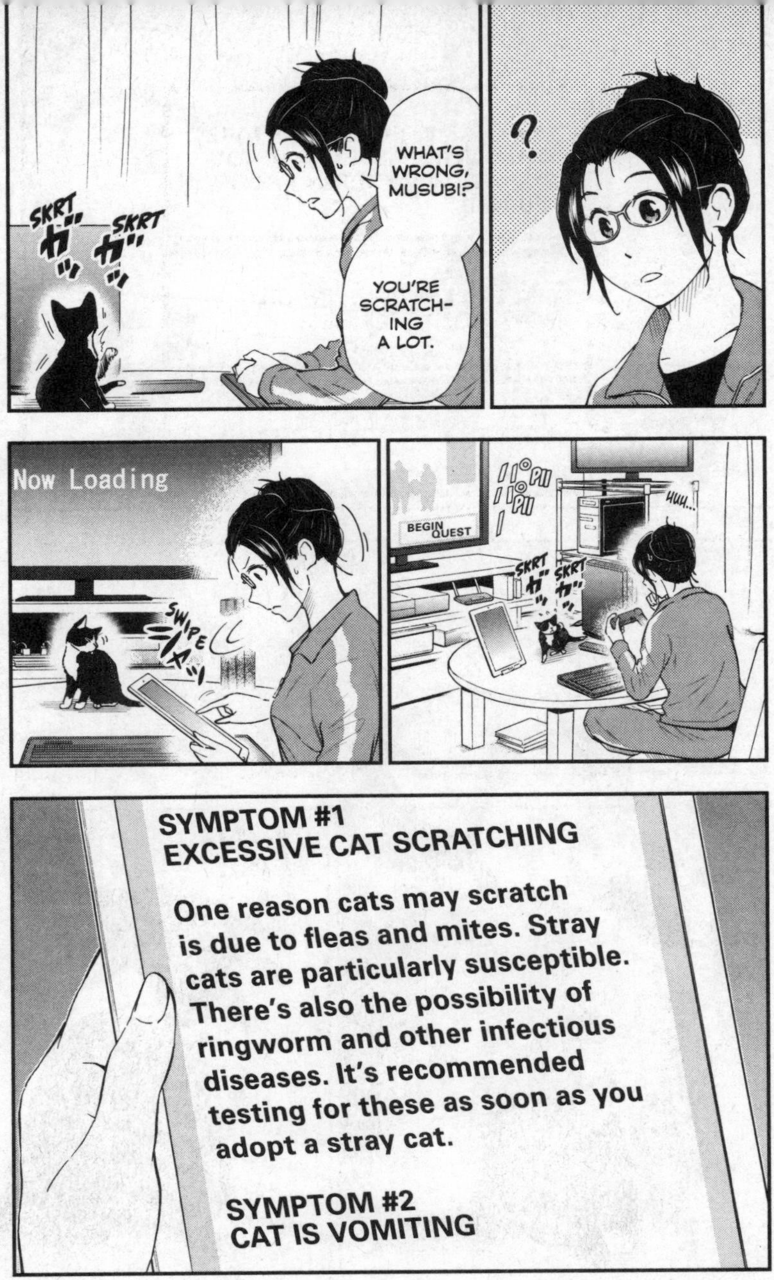
?
WHAT'S WRONG, MUSUBI?
YOU'RE SCRATCH- ING A LOT.
SKRT
SKRT
PII
PII
HUU...
BEGIN QUEST
SKRT
SKRT
Now Loading
SWIPE
SYMPTOM #1
EXCESSIVE CAT SCRATCHING
One reason cats may scratch is due to fleas and mites. Stray cats are particularly susceptible. There's also the possibility of ringworm and other infectious diseases. It's recommended testing for these as soon as you adopt a stray cat.
SYMPTOM #2
CAT IS VOMITING

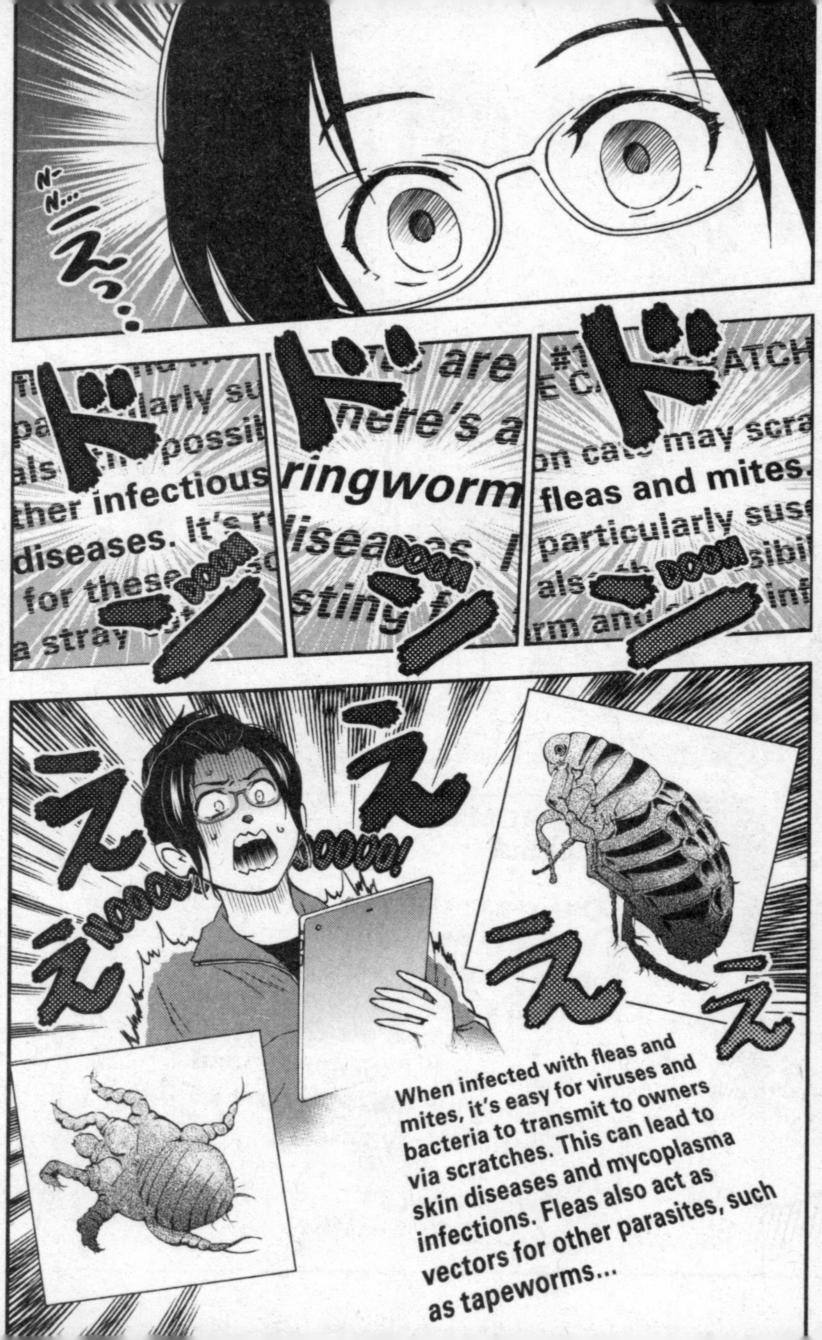
N-N...
んっ…
fleas and mites.
particularly sus
ドーン
DOOM
ringworm
ドーン
DOOM
infectious
diseases.
ドーン
DOOM
えええええ
NOOOOOOOOO!
When infected with fleas and mites, it's easy for viruses and bacteria to transmit to owners via scratches. This can lead to skin diseases and mycoplasma infections. Fleas also act as vectors for other parasites, such as tapeworms...

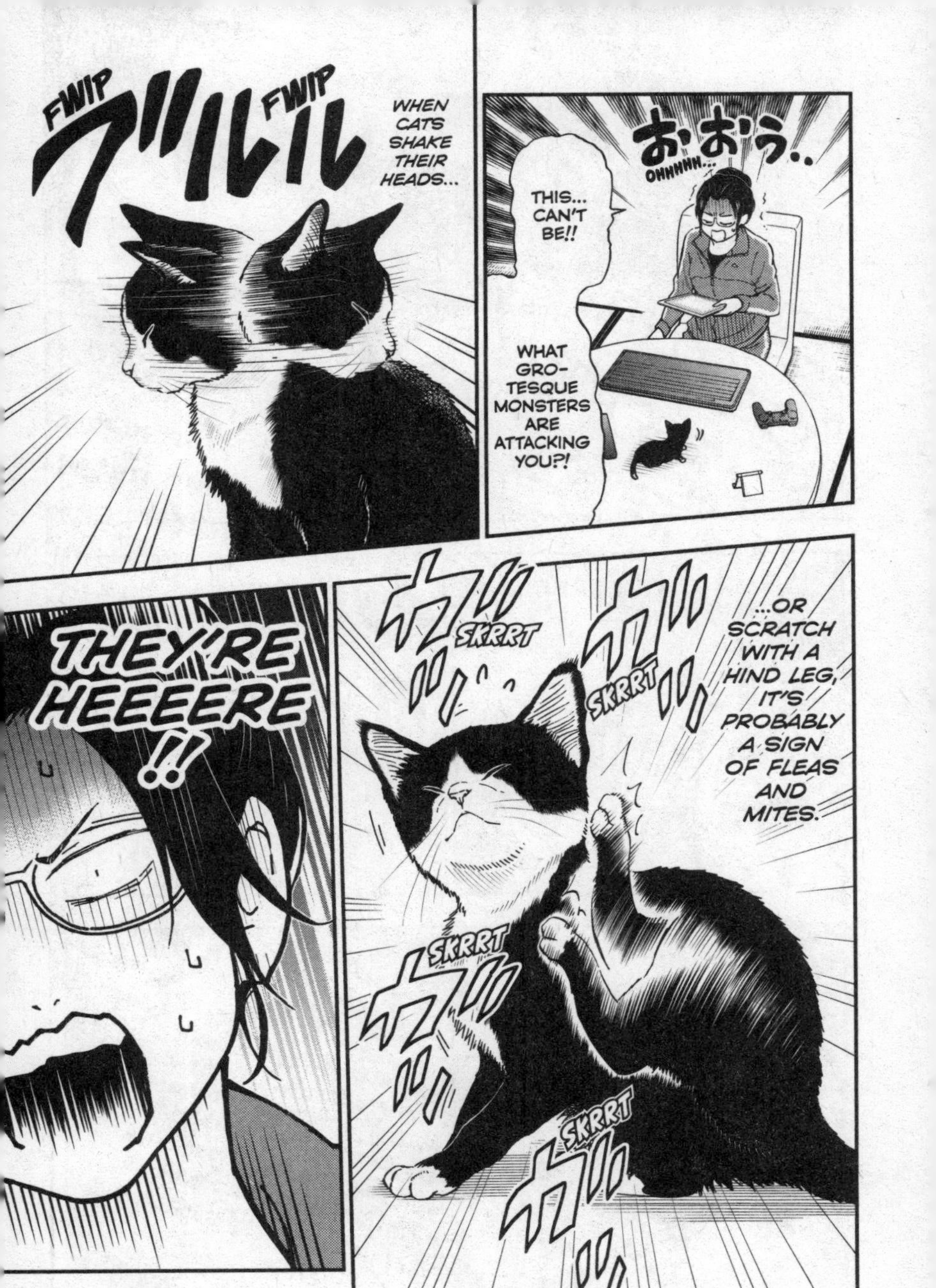
おおう..
OHHHHH...
THIS... CAN'T BE!!
WHAT GRO-TESQUE MONSTERS ARE ATTACKING YOU?!
FWIP
ブルル
FWIP
WHEN CATS SHAKE THEIR HEADS...
ウ
SKRRT
ウ
SKRRT
...OR SCRATCH WITH A HIND LEG, IT'S PROBABLY A SIGN OF FLEAS AND MITES.
SKRRT
ウ
SKRRT
ウ
THEY'RE HEEEEERE!!

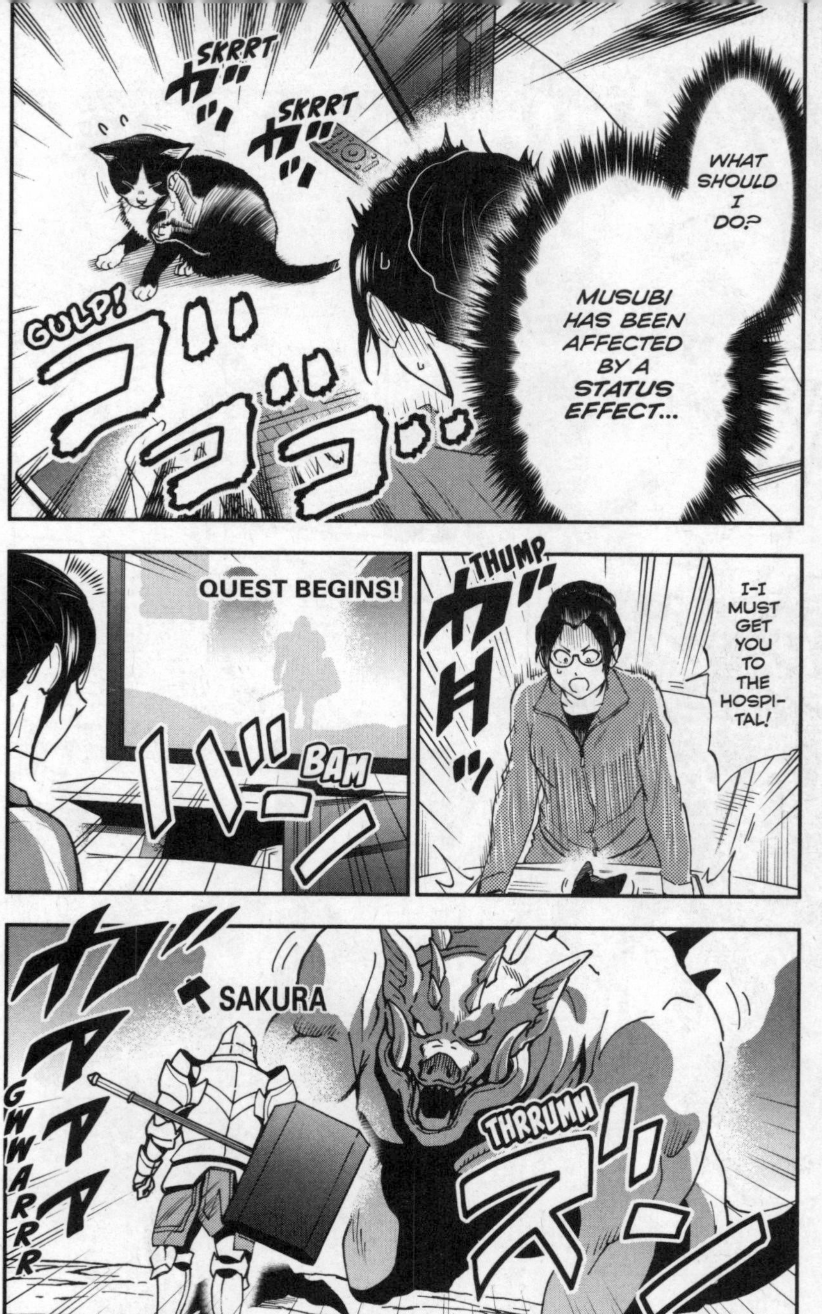
WHAT SHOULD I DO?
SKRRT
SKRRT
MUSUBI HAS BEEN AFFECTED BY A STATUS EFFECT...
GULP!
THUMP
I-I MUST GET YOU TO THE HOSPITAL!
QUEST BEGINS!
BAM
SAKURA
THRRUMM
GWWARRRR

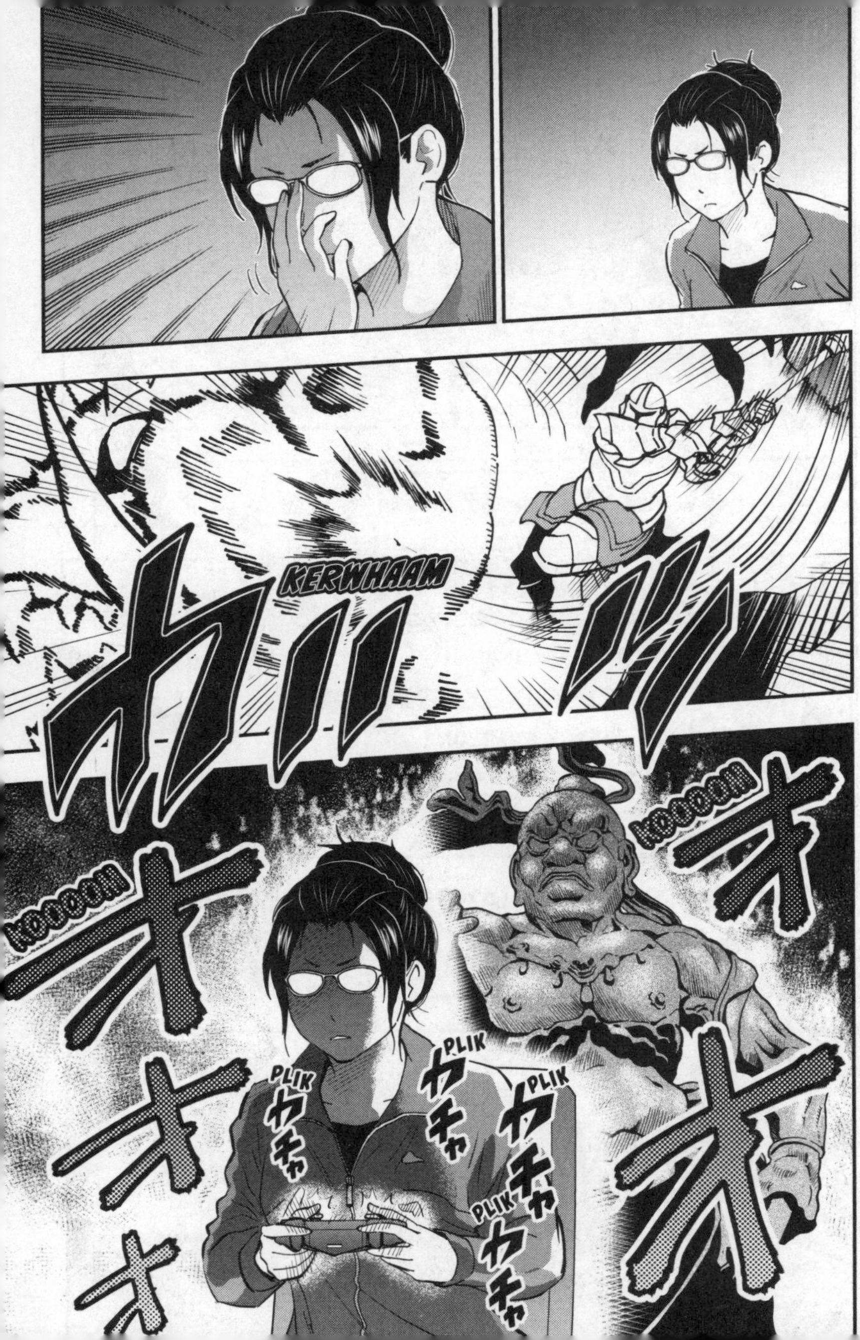
KERWHAAM
KOOOOM
KOOOOM
PLIK
PLIK
PLIK
PLIK

QUEST CLEARED

POPEYE T.A.

SAKURA

LILI

THOOOMP

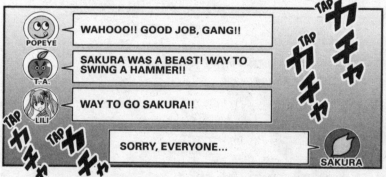

WAHOOO!! GOOD JOB, GANG!!

POPEYE

SAKURA WAS A BEAST! WAY TO SWING A HAMMER!!

T.A.

WAY TO GO SAKURA!!

LILI

SORRY, EVERYONE...

SAKURA

I'M LOGGING OFF. I HAVE TO RUN!!

BADUMP!

SAKURA

BADUMP!

WHERE'S THE NEAREST VET?!

WAMP

WAMP

?

ruyama Veterinary Hospital

SKREEEEECH

Maruyama Veterinary Hospital

Clinic Guide (Hours)

診察時間	月	火	水	木	金	土	日
9:00~ 12:00	●	●	×	●	●	●	●
16:00~ 20:00	●	●	×	●	●	●	●

Dogs, Cats, Birds, Rabbits, Hamsters, Marmots, and other animals
TEL △△△△－○○－××××

AH! E-EXCUSE ME!!

ARE YOU ALREADY CLOSED?!

本日の診察は終了しました

TMP TMP TMP

YES...

SIGN ON DOOR: TODAY'S EXAMS FINISHED

105

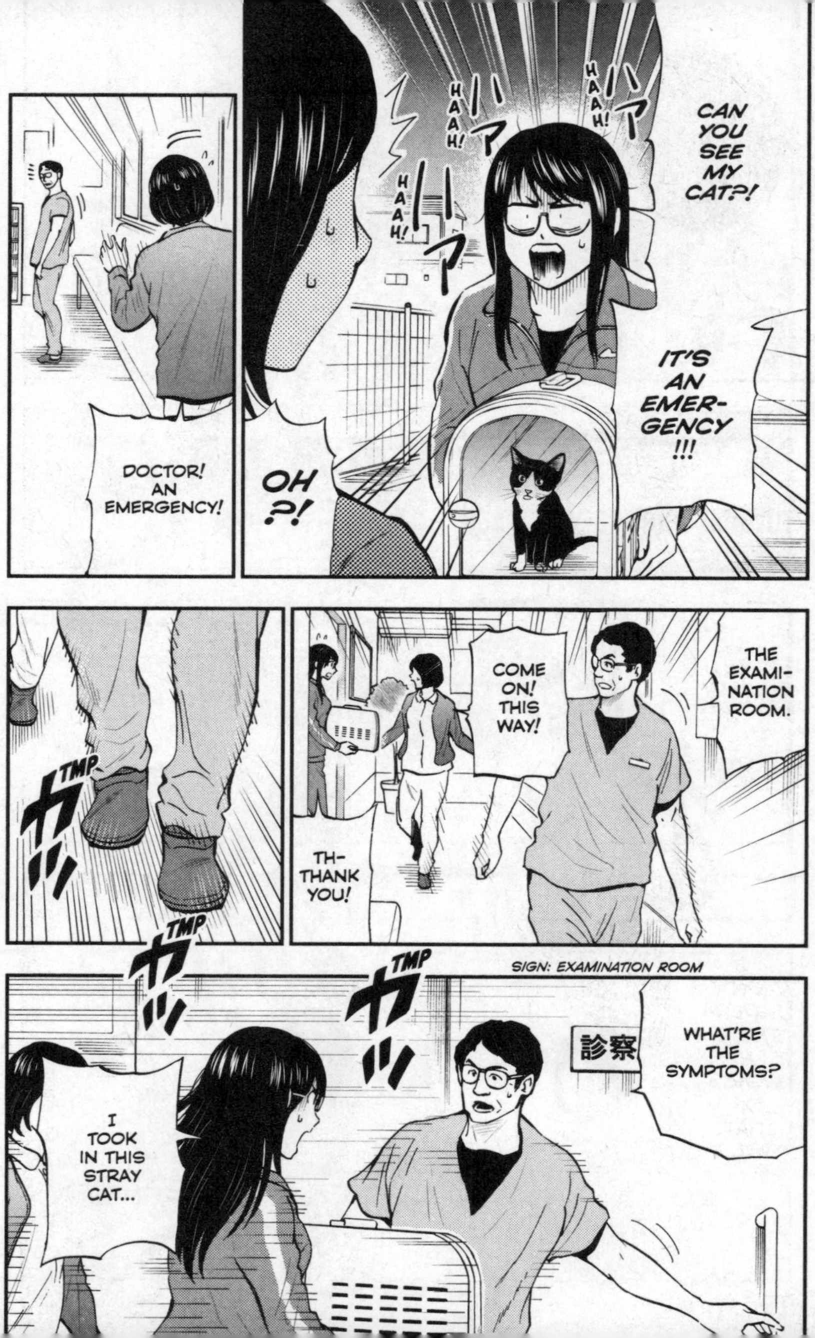

CAN YOU SEE MY CAT?!
HAAH!
HAAH!
HAAH!
IT'S AN EMERGENCY!!!
OH ?!
DOCTOR! AN EMERGENCY!
THE EXAMINATION ROOM.
COME ON! THIS WAY!
TH-THANK YOU!
TMP
TMP
SIGN: EXAMINATION ROOM
TMP
診察
WHAT'RE THE SYMPTOMS?
I TOOK IN THIS STRAY CAT...

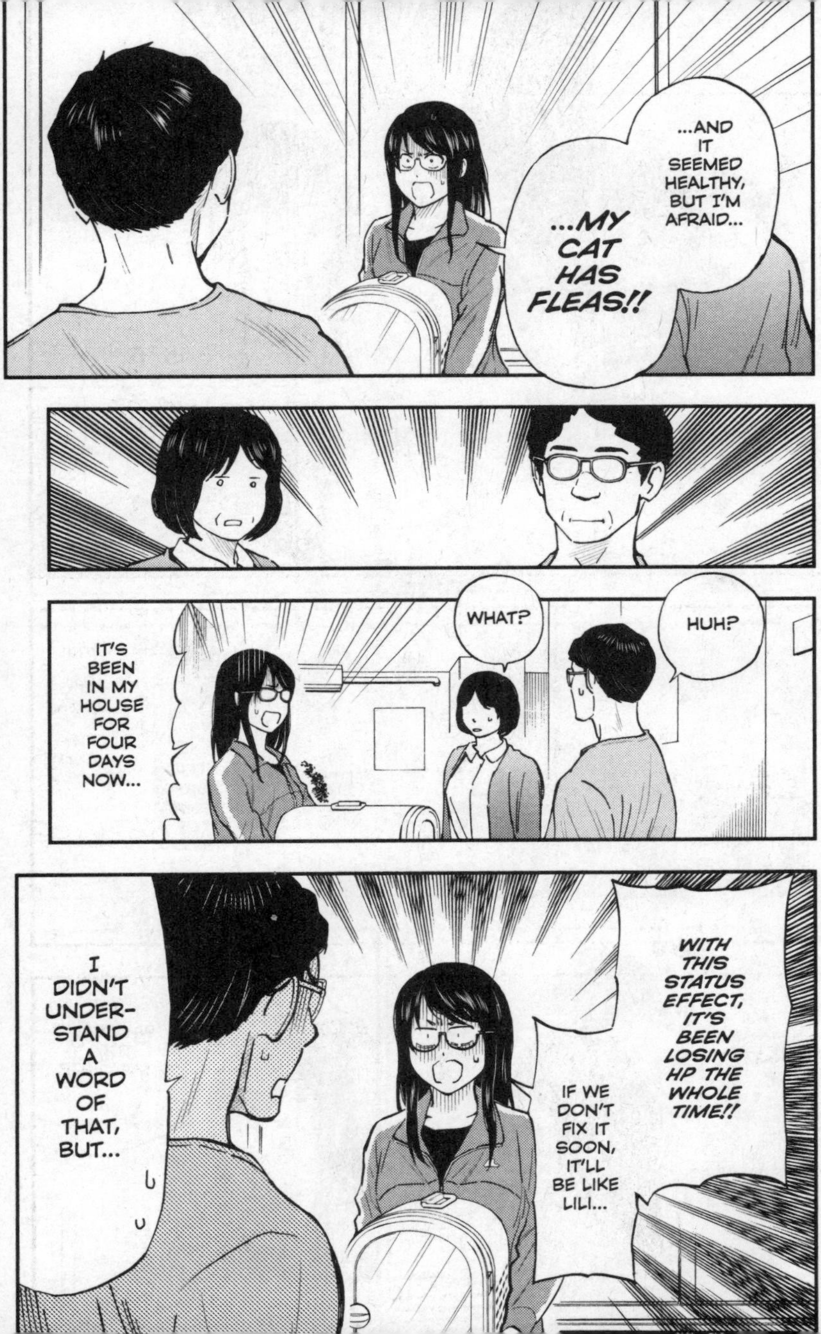
...AND IT SEEMED HEALTHY, BUT I'M AFRAID...
...MY CAT HAS FLEAS!!
HUH?
WHAT?
IT'S BEEN IN MY HOUSE FOR FOUR DAYS NOW...
WITH THIS STATUS EFFECT, IT'S BEEN LOSING HP THE WHOLE TIME!!
IF WE DON'T FIX IT SOON, IT'LL BE LIKE LILI...
I DIDN'T UNDERSTAND A WORD OF THAT, BUT...

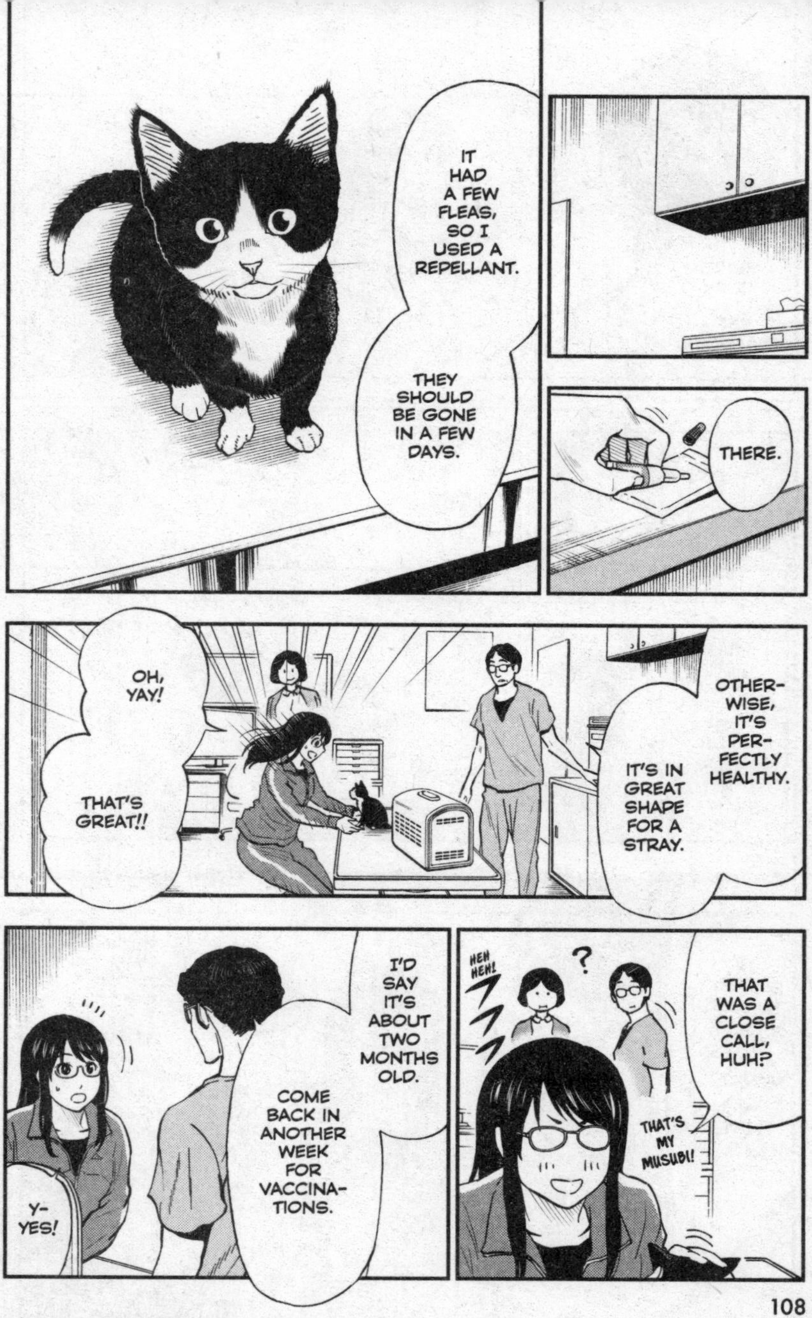
THERE.
IT HAD A FEW FLEAS, SO I USED A REPELLANT.
THEY SHOULD BE GONE IN A FEW DAYS.
OTHERWISE, IT'S PERFECTLY HEALTHY.
IT'S IN GREAT SHAPE FOR A STRAY.
OH, YAY!
THAT'S GREAT!!
THAT WAS A CLOSE CALL, HUH?
?
HEH HEH!
THAT'S MY MUSUBI!
I'D SAY IT'S ABOUT TWO MONTHS OLD.
COME BACK IN ANOTHER WEEK FOR VACCINATIONS.
Y-YES!

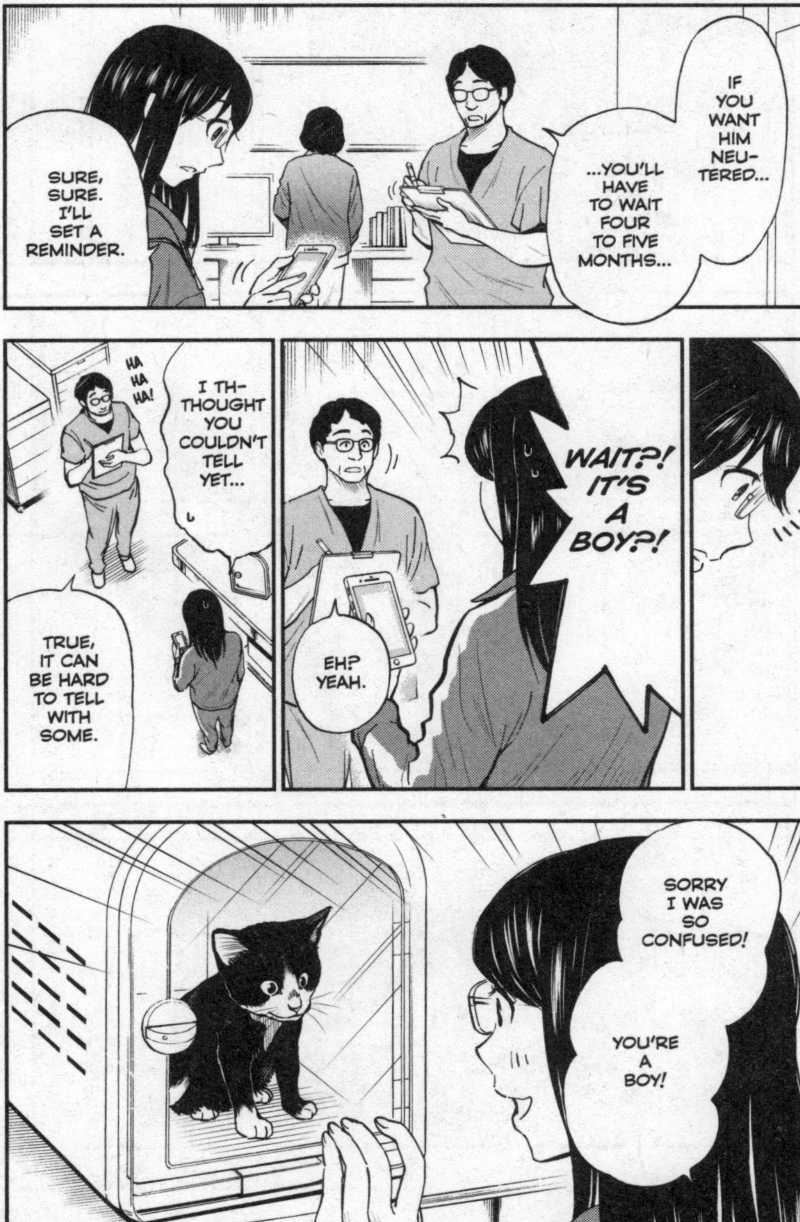
IF YOU WANT HIM NEU-TERED...
...YOU'LL HAVE TO WAIT FOUR TO FIVE MONTHS...
SURE, SURE. I'LL SET A REMINDER.
WAIT?! IT'S A BOY?!
EH? YEAH.
I TH-THOUGHT YOU COULDN'T TELL YET...
HA HA HA!
TRUE, IT CAN BE HARD TO TELL WITH SOME.
SORRY I WAS SO CONFUSED!
YOU'RE A BOY!

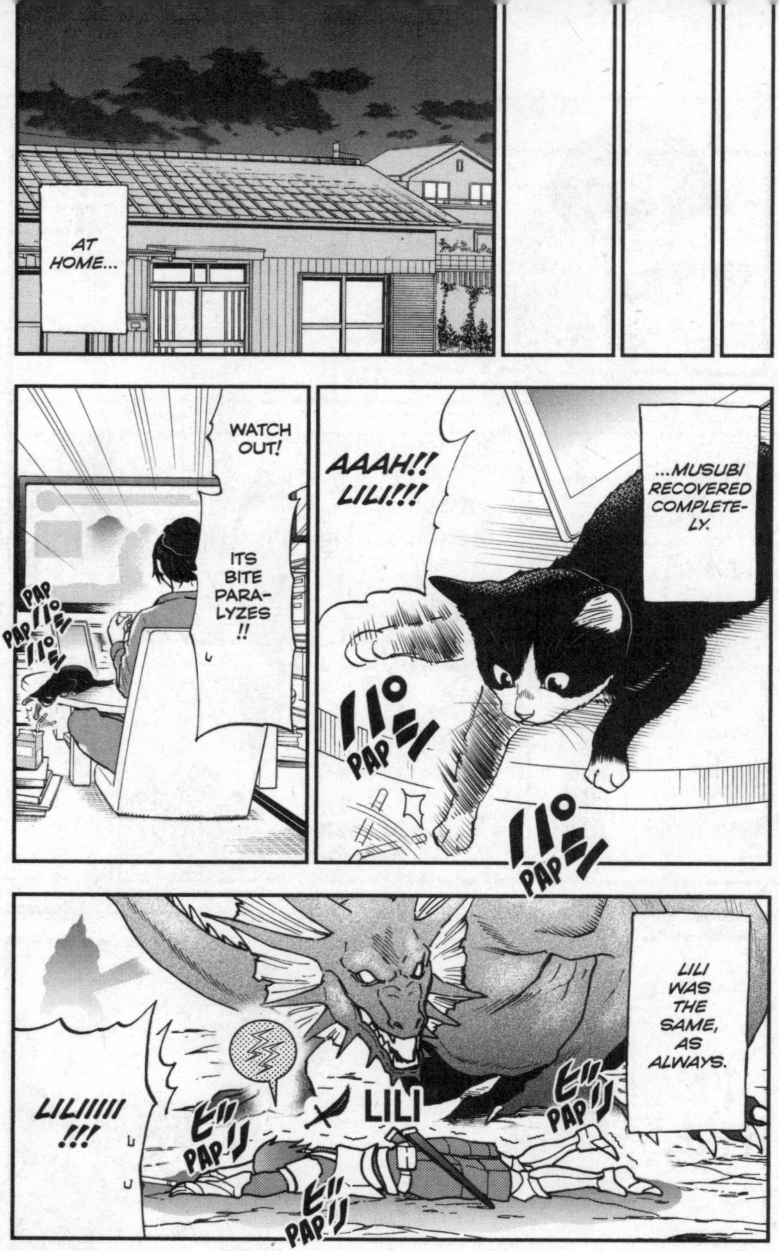
AT HOME...
...MUSUBI RECOVERED COMPLETE-LY.
AAAH!! LILI!!!
PAP
PAP
WATCH OUT!
ITS BITE PARA-LYZES !!
PAP
PAP
LILI WAS THE SAME, AS ALWAYS.
PAP
LILI
PAP
LILIIIIII !!!
PAP

Chapter 4: Bonus Stage

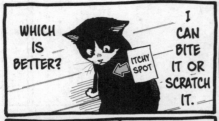

AH...
IT'S ITCHY HERE.
I CAN BITE IT OR SCRATCH IT.
ITCHY SPOT
WHICH IS BETTER?
BITE IT? BUT MOM ALWAYS SCRATCHED WITH HER FEET.
HMMM...
OH!
ITCHY SPOT 1
NOW IT'S ITCHY THERE, TOO!
ITCHY SPOT 2
DO I DO THE FIRST ONE FIRST?
OH...
OHHH...
MUSUBI! DINNER TIME!!!
MEH.
I'M FINE.

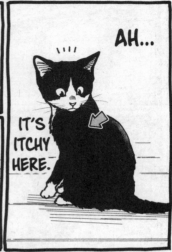

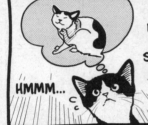

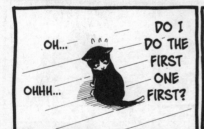

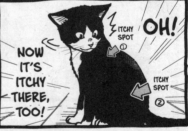

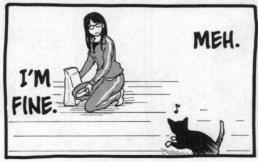

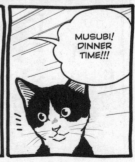

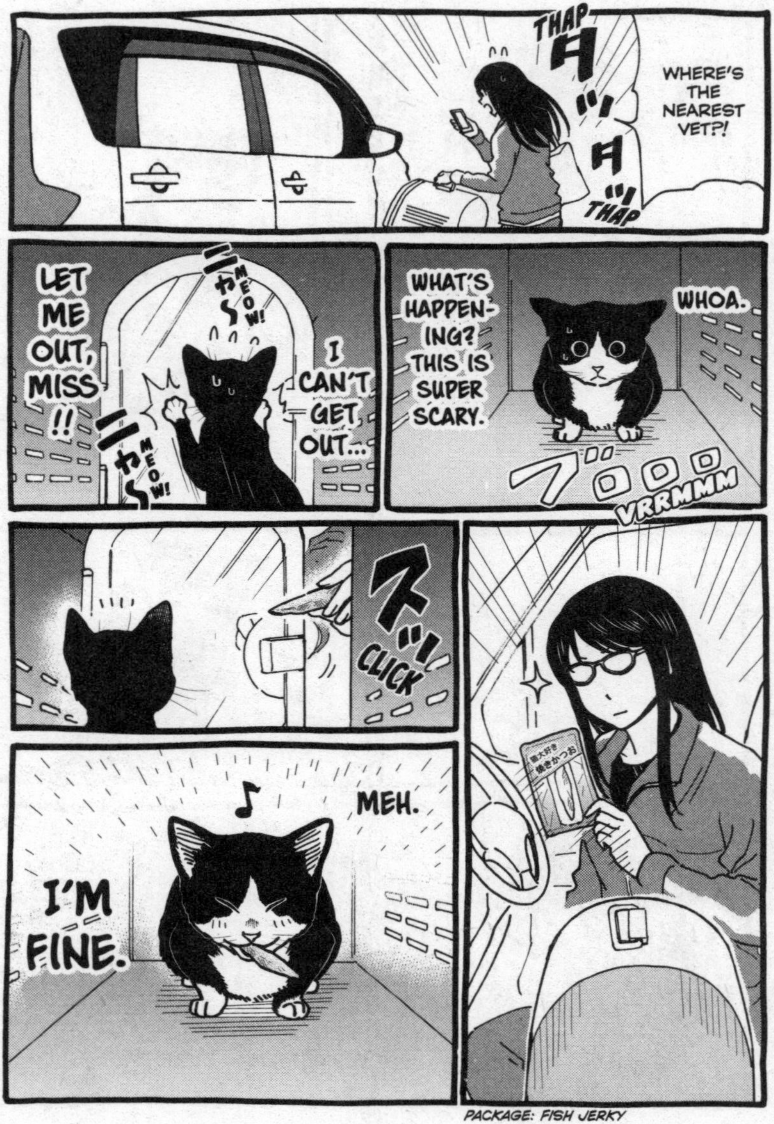
THAP
THAP
WHERE'S THE NEAREST VET?!
WHAT'S HAPPEN-ING? THIS IS SUPER SCARY.
WHOA.
VRRMMM
LET ME OUT, MISS!!
MEOW!
MEOW!
I CAN'T GET OUT...
CLICK
MEH.
I'M FINE.

PACKAGE: FISH JERKY

CAT +
GAMER

Chapter 5: Lucky Cat

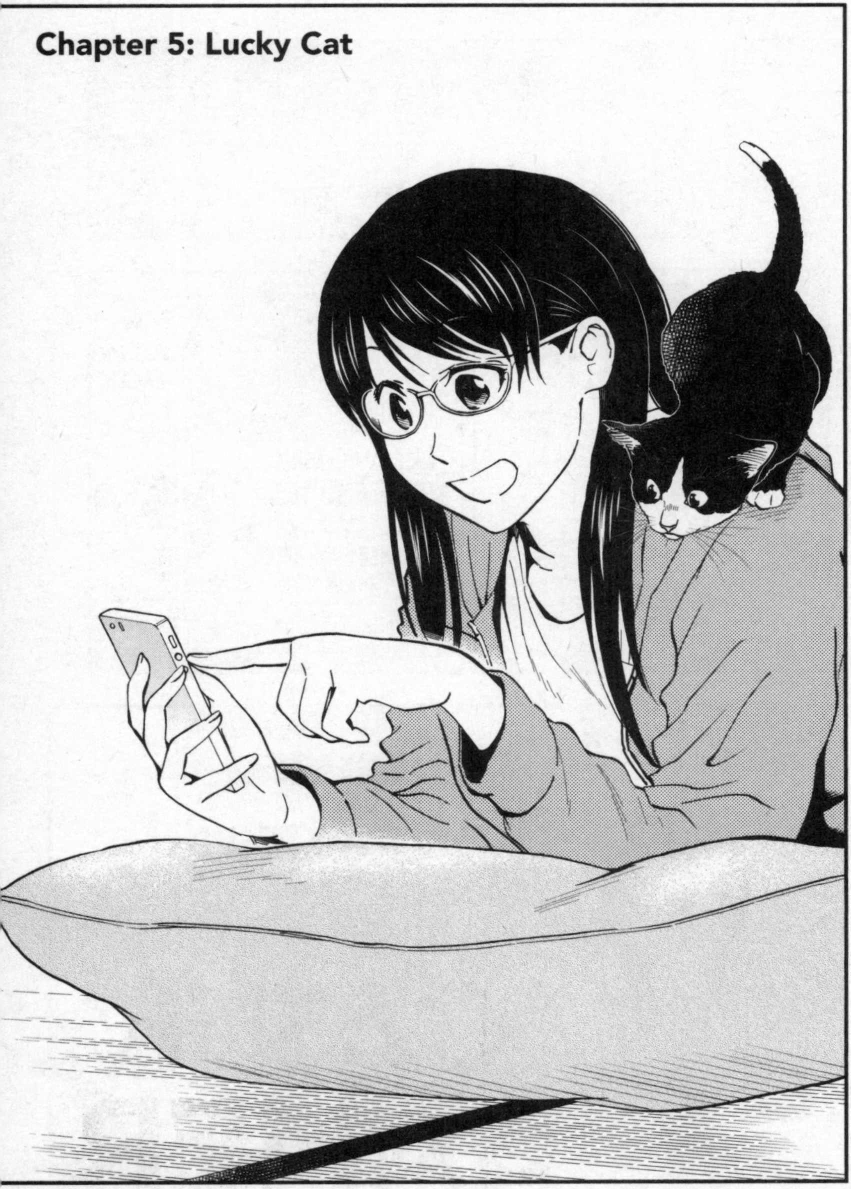

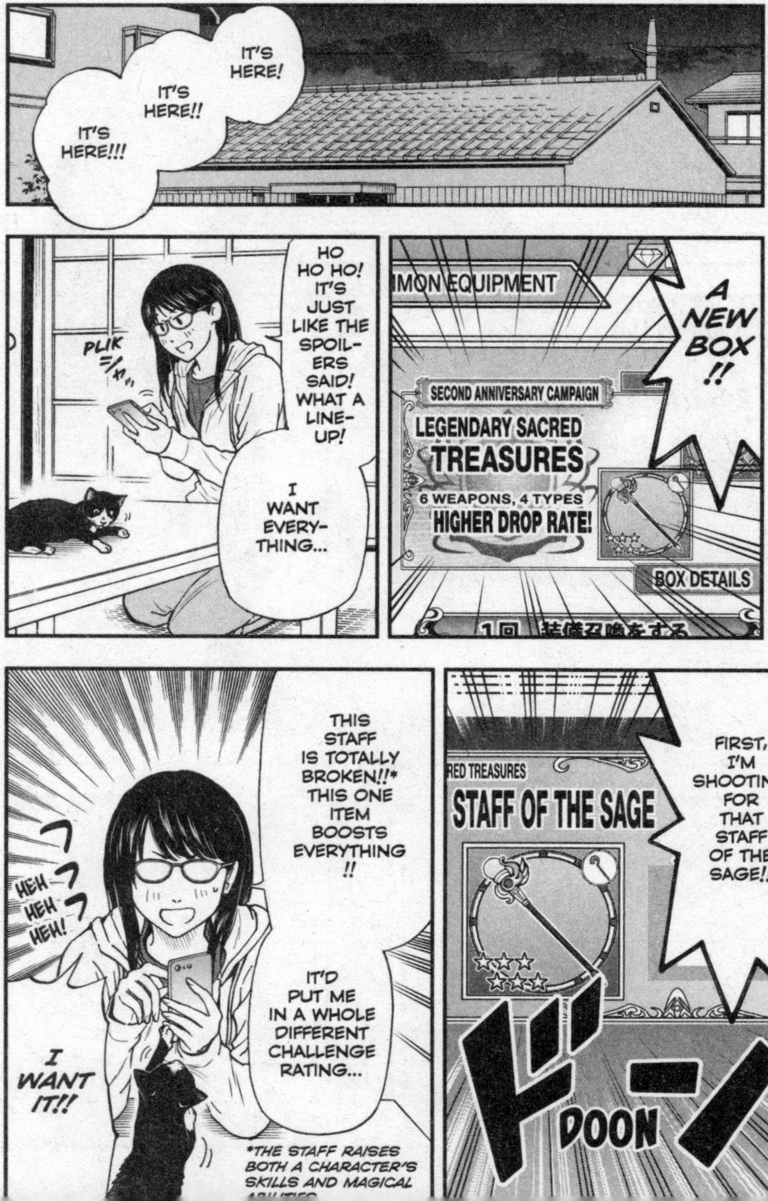
IT'S HERE!
IT'S HERE!!
IT'S HERE!!!
A NEW BOX!!
MON EQUIPMENT
SECOND ANNIVERSARY CAMPAIGN
LEGENDARY SACRED TREASURES
6 WEAPONS, 4 TYPES
HIGHER DROP RATE!
BOX DETAILS
PLIK
HO HO HO! IT'S JUST LIKE THE SPOIL-ERS SAID! WHAT A LINE-UP!
I WANT EVERY-THING...
FIRST, I'M SHOOTING FOR THAT STAFF OF THE SAGE!!
RED TREASURES
STAFF OF THE SAGE
DOON
THIS STAFF IS TOTALLY BROKEN!!* THIS ONE ITEM BOOSTS EVERYTHING!!
IT'D PUT ME IN A WHOLE DIFFERENT CHALLENGE RATING...
HEH HEH HEH!
I WANT IT!!
*THE STAFF RAISES BOTH A CHARACTER'S SKILLS AND MAGICAL

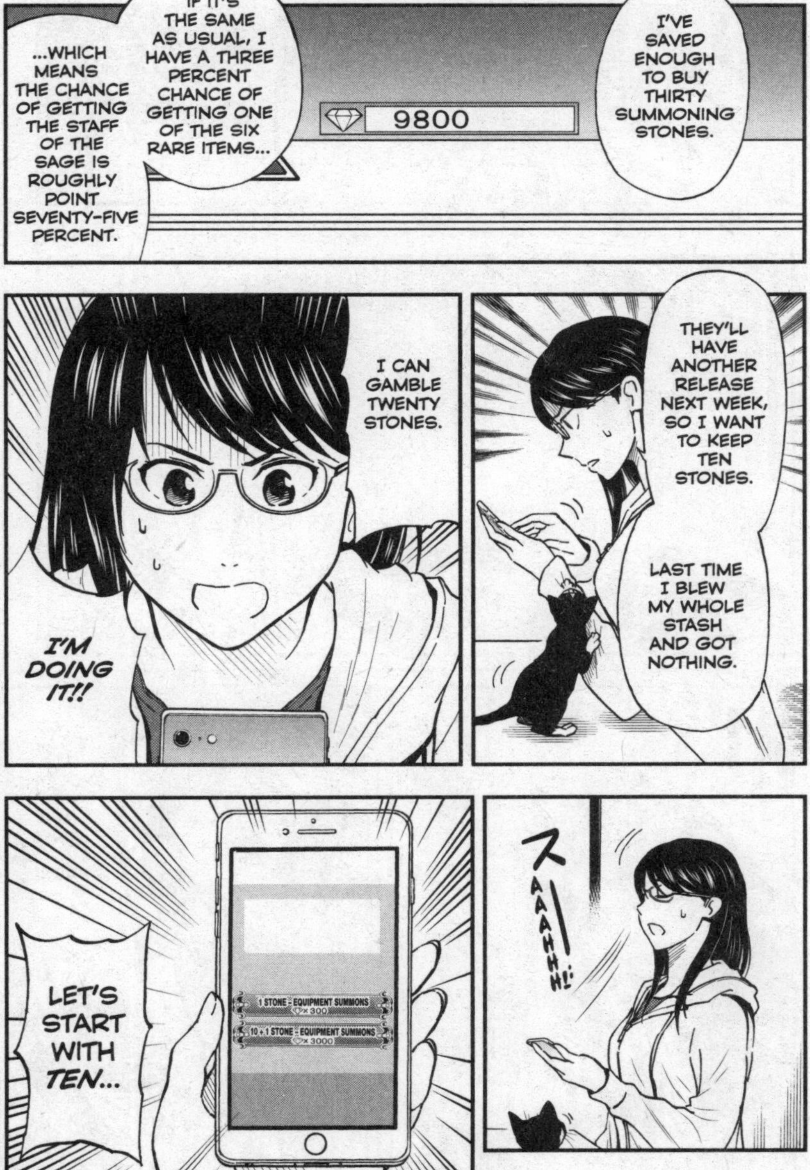
I'VE SAVED ENOUGH TO BUY THIRTY SUMMONING STONES.
9800
IF IT'S THE SAME AS USUAL, I HAVE A THREE PERCENT CHANCE OF GETTING ONE OF THE SIX RARE ITEMS...
...WHICH MEANS THE CHANCE OF GETTING THE STAFF OF THE SAGE IS ROUGHLY POINT SEVENTY-FIVE PERCENT.
THEY'LL HAVE ANOTHER RELEASE NEXT WEEK, SO I WANT TO KEEP TEN STONES.
LAST TIME I BLEW MY WHOLE STASH AND GOT NOTHING.
I CAN GAMBLE TWENTY STONES.
I'M DOING IT!!
ス
AAAHH!
1 STONE - EQUIPMENT SUMMONS
×300
10 + 1 STONE - EQUIPMENT SUMMONS
×3000
LET'S START WITH TEN...

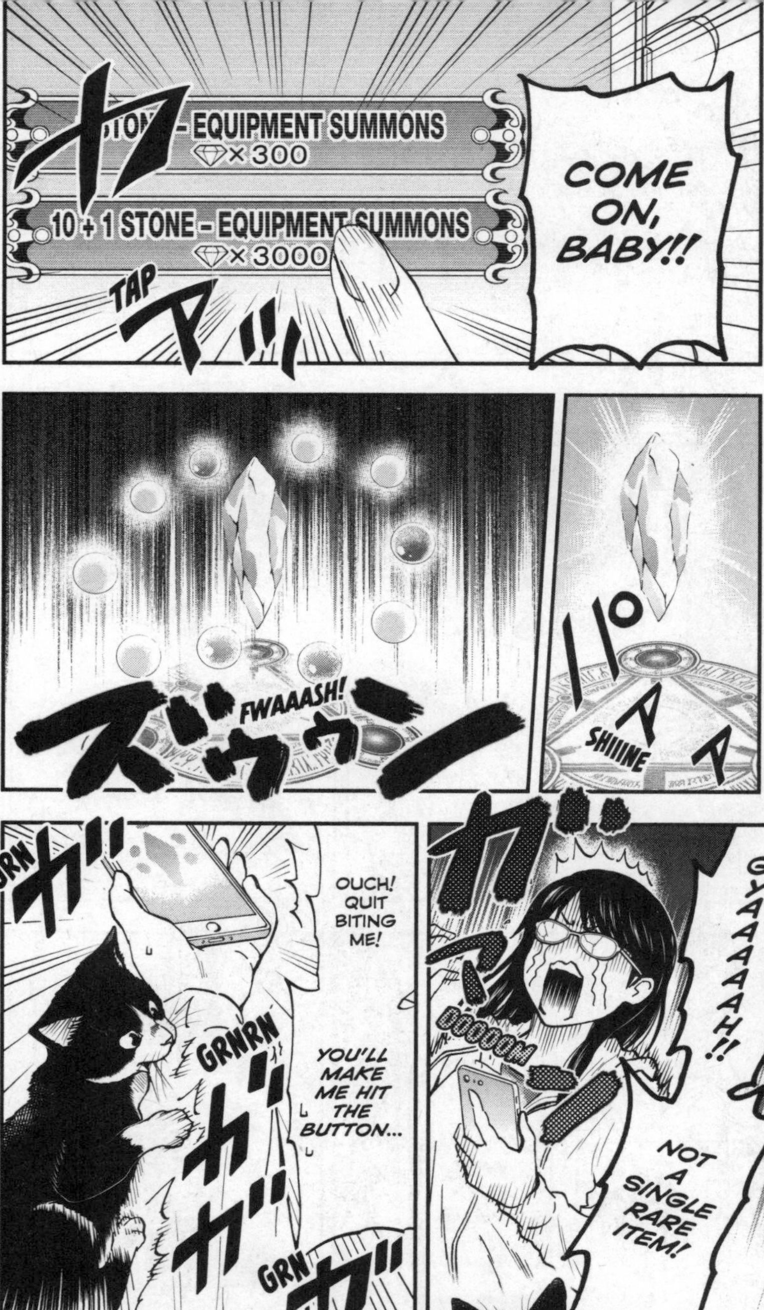
COME ON, BABY!!
– EQUIPMENT SUMMONS
× 300
10 + 1 STONE – EQUIPMENT SUMMONS
× 3000
TAP
SHIINE
FWAAASH!
GYAAAAAAH!!
NOT A SINGLE RARE ITEM!
DOOOOOM
OUCH! QUIT BITING ME!
GRN
GRNRN
YOU'LL MAKE ME HIT THE BUTTON...
GRN

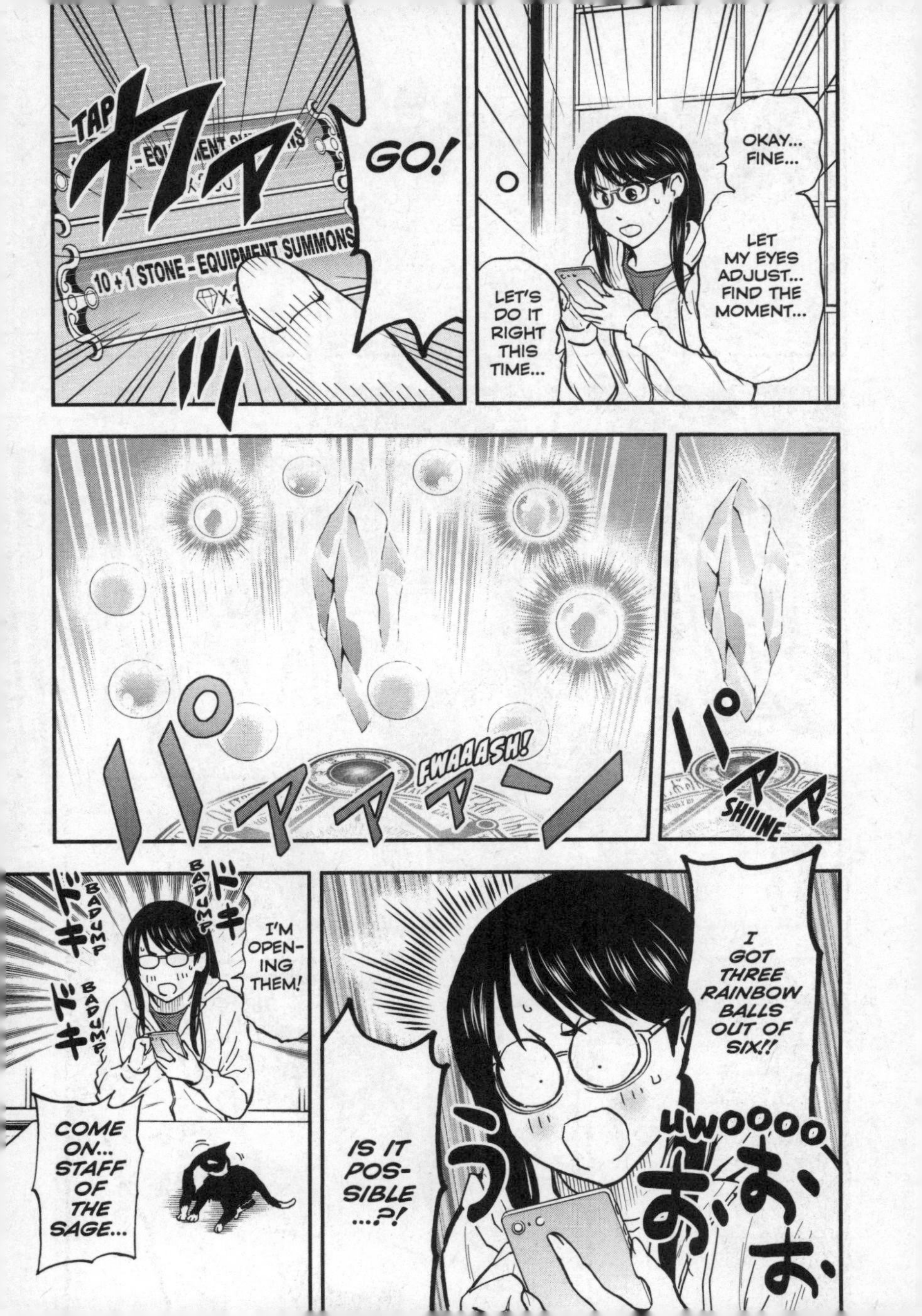
OKAY... FINE...
LET MY EYES ADJUST... FIND THE MOMENT...
LET'S DO IT RIGHT THIS TIME...
GO!
TAP
10 + 1 STONE - EQUIPMENT SUMMONS
SHIIINE
FWAAASH!
I GOT THREE RAINBOW BALLS OUT OF SIX!!
UWOOOO
IS IT POSSIBLE ...?!
BADUMP
BADUMP
I'M OPENING THEM!
COME ON... STAFF OF THE SAGE...

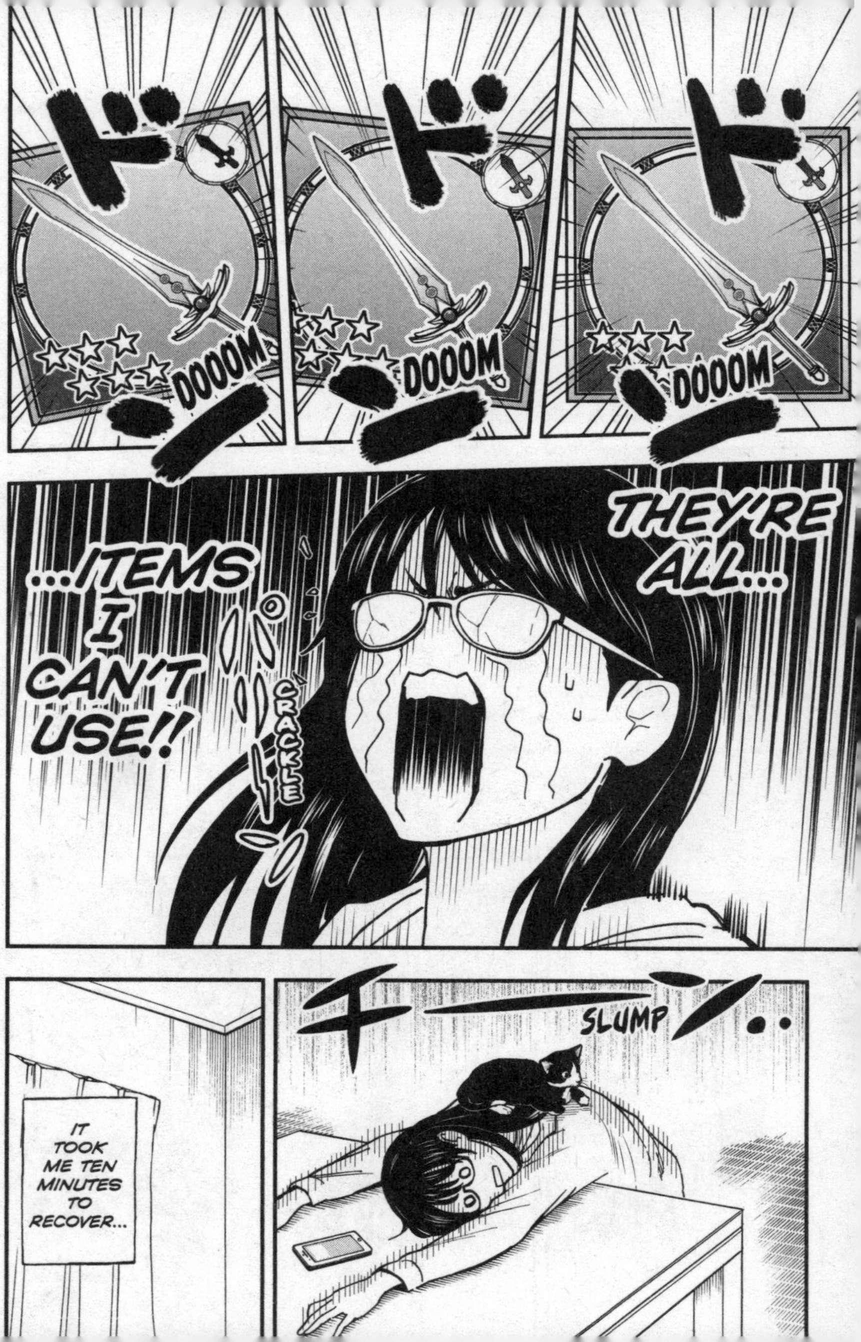
DOOOM
DOOOM
DOOOM
THEY'RE ALL...
...ITEMS I CAN'T USE!!
CRACKLE
SLUMP
IT TOOK ME TEN MINUTES TO RECOVER...

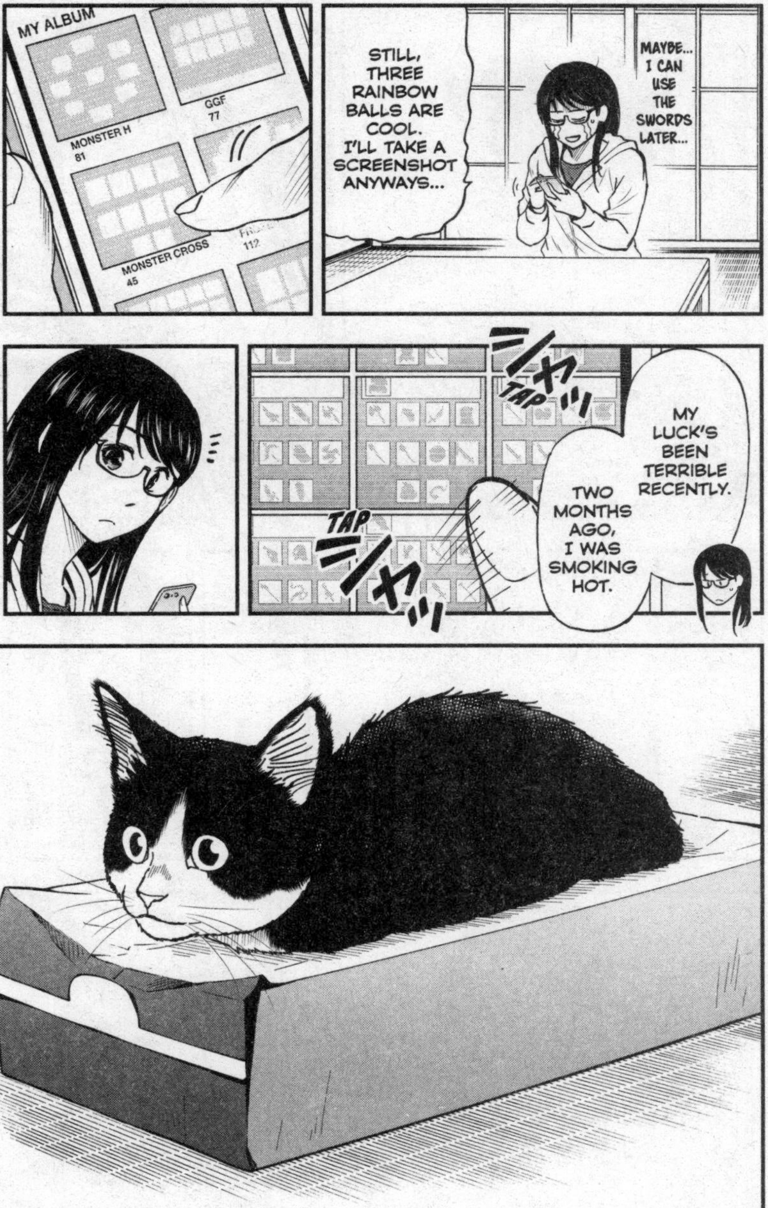
MAYBE... I CAN USE THE SWORDS LATER...
STILL, THREE RAINBOW BALLS ARE COOL. I'LL TAKE A SCREENSHOT ANYWAYS...
GGF
77
MY ALBUM
MONSTER H
81
112
MONSTER CROSS
45
シャッ
TAP
MY LUCK'S BEEN TERRIBLE RECENTLY.
TWO MONTHS AGO, I WAS SMOKING HOT.
TAP
シャッ

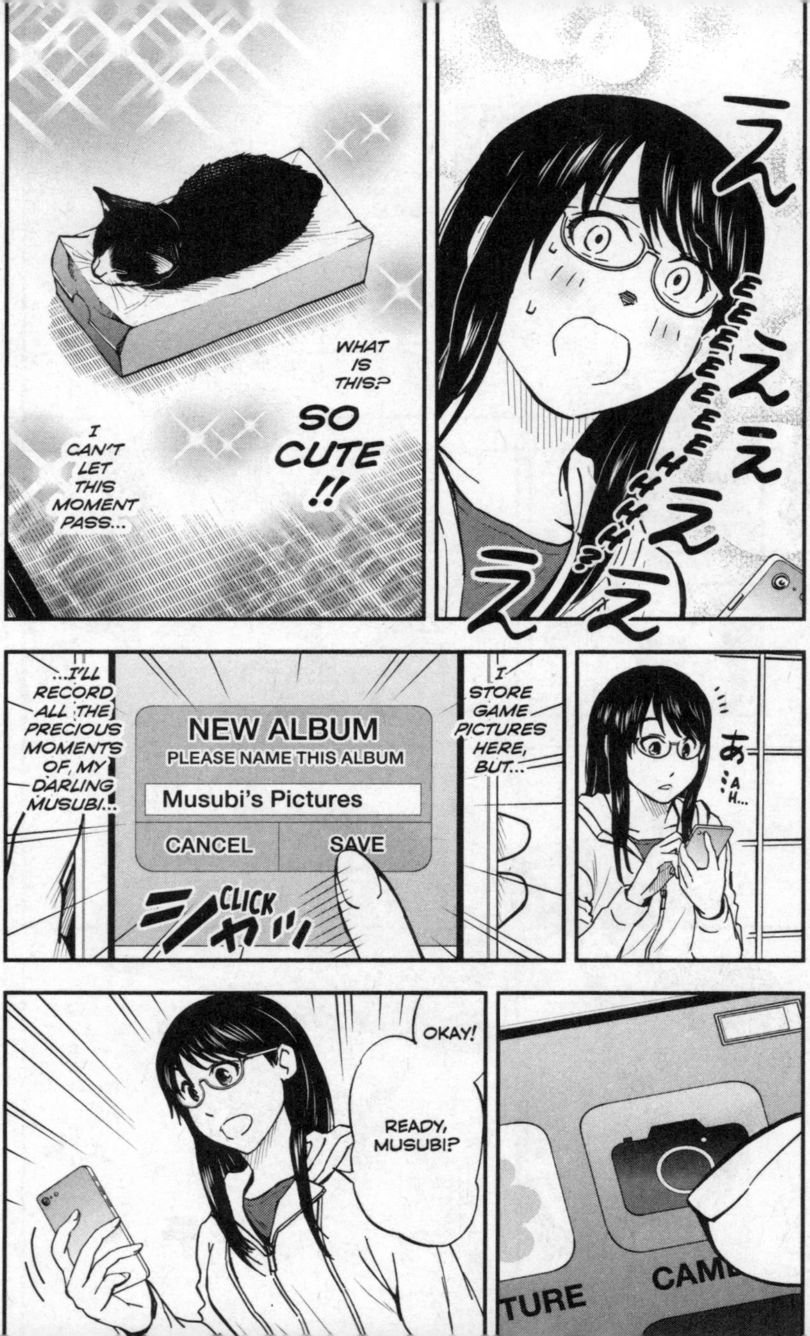

EEEEEEEEHHHHH?!
WHAT IS THIS?
SO CUTE!!
I CAN'T LET THIS MOMENT PASS...
あ
AH...
I STORE GAME PICTURES HERE, BUT...
NEW ALBUM
PLEASE NAME THIS ALBUM
Musubi's Pictures
CANCEL
SAVE
...I'LL RECORD ALL THE PRECIOUS MOMENTS OF, MY DARLING MUSUBI...
シャッ
CLICK
CAME
TURE
OKAY!
READY, MUSUBI?

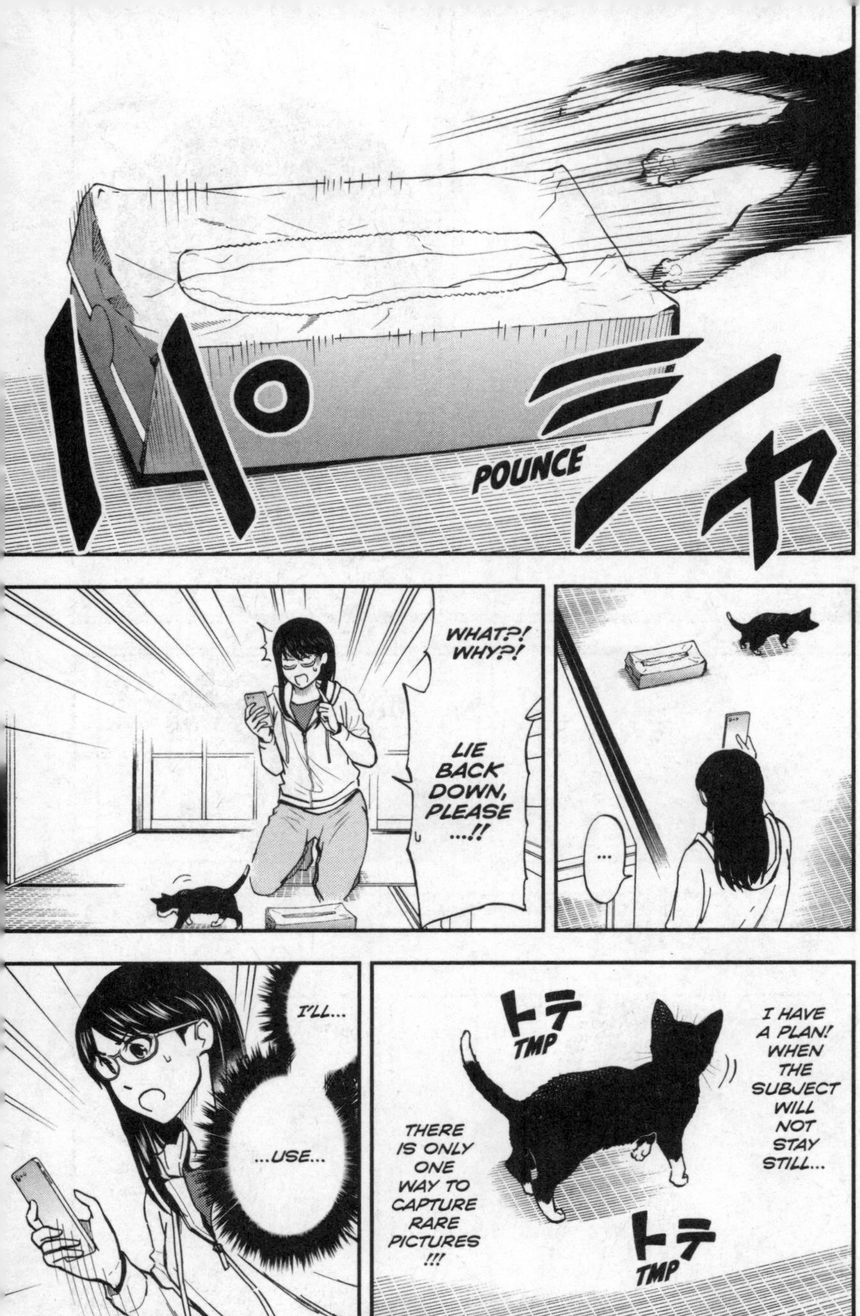
POUNCE
...
WHAT?! WHY?!
LIE BACK DOWN, PLEASE ...!!
I HAVE A PLAN! WHEN THE SUBJECT WILL NOT STAY STILL...
トテ
TMP
THERE IS ONLY ONE WAY TO CAPTURE RARE PICTURES !!!
トテ
TMP
I'LL...
...USE...

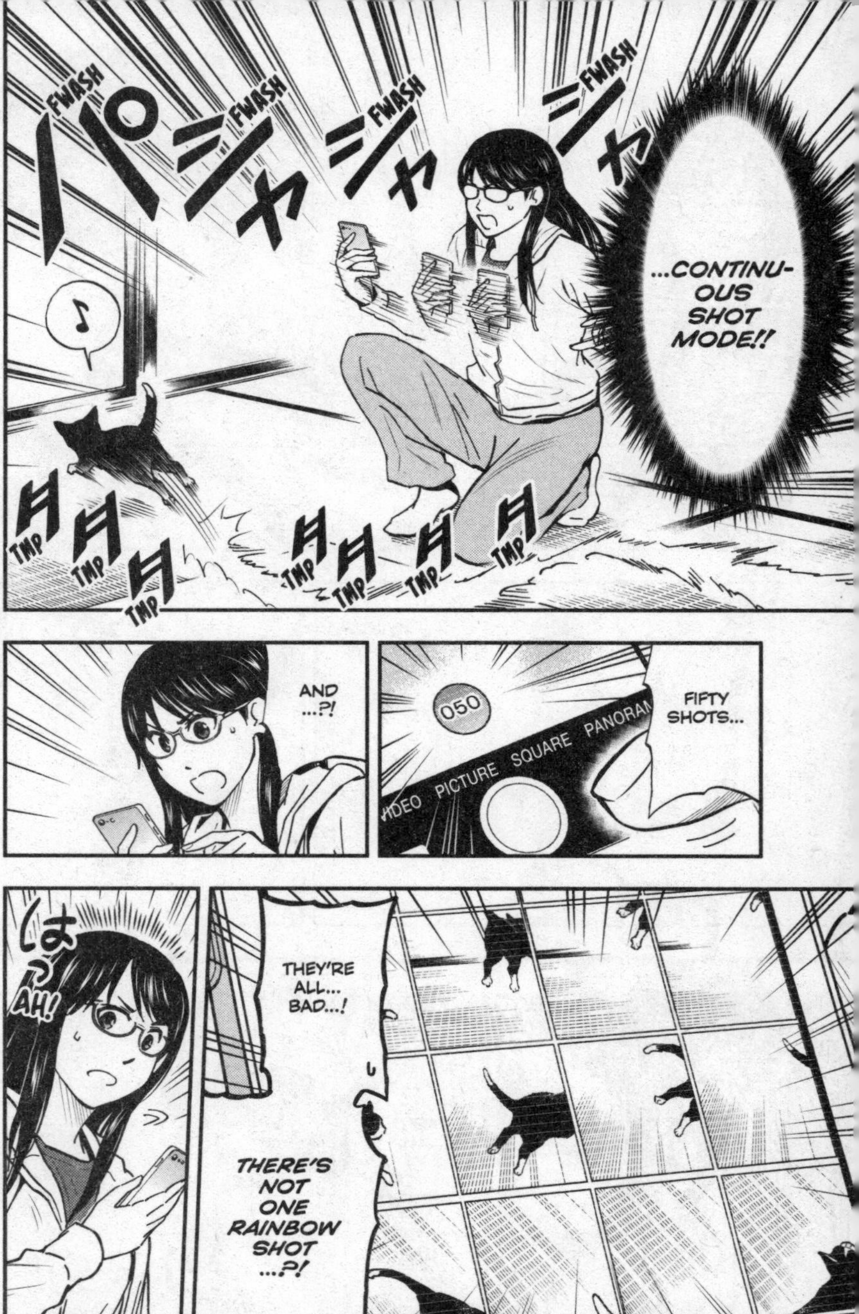

FWASH
FWASH
FWASH
FWASH
♪
...CONTINU-OUS SHOT MODE!!
TMP
TMP
TMP
TMP
TMP
TMP
TMP
050
VIDEO PICTURE SQUARE PANORAM
FIFTY SHOTS...
AND ...?!
THEY'RE ALL... BAD...!
THERE'S NOT ONE RAINBOW SHOT ...?!
AH!

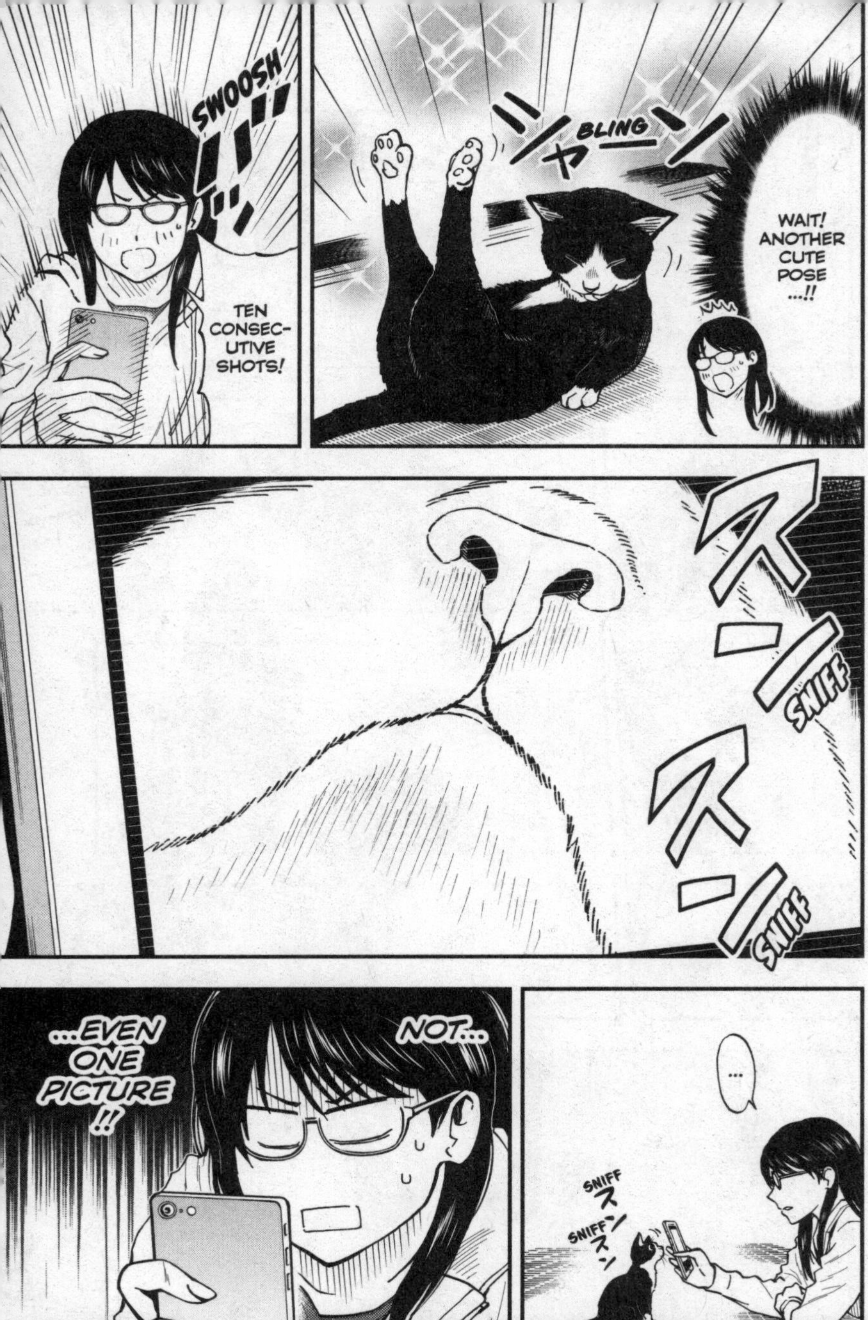
BLING
WAIT! ANOTHER CUTE POSE ...!!
SWOOSH
TEN CONSECUTIVE SHOTS!
SNIFF
SNIFF
...
SNIFF
SNIFF
NOT...
...EVEN ONE PICTURE !!

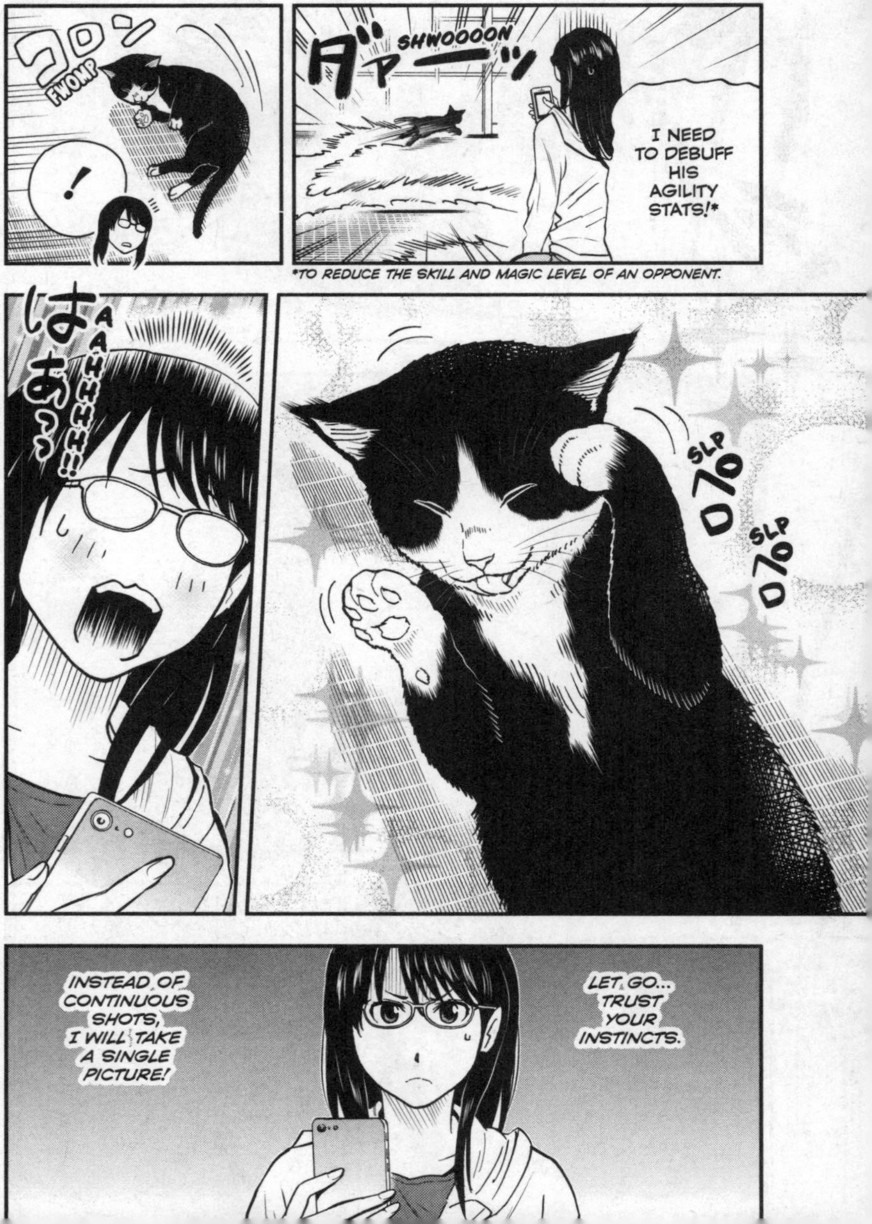
ダァーッ
SHWOOOON
I NEED TO DEBUFF HIS AGILITY STATS!*
コロン
FWOMP
!
*TO REDUCE THE SKILL AND MAGIC LEVEL OF AN OPPONENT.
SLP
SLP
はあっ
AAHHHHH!!
LET GO... TRUST YOUR INSTINCTS.
INSTEAD OF CONTINUOUS SHOTS, I WILL TAKE A SINGLE PICTURE!

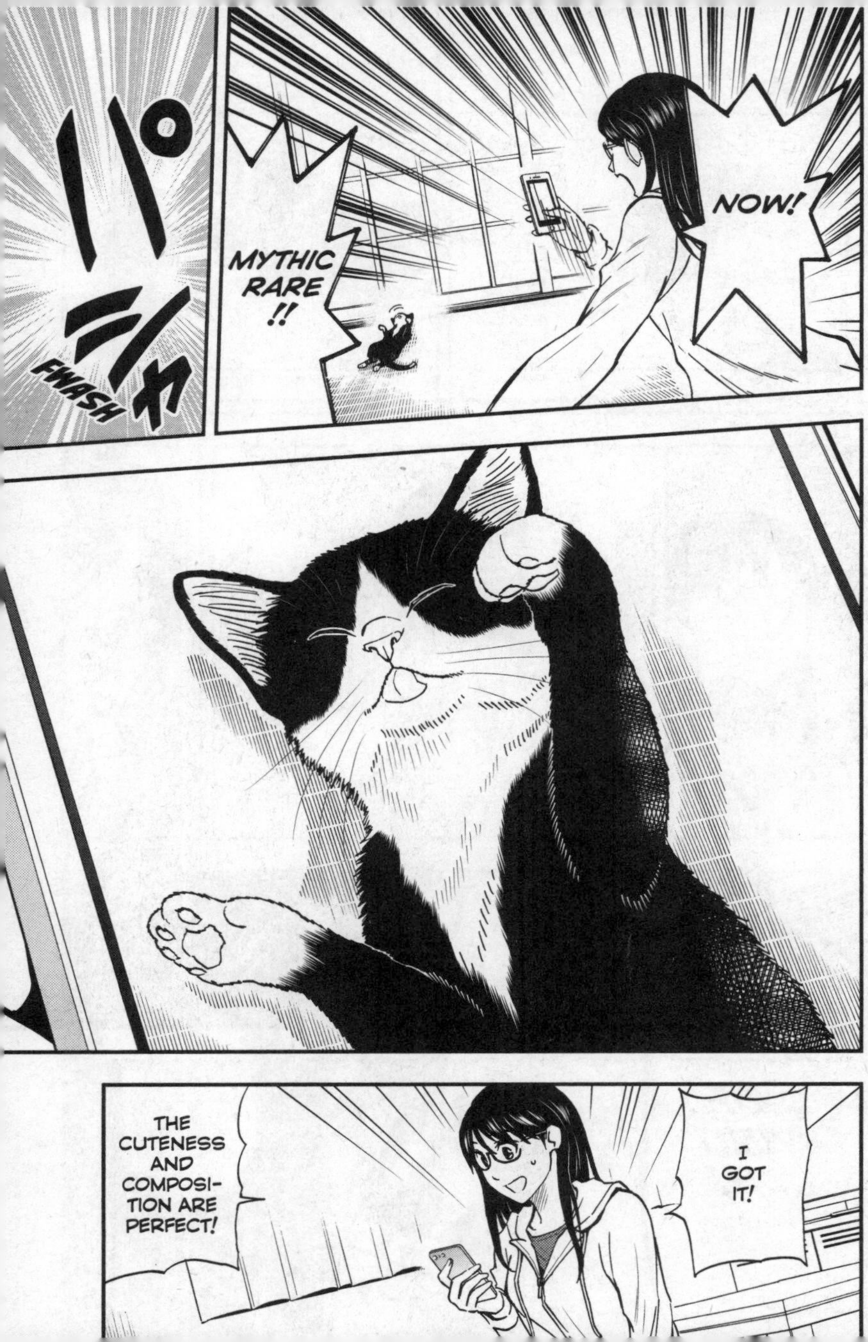
NOW!
MYTHIC RARE !!
パシャ
FWASH
I GOT IT!
THE CUTENESS AND COMPOSITION ARE PERFECT!

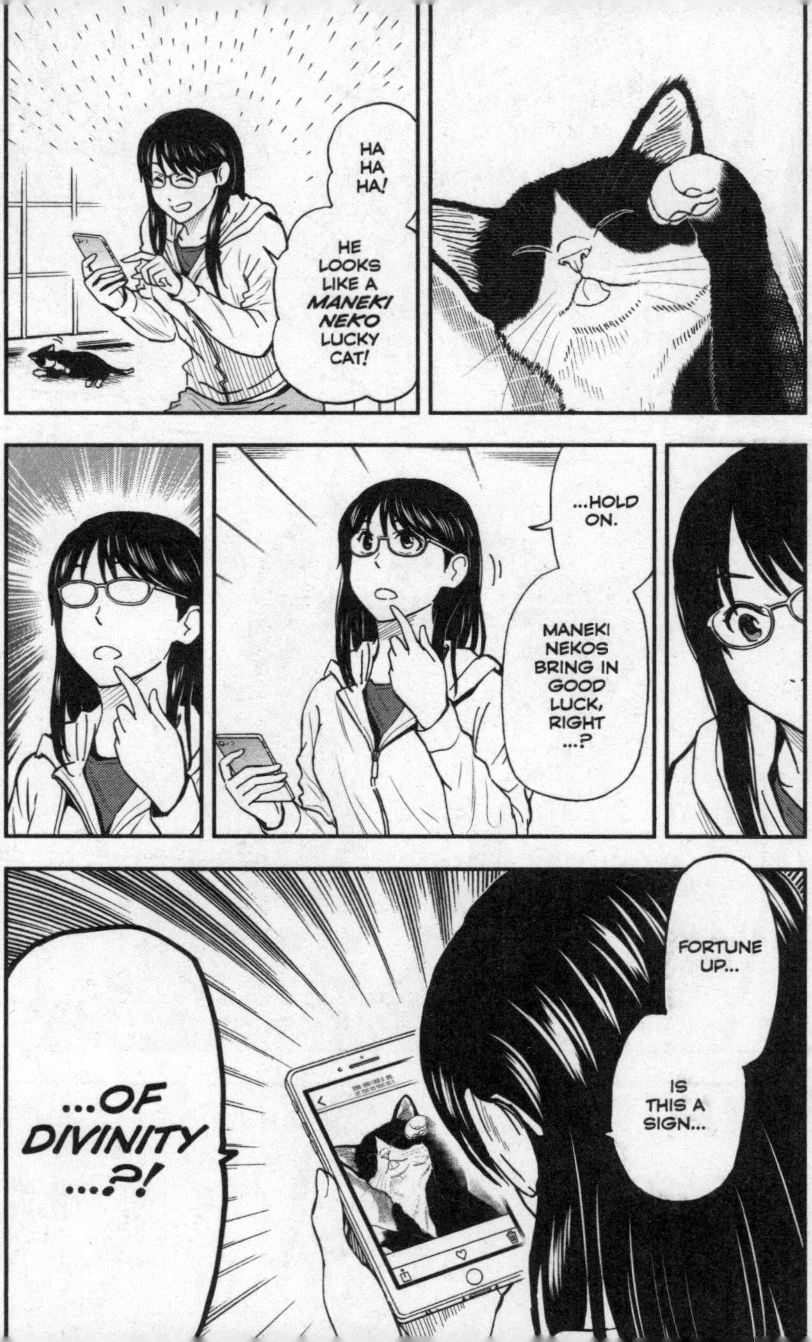
HA HA HA!
HE LOOKS LIKE A *MANEKI NEKO* LUCKY CAT!
...HOLD ON.
MANEKI NEKOS BRING IN GOOD LUCK, RIGHT ...?
FORTUNE UP...
IS THIS A SIGN...
...OF DIVINITY ...?!

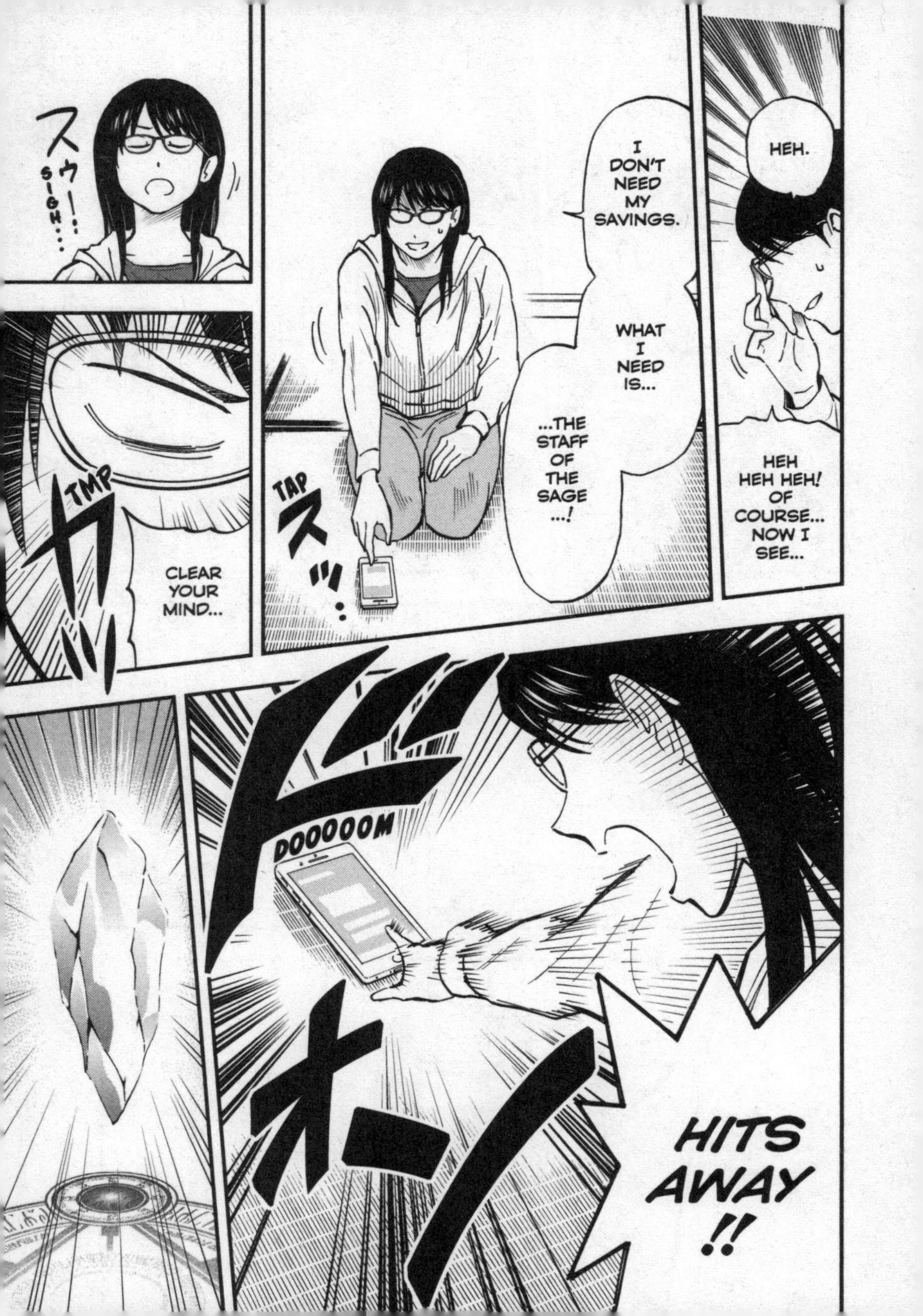
HEH.
HEH HEH HEH! OF COURSE... NOW I SEE...
I DON'T NEED MY SAVINGS.
WHAT I NEED IS...
...THE STAFF OF THE SAGE ...!
TAP
SIGH...
TMP
CLEAR YOUR MIND...
DOOOOOM
HITS AWAY!!

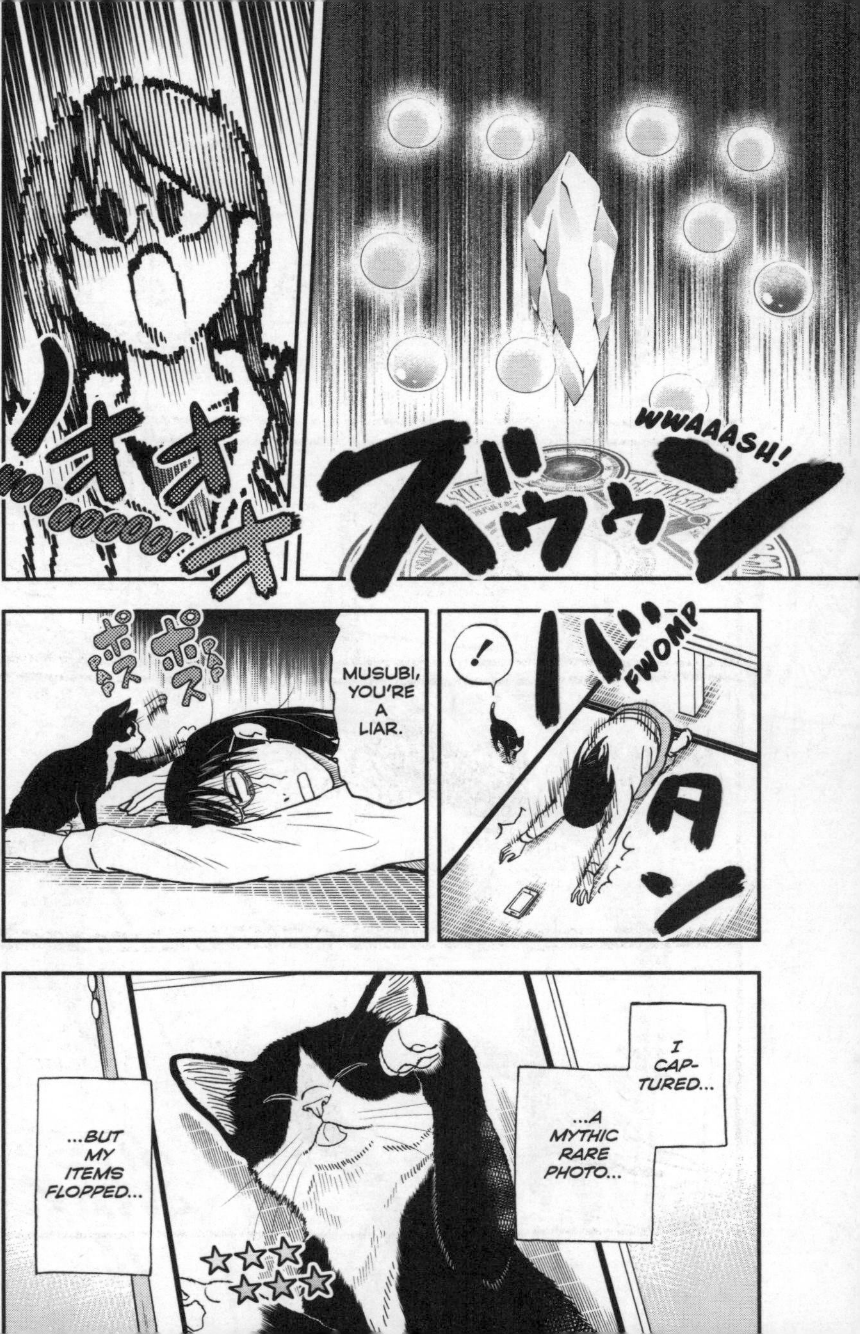

WWAAASH!
ズゥゥン
ノオオオオ
HOOOOOOOO!
!
バッ
FWOMP
タン
ポス ポス
MUSUBI, YOU'RE A LIAR.
I CAPTURED...
...A MYTHIC RARE PHOTO...
...BUT MY ITEMS FLOPPED...

Chapter 5: Bonus Stage

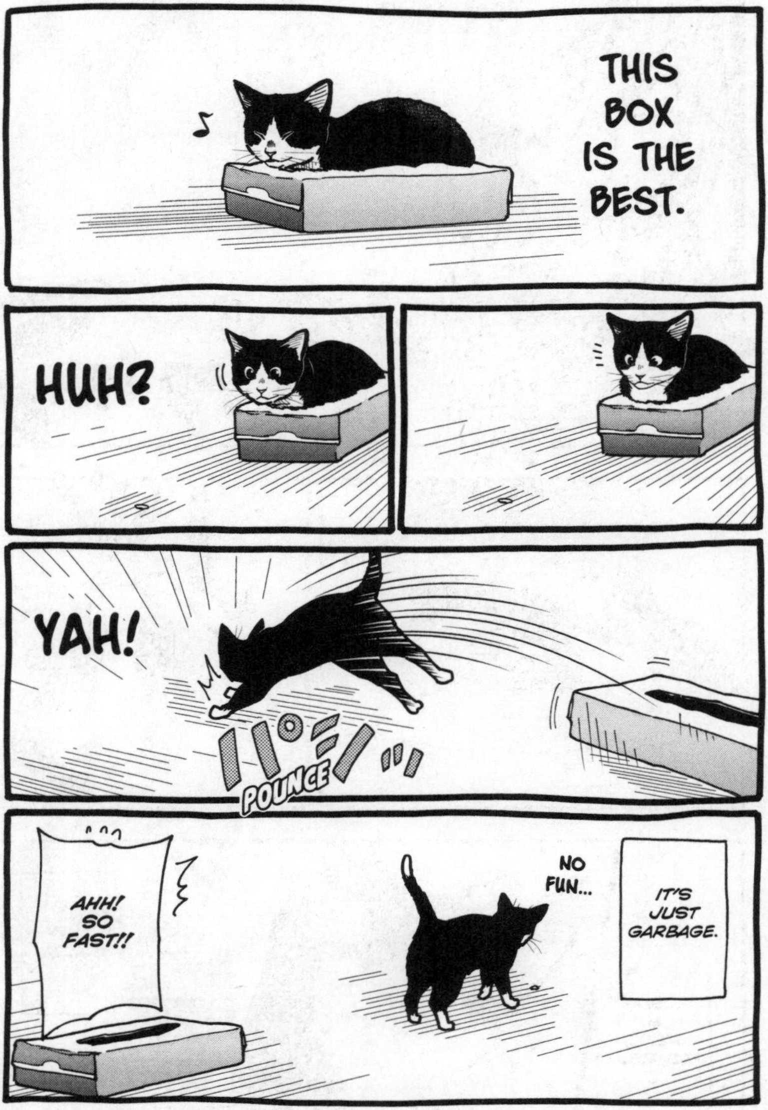
THIS BOX IS THE BEST.
HUH?
YAH!
POUNCE
IT'S JUST GARBAGE.
NO FUN...
AHH! SO FAST!!

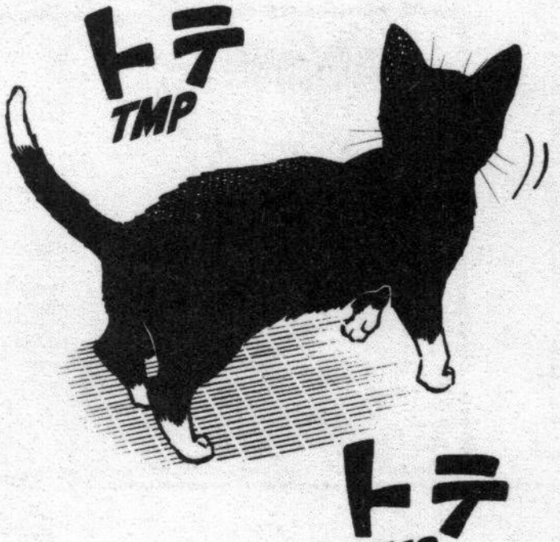
トテ
TMP
トテ
TMP

Chapter 6: Copper Sword

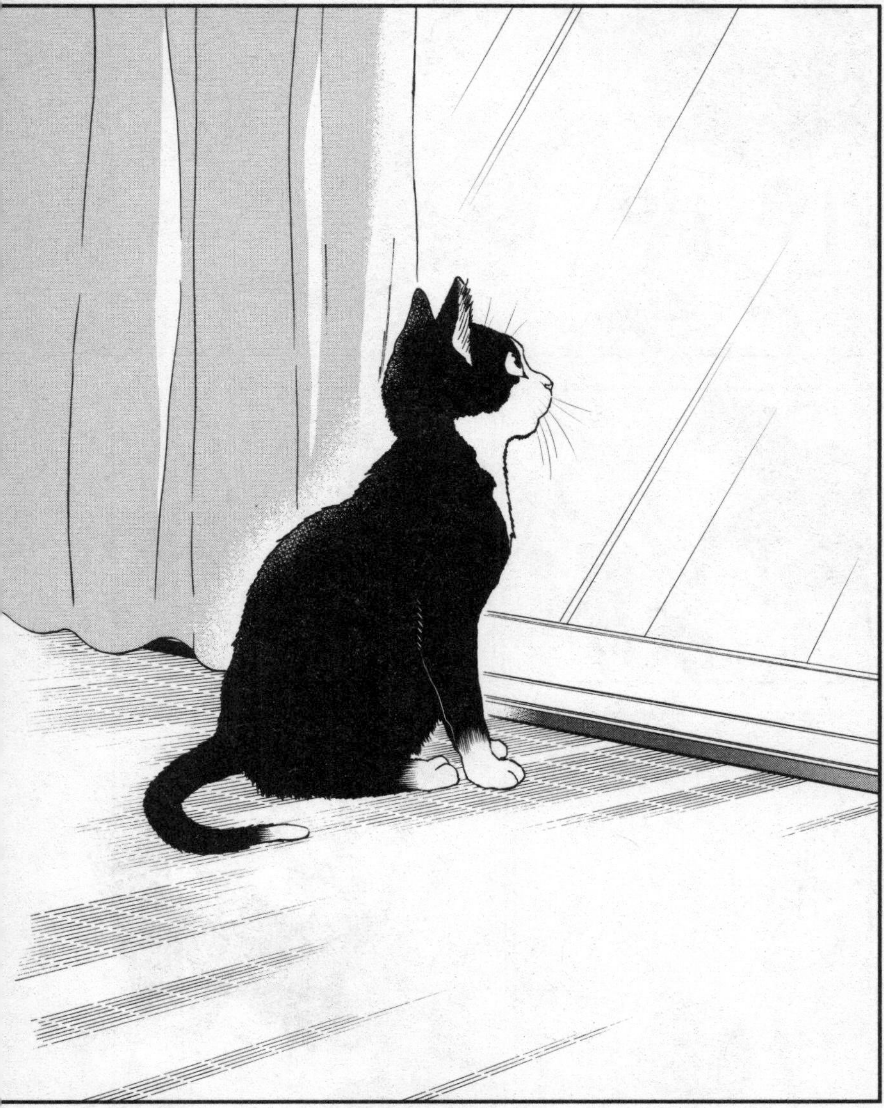

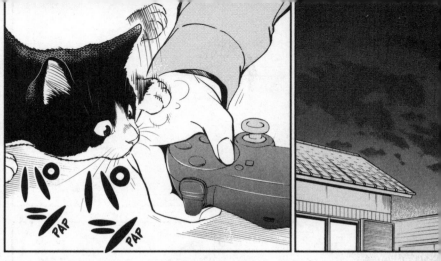

CLK ス

ギュ
SWP

AH...

IT'S
ALMOST
TIME...

モフ
PAT

モフ
PAT

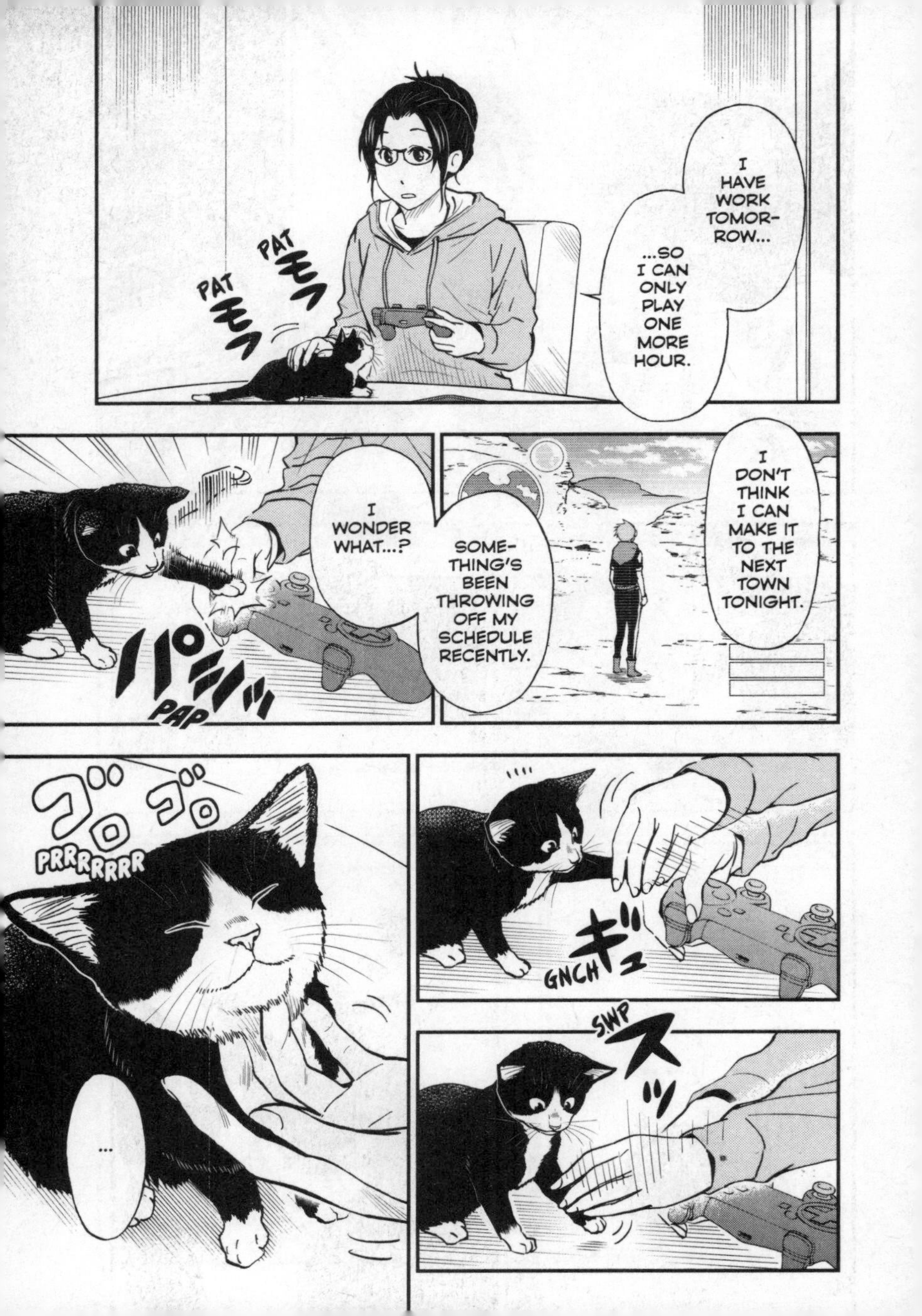
I HAVE WORK TOMORROW...
...SO I CAN ONLY PLAY ONE MORE HOUR.
PAT モフ
PAT モフ
I DON'T THINK I CAN MAKE IT TO THE NEXT TOWN TONIGHT.
SOMETHING'S BEEN THROWING OFF MY SCHEDULE RECENTLY.
I WONDER WHAT...?
パシッ
PAP
ギュ
GNCH
スッ
SWP
ゴロゴロ
PRRRRRRR
...

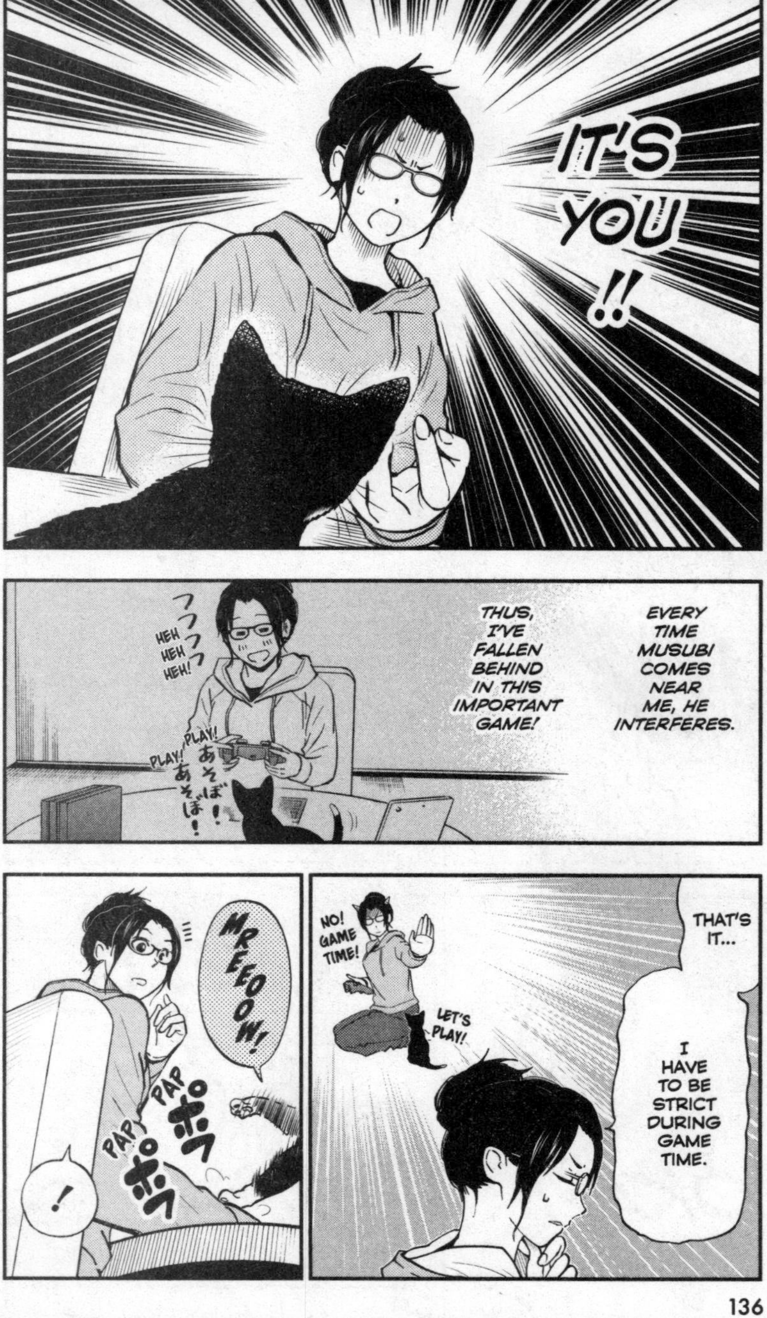
IT'S YOU!!
EVERY TIME MUSUBI COMES NEAR ME, HE INTERFERES.
THUS, I'VE FALLEN BEHIND IN THIS IMPORTANT GAME!
フフフ
HEH HEH HEH!
あそぼ!
PLAY!
あそぼ!
PLAY!
THAT'S IT...
I HAVE TO BE STRICT DURING GAME TIME.
NO! GAME TIME!
LET'S PLAY!
MREEOOW!
ポフ
PAP
ポフ
PAP
!

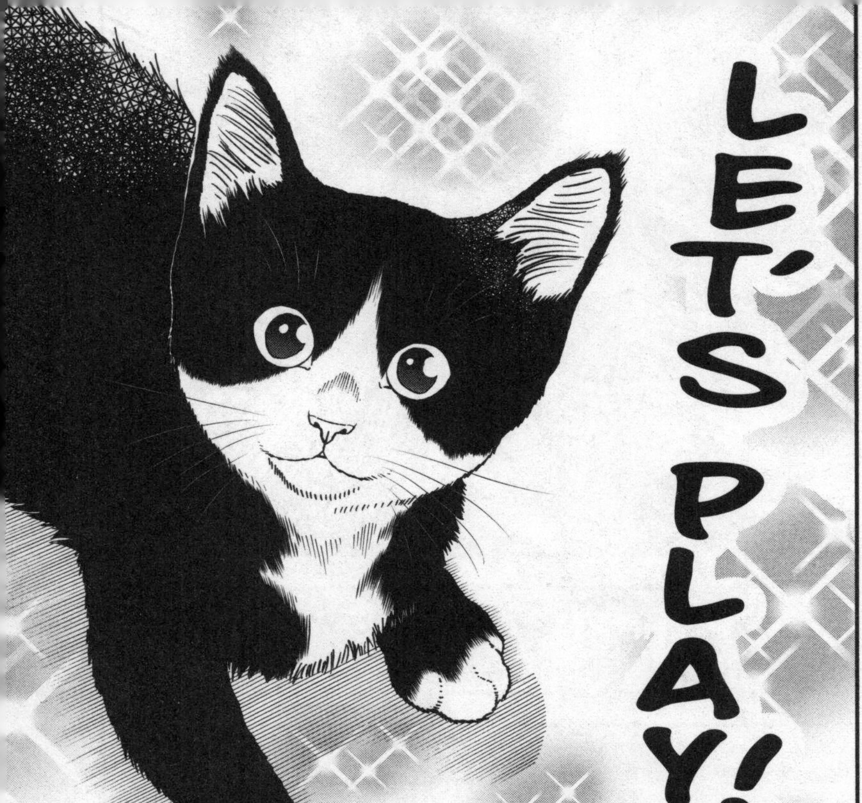
LET'S PLAY!
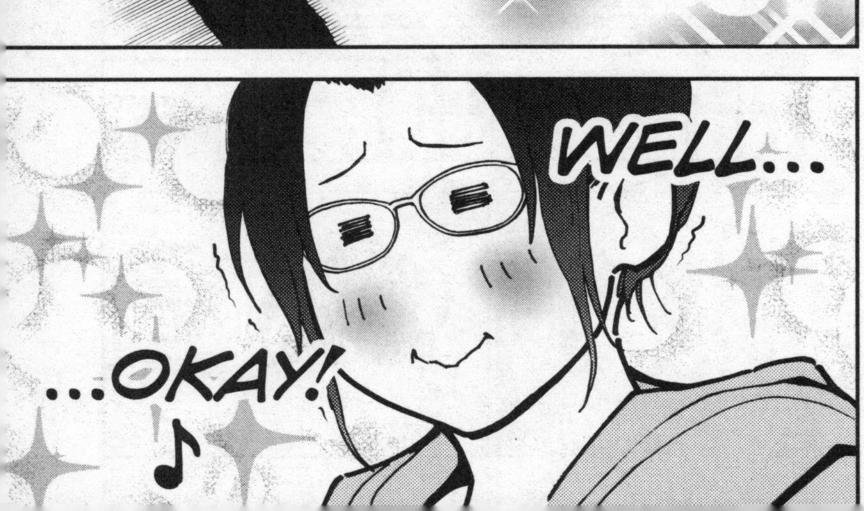
WELL...
...OKAY! ♪

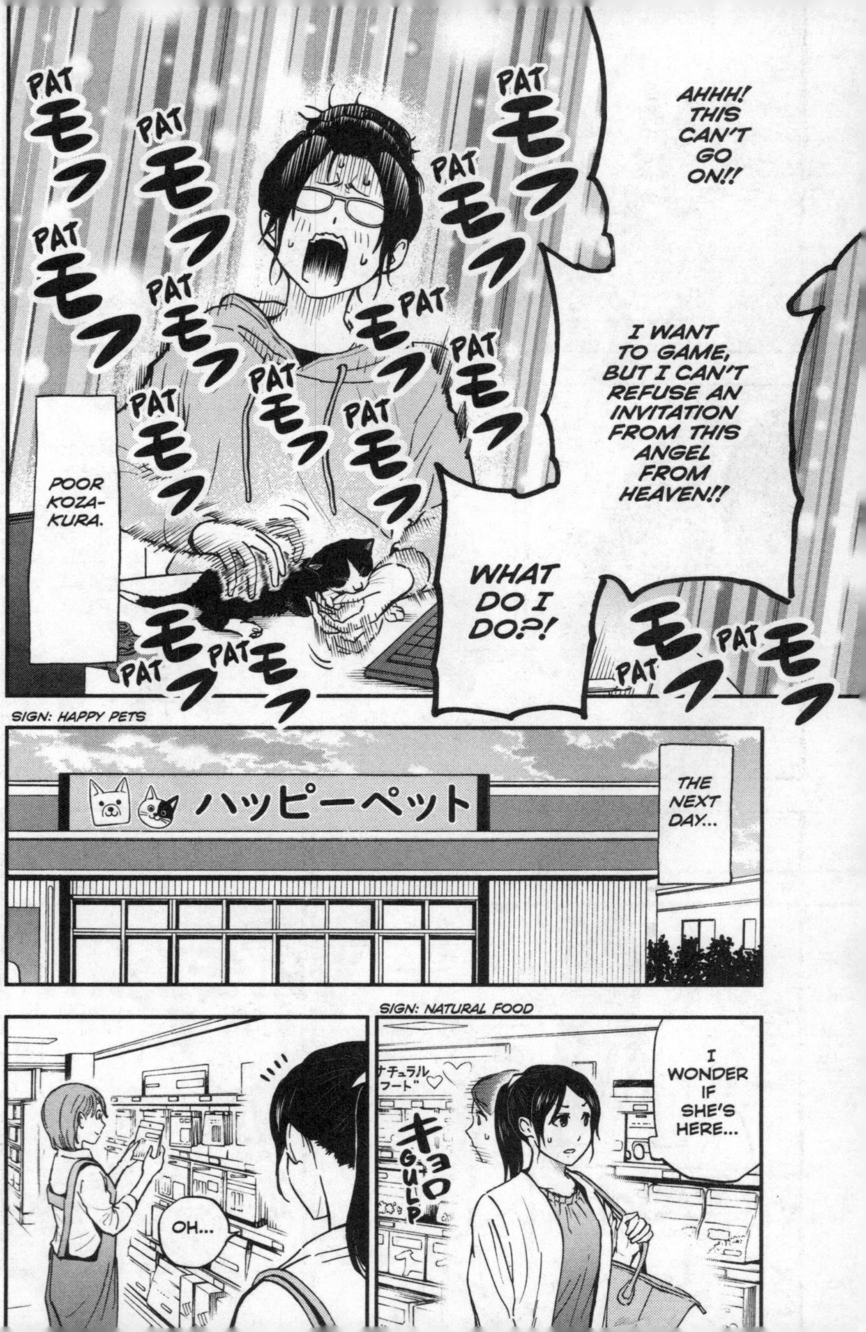
AHHH! THIS CAN'T GO ON!!
I WANT TO GAME, BUT I CAN'T REFUSE AN INVITATION FROM THIS ANGEL FROM HEAVEN!!
PAT モフ PAT モフ PAT モフ PAT モフ PAT モフ PAT モフ
WHAT DO I DO?!
PAT モフ PAT モフ PAT モフ PAT モフ PAT モフ PAT モフ PAT モフ PAT モフ
POOR KOZAKURA.
SIGN: HAPPY PETS
THE NEXT DAY...
ハッピーペット
SIGN: NATURAL FOOD
I WONDER IF SHE'S HERE...
ナチュラルフード♡
キョロ
GULP
OH...

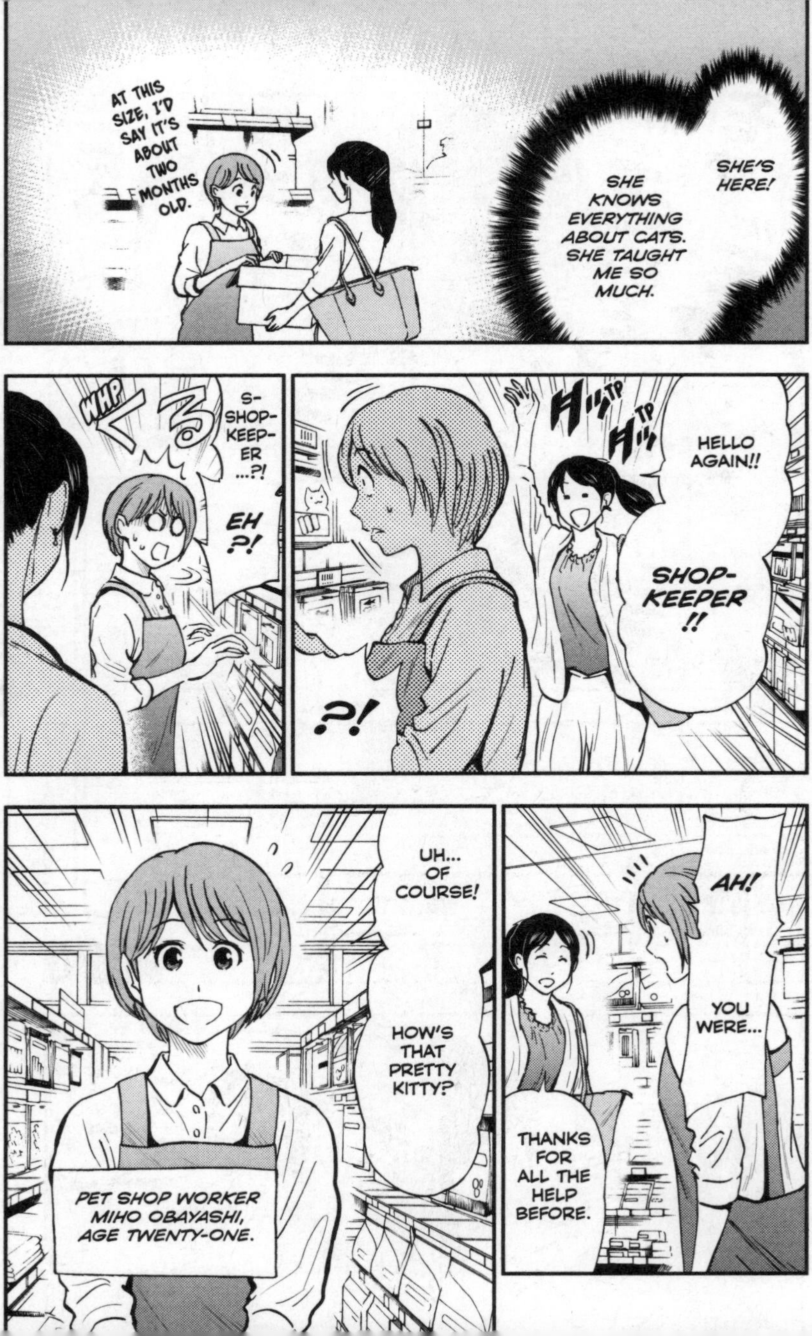
SHE'S HERE!
SHE KNOWS EVERYTHING ABOUT CATS. SHE TAUGHT ME SO MUCH.
AT THIS SIZE, I'D SAY IT'S ABOUT TWO MONTHS OLD.
TP
TP
HELLO AGAIN!!
SHOP-KEEPER!!
?!
WHP
くる
S-SHOP-KEEPER...?!
EH?!
AH!
YOU WERE...
THANKS FOR ALL THE HELP BEFORE.
UH... OF COURSE!
HOW'S THAT PRETTY KITTY?
PET SHOP WORKER MIHO OBAYASHI, AGE TWENTY-ONE.

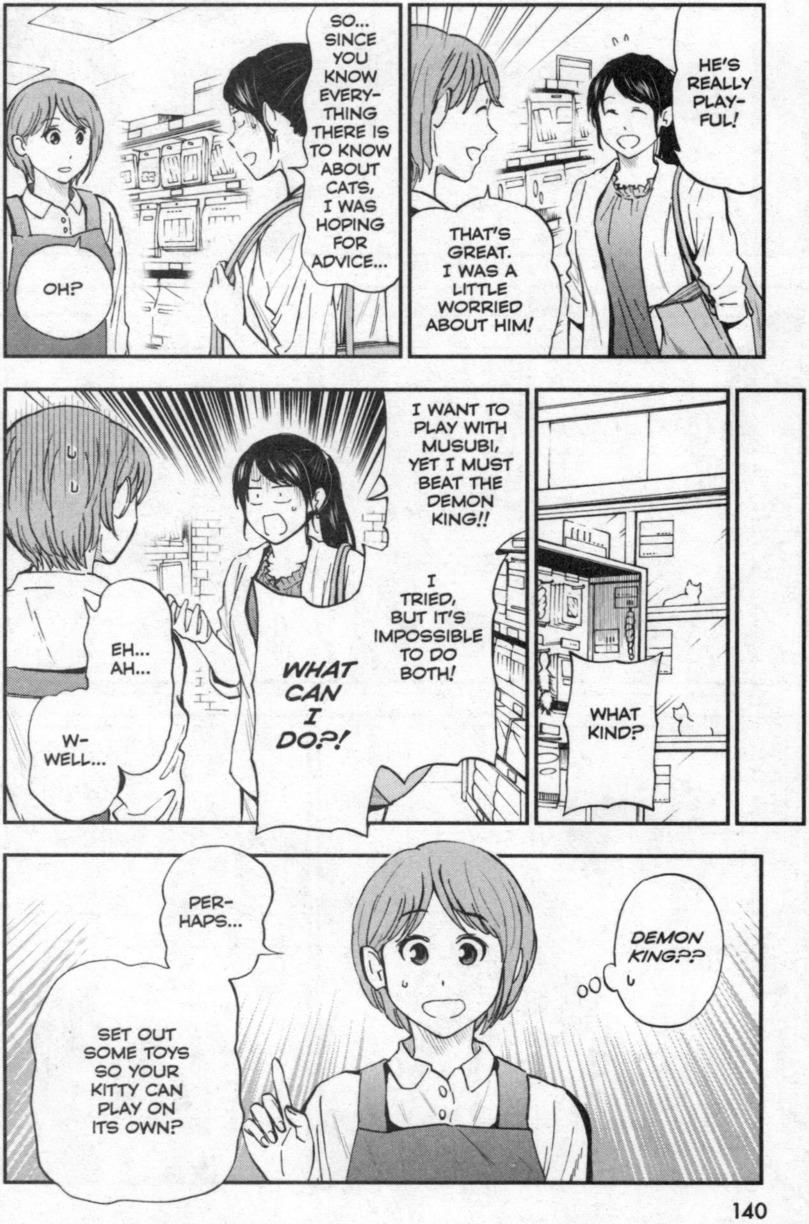
HE'S REALLY PLAYFUL!
THAT'S GREAT. I WAS A LITTLE WORRIED ABOUT HIM!
SO... SINCE YOU KNOW EVERYTHING THERE IS TO KNOW ABOUT CATS, I WAS HOPING FOR ADVICE...
OH?
WHAT KIND?
I WANT TO PLAY WITH MUSUBI, YET I MUST BEAT THE DEMON KING!!
I TRIED, BUT IT'S IMPOSSIBLE TO DO BOTH!
WHAT CAN I DO?!
EH... AH...
W-WELL...
DEMON KING??
PER-HAPS...
SET OUT SOME TOYS SO YOUR KITTY CAN PLAY ON ITS OWN?

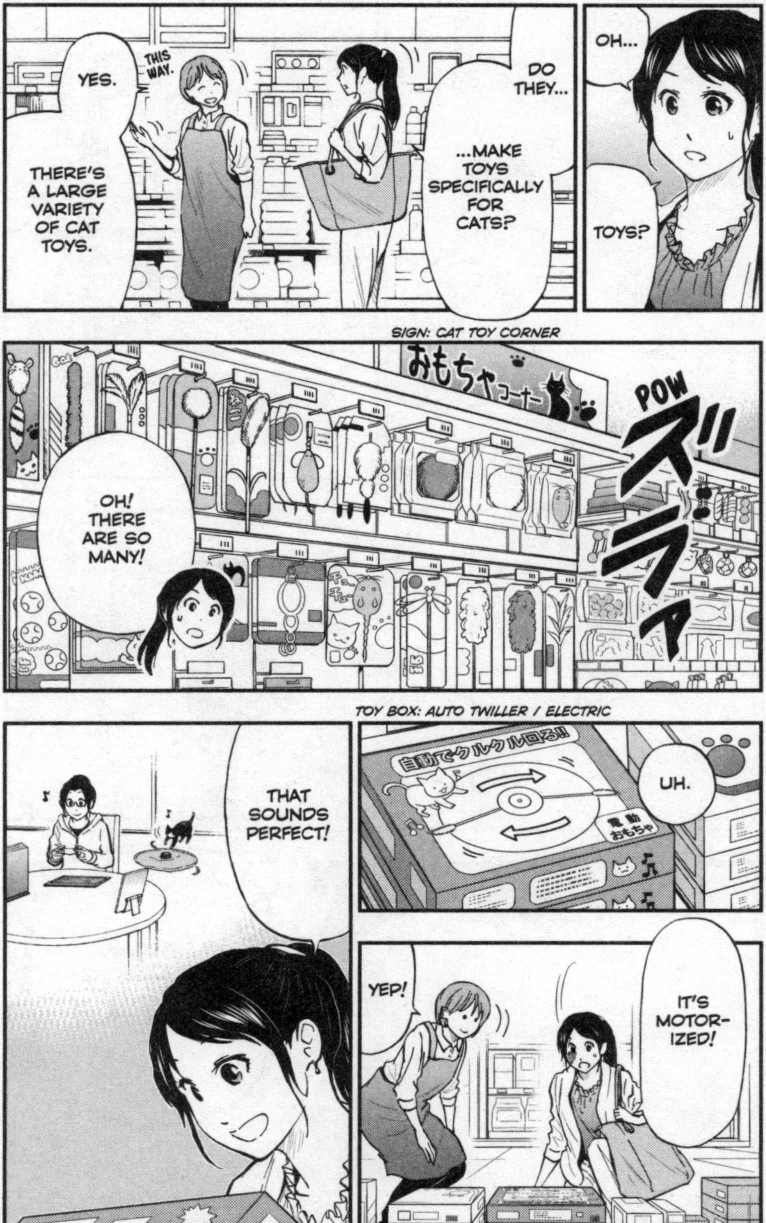
OH...
TOYS?
DO THEY...
...MAKE TOYS SPECIFICALLY FOR CATS?
YES.
THIS WAY.
THERE'S A LARGE VARIETY OF CAT TOYS.
SIGN: CAT TOY CORNER
おもちゃコーナー
POW
ズラァ
OH! THERE ARE SO MANY!
TOY BOX: AUTO TWILLER / ELECTRIC
自動でクルクル回る!!
電動おもちゃ
UH.
IT'S MOTOR-IZED!
YEP!
THAT SOUNDS PERFECT!

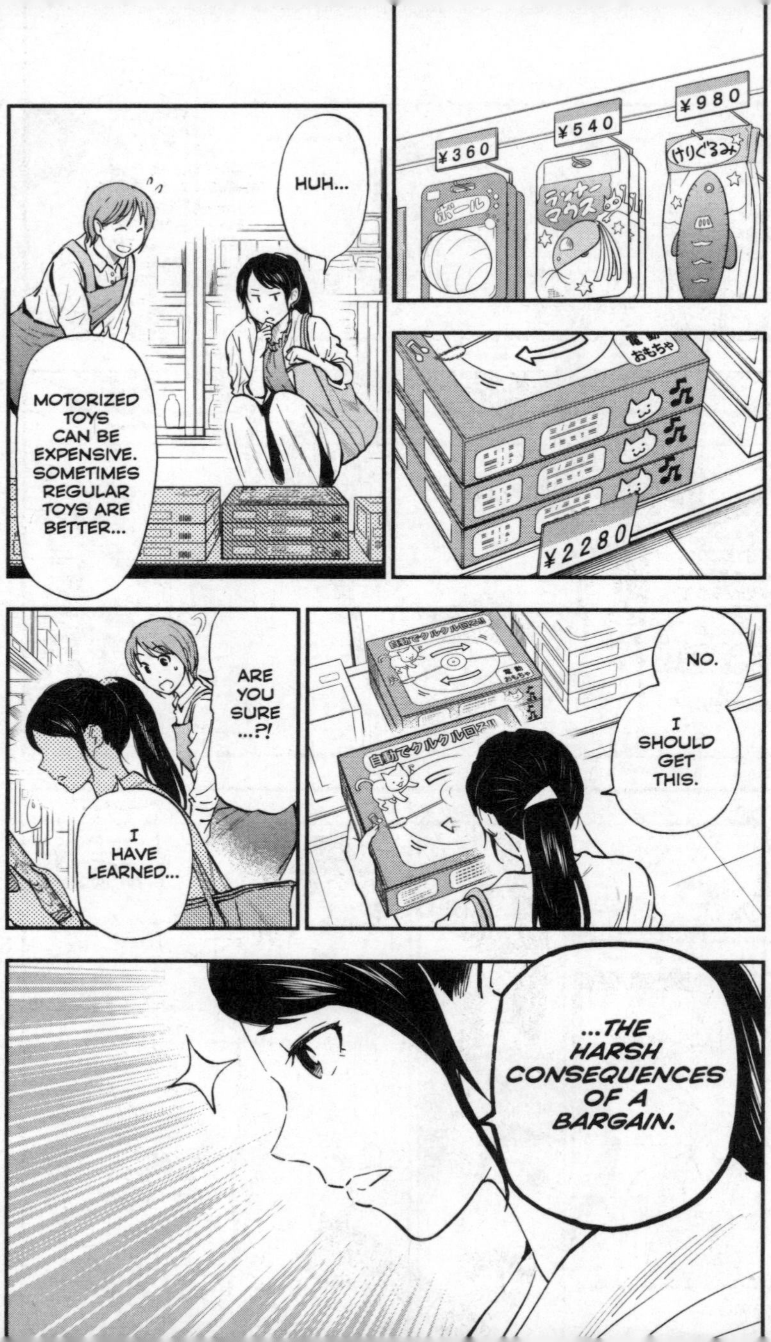
¥360
ボール
¥540
ランナーマウス
¥980
けりぐるみ
電動おもちゃ
¥2280
HUH...
MOTORIZED TOYS CAN BE EXPENSIVE. SOMETIMES REGULAR TOYS ARE BETTER...
自動でクルクル回る!!
電動おもちゃ
NO.
I SHOULD GET THIS.
ARE YOU SURE ...?!
I HAVE LEARNED...
...THE HARSH CONSEQUENCES OF A BARGAIN.

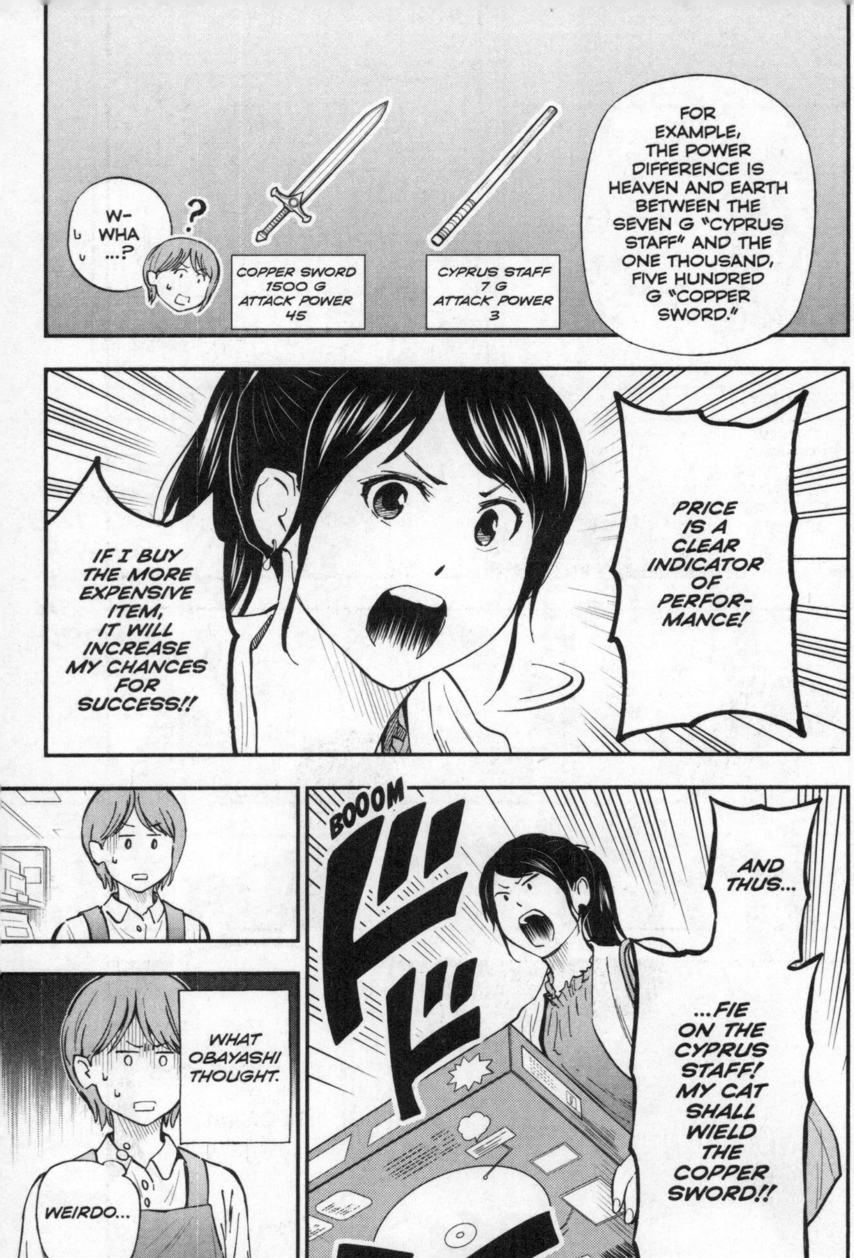
FOR EXAMPLE, THE POWER DIFFERENCE IS HEAVEN AND EARTH BETWEEN THE SEVEN G "CYPRUS STAFF" AND THE ONE THOUSAND, FIVE HUNDRED G "COPPER SWORD."
CYPRUS STAFF 7 G ATTACK POWER 3
COPPER SWORD 1500 G ATTACK POWER 45
W-WHA ...?
?
PRICE IS A CLEAR INDICATOR OF PERFOR-MANCE!
IF I BUY THE MORE EXPENSIVE ITEM, IT WILL INCREASE MY CHANCES FOR SUCCESS!!
AND THUS...
...FIE ON THE CYPRUS STAFF! MY CAT SHALL WIELD THE COPPER SWORD!!
BOOOM
ドド
WHAT OBAYASHI THOUGHT.
WEIRDO...

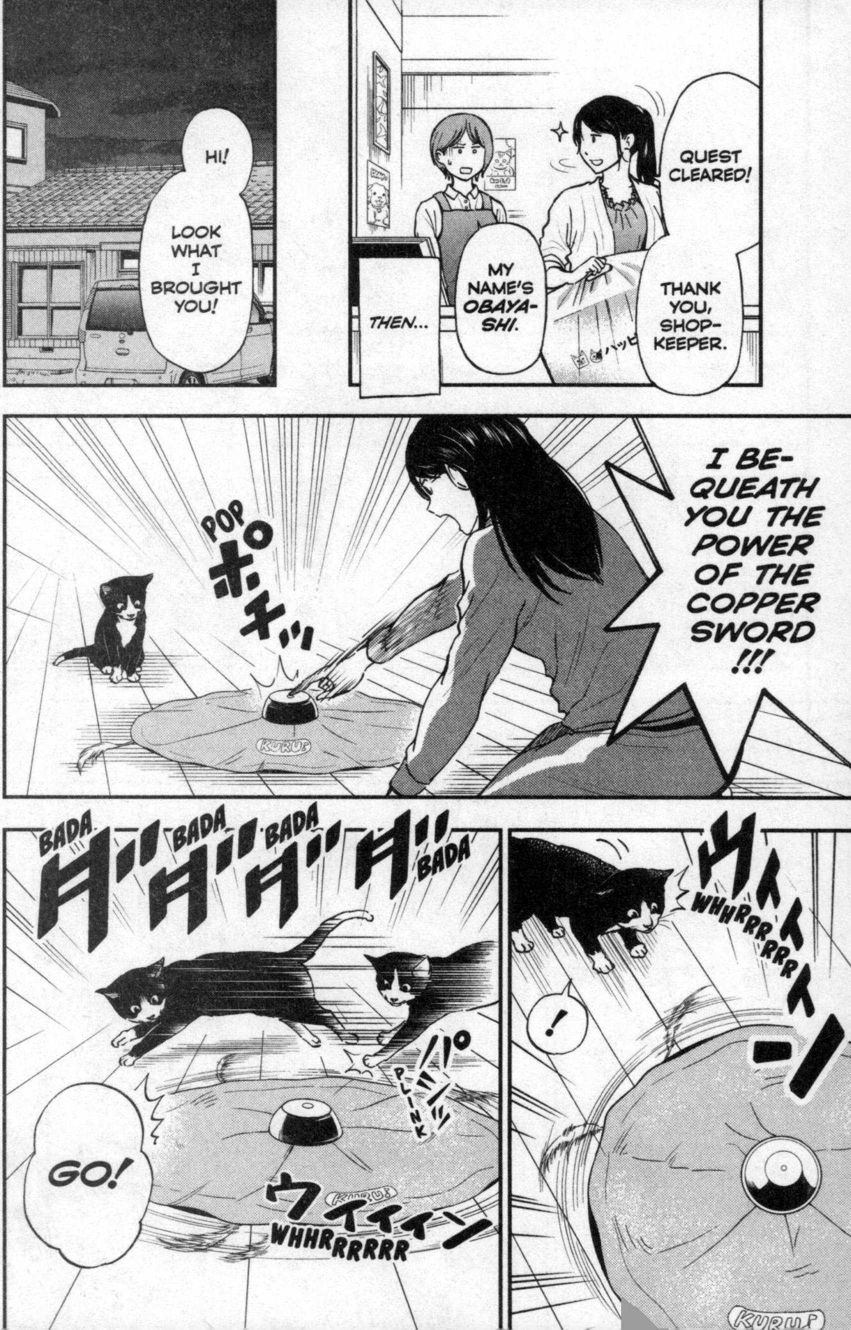
QUEST CLEARED!
THANK YOU, SHOPKEEPER.
MY NAME'S OBAYASHI.
THEN...
HI!
LOOK WHAT I BROUGHT YOU!
I BEQUEATH YOU THE POWER OF THE COPPER SWORD!!!
POP
ポチッ
KURU!
ウイイイーン
WHHRRRRRR
!
KURU!
BADA BADA BADA BADA
PLINK
GO!
ウイイイーン
WHHRRRRRR
KURU!

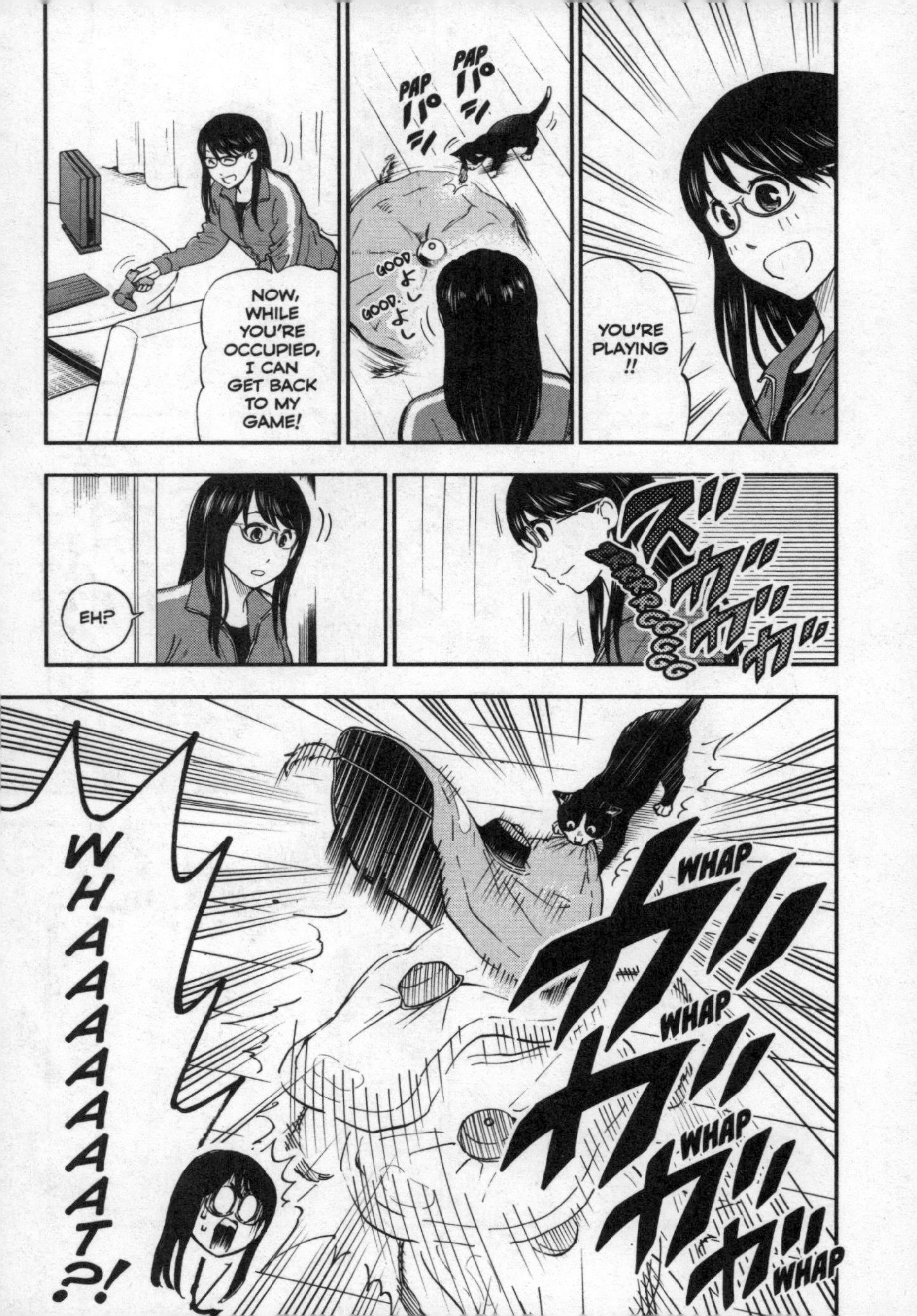
YOU'RE PLAYING !!
PAP
PAP
GOOD よし
GOOD よし
NOW, WHILE YOU'RE OCCUPIED, I CAN GET BACK TO MY GAME!
EH?
WHAP
WHAP
WHAP
WHAP
WHAAAAAAAAAT?!

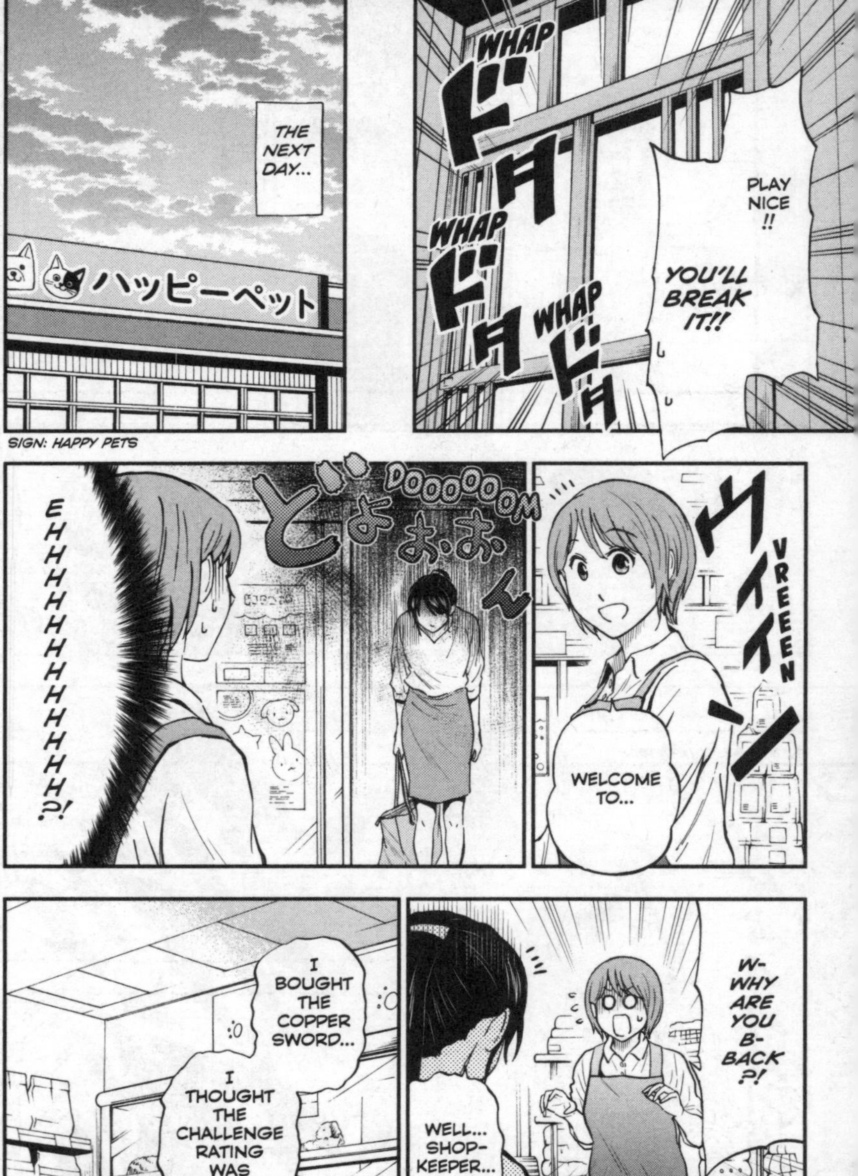

WHAP
WHAP
WHAP
PLAY NICE!!
YOU'LL BREAK IT!!
THE NEXT DAY...
ハッピーペット
VREEEN
WELCOME TO...
DOOOOOOOM
EHHHHHHHHHHHHH?!
W-WHY ARE YOU B-BACK?!
WELL... SHOP-KEEPER...
I BOUGHT THE COPPER SWORD...
I THOUGHT THE CHALLENGE RATING WAS PERFECT...

SIGN: HAPPY PETS

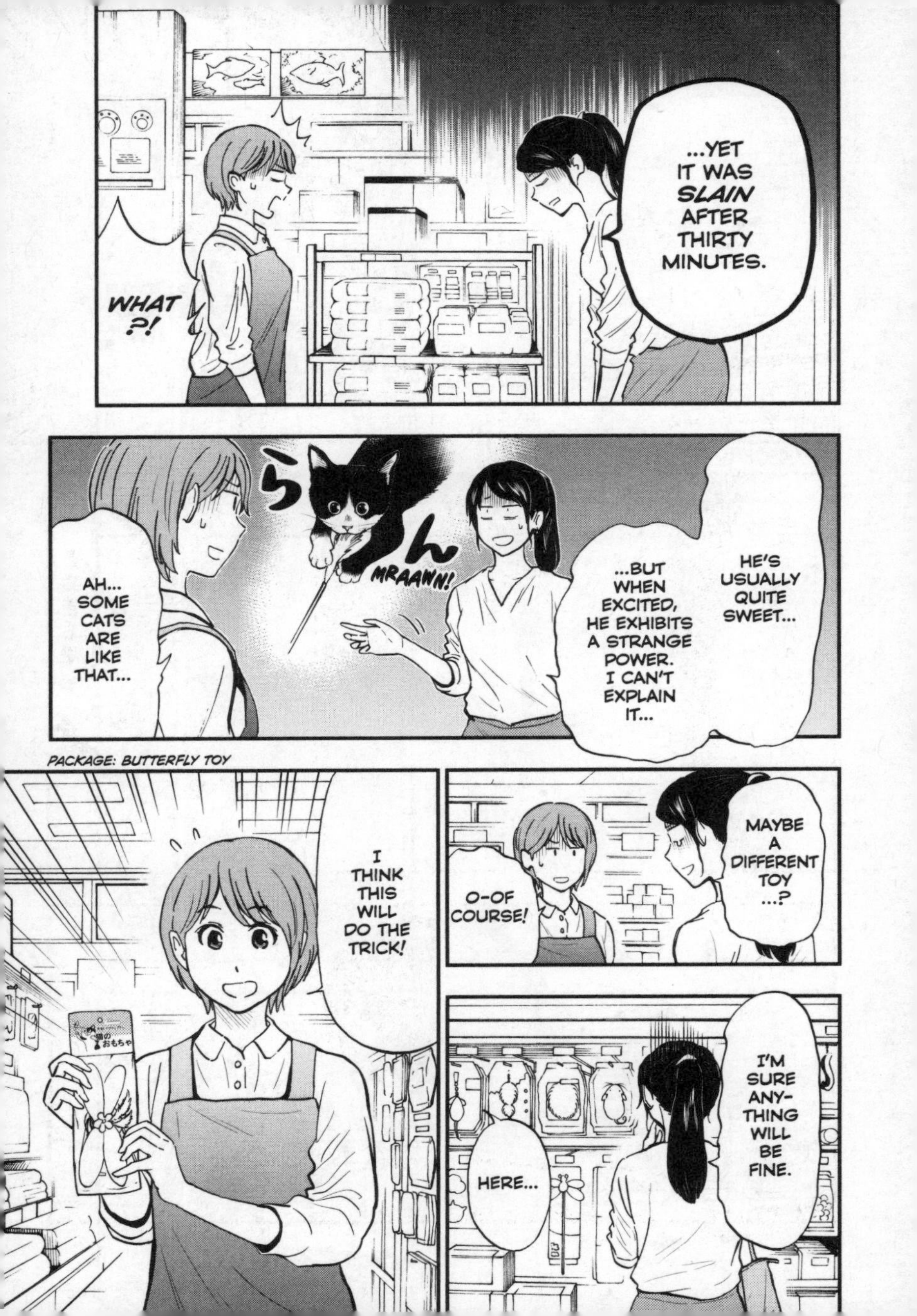
...YET IT WAS SLAIN AFTER THIRTY MINUTES.
WHAT?!
HE'S USUALLY QUITE SWEET...
...BUT WHEN EXCITED, HE EXHIBITS A STRANGE POWER. I CAN'T EXPLAIN IT...
MRAAWN!
AH... SOME CATS ARE LIKE THAT...
MAYBE A DIFFERENT TOY ...?
O-OF COURSE!
I'M SURE ANYTHING WILL BE FINE.
HERE...
I THINK THIS WILL DO THE TRICK!
猫の おもちゃ
PACKAGE: BUTTERFLY TOY

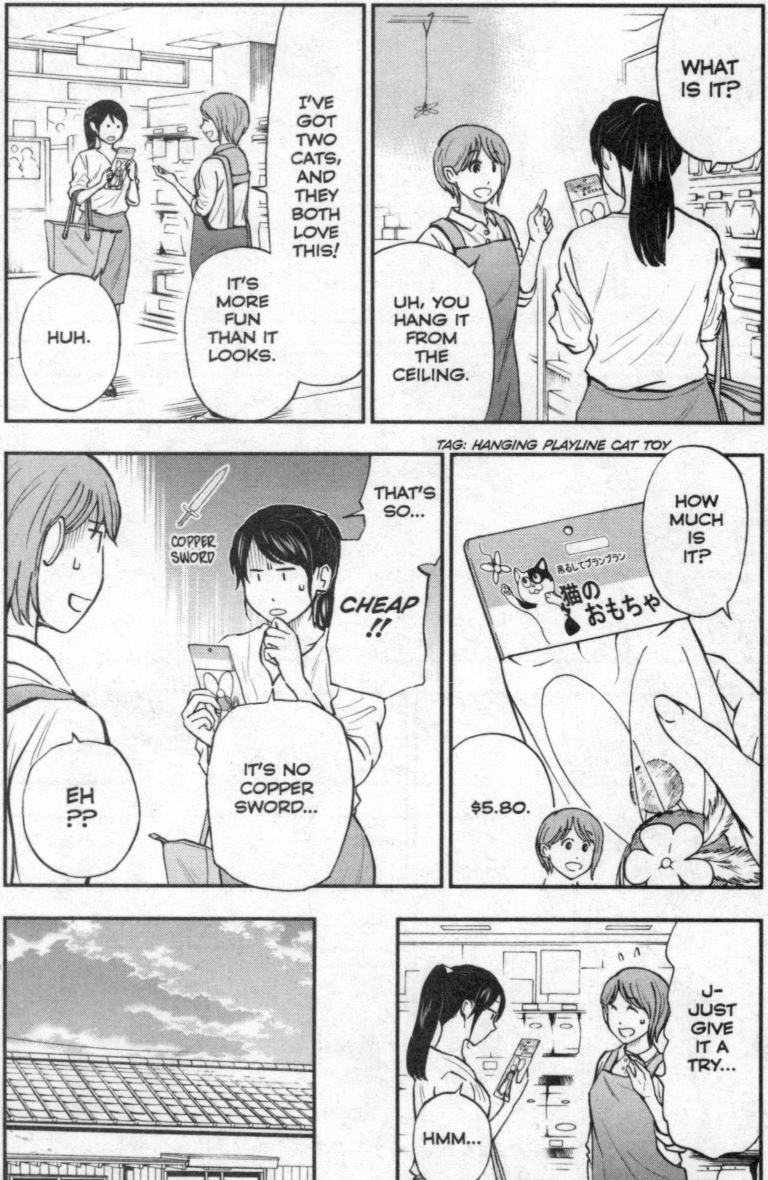
WHAT IS IT?
UH, YOU HANG IT FROM THE CEILING.
I'VE GOT TWO CATS, AND THEY BOTH LOVE THIS!
IT'S MORE FUN THAN IT LOOKS.
HUH.
TAG: HANGING PLAYLINE CAT TOY
HOW MUCH IS IT?
吊るしてブランブラン
猫のおもちゃ
$5.80.
THAT'S SO...
CHEAP !!
COPPER SWORD
IT'S NO COPPER SWORD...
EH ??
J-JUST GIVE IT A TRY...
HMM...

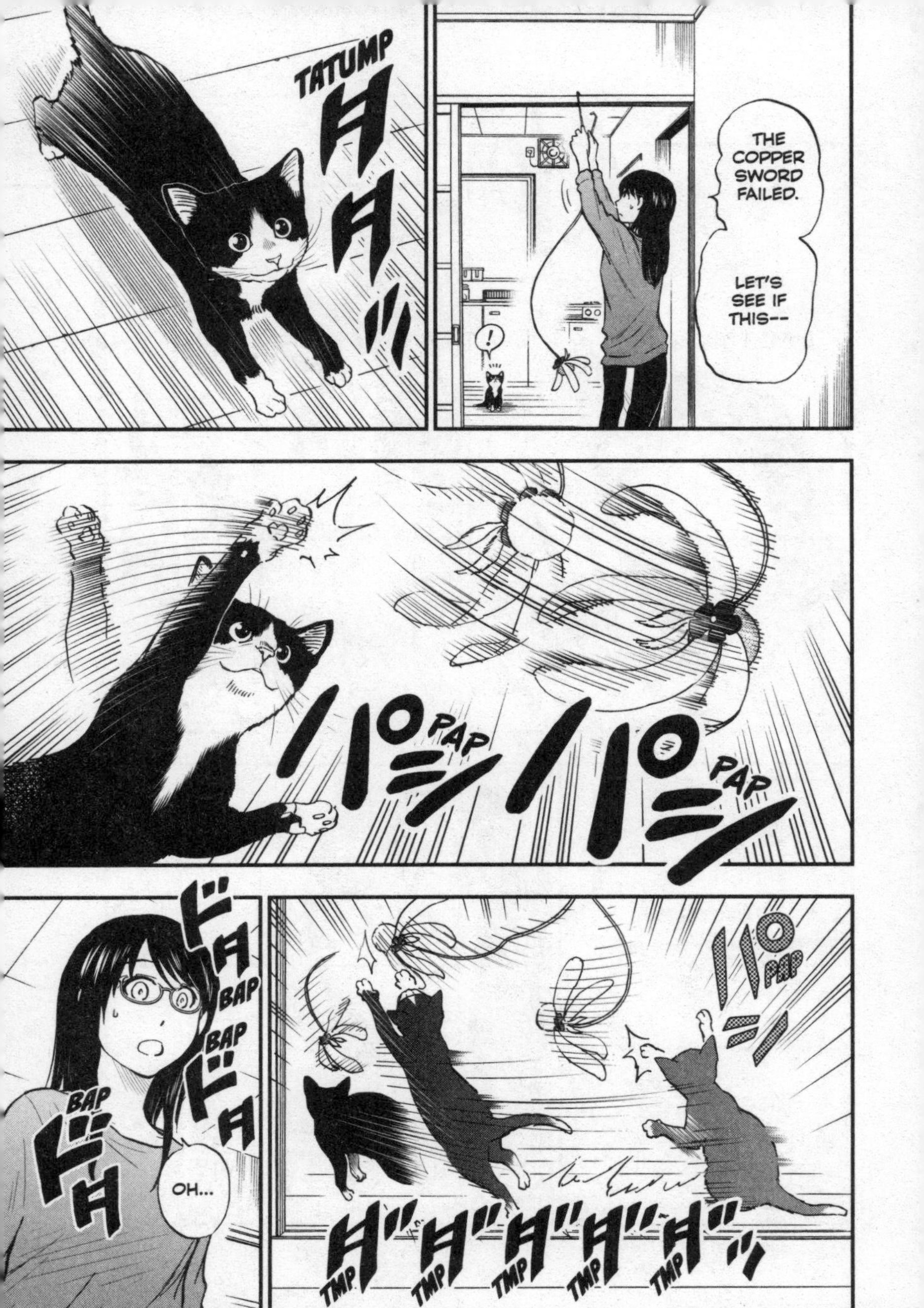
THE COPPER SWORD FAILED.
LET'S SEE IF THIS--
!
TATUMP
PAP
PAP
PAP
TMP
TMP
TMP
TMP
TMP
BAP
BAP
BAP
OH...

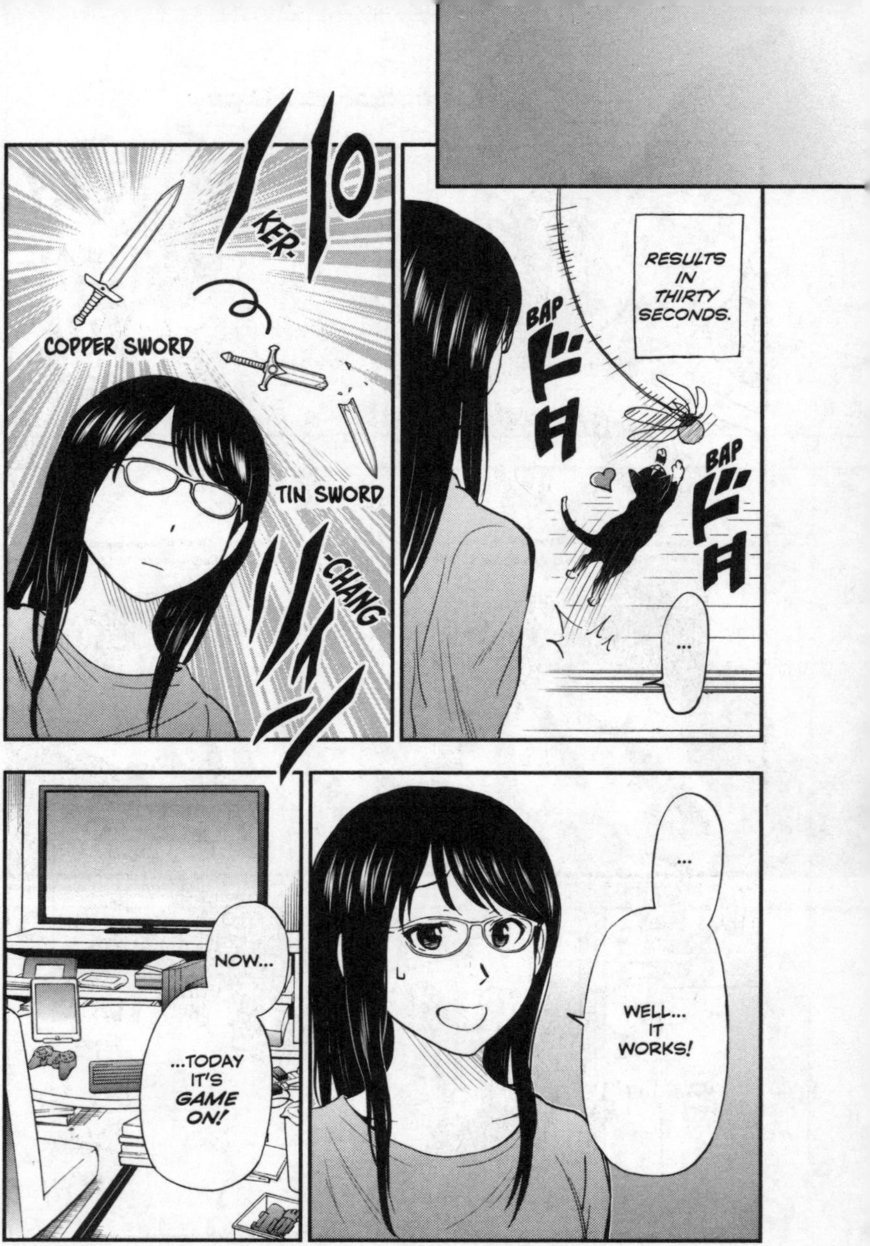

RESULTS IN THIRTY SECONDS.
BAP
ドタ
BAP
ドタ
...
COPPER SWORD
KER-
TIN SWORD
-CHANG
...
WELL... IT WORKS!
NOW...
...TODAY IT'S GAME ON!

Chapter 6: Bonus Stage

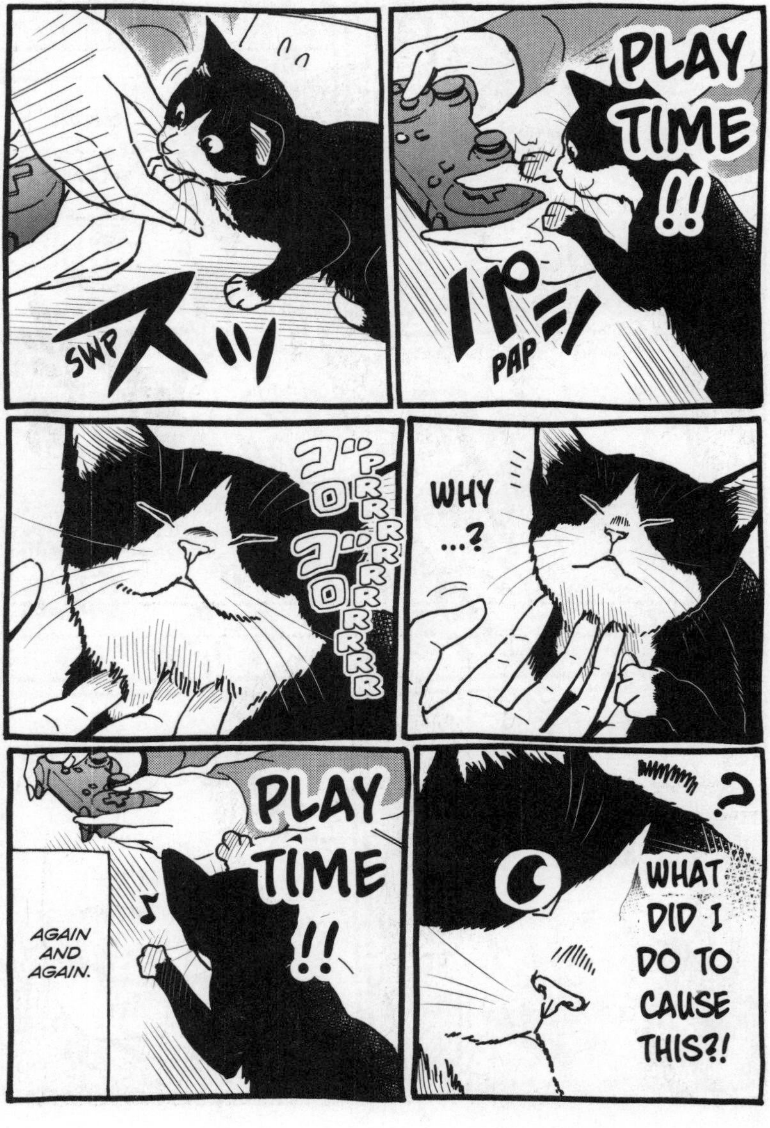

PLAY TIME !!
PAP
SWP
WHY ...?
PRRRRRRRRRRRR
?
WHAT DID I DO TO CAUSE THIS?!
PLAY TIME !!
AGAIN AND AGAIN.

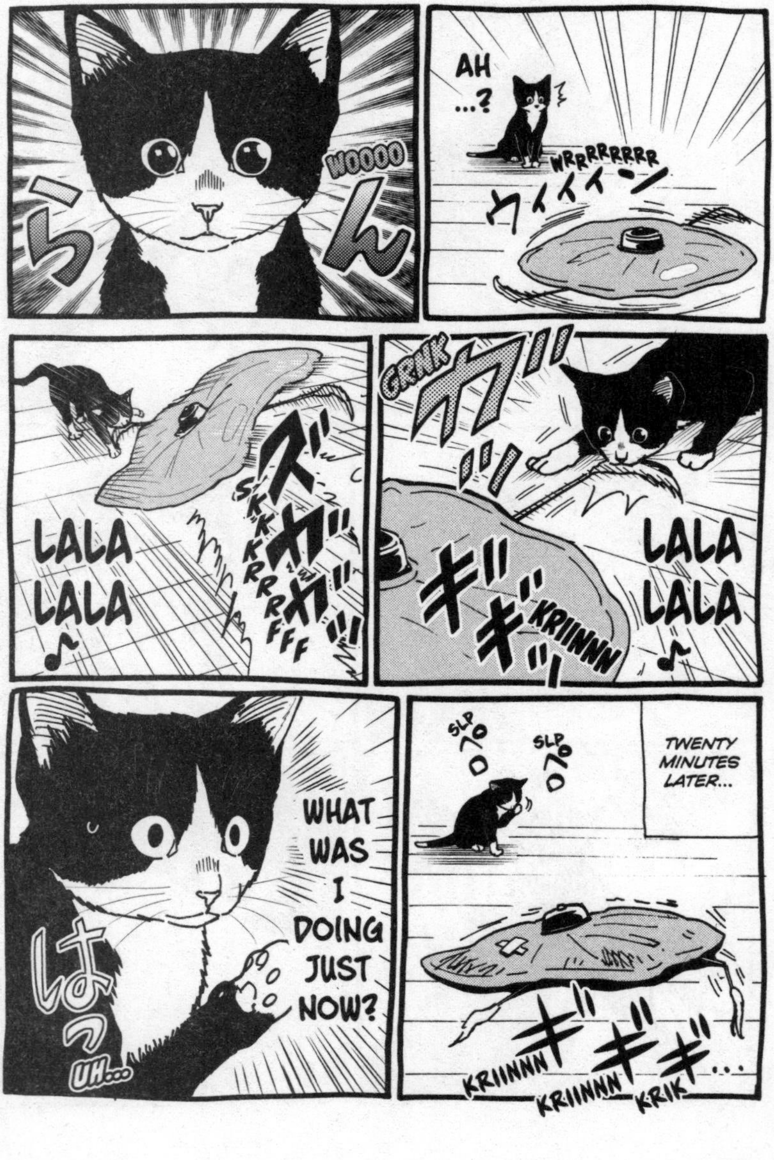
AH ...?
WRRRRRRRR
ウイイーン
WOOOO
GRNK
KRIINNN
LALA LALA ♪
LALA LALA ♪
SKKKRRRRFFF
TWENTY MINUTES LATER...
SLP
SLP
KRIINNN
KRIINNN
KRIK
...
WHAT WAS I DOING JUST NOW?
UH...

CAT +
GAMER

Chapter 7: Check

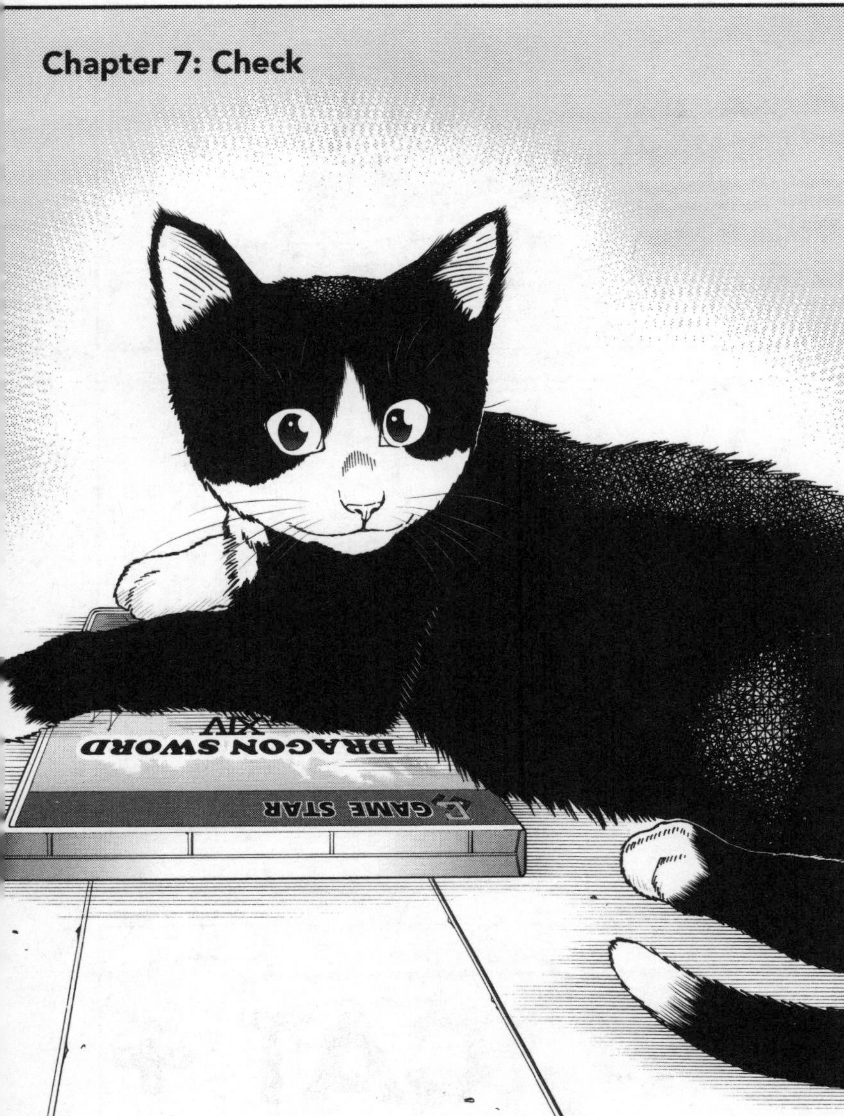
DRAGON SWORD XIV
GAME STAR

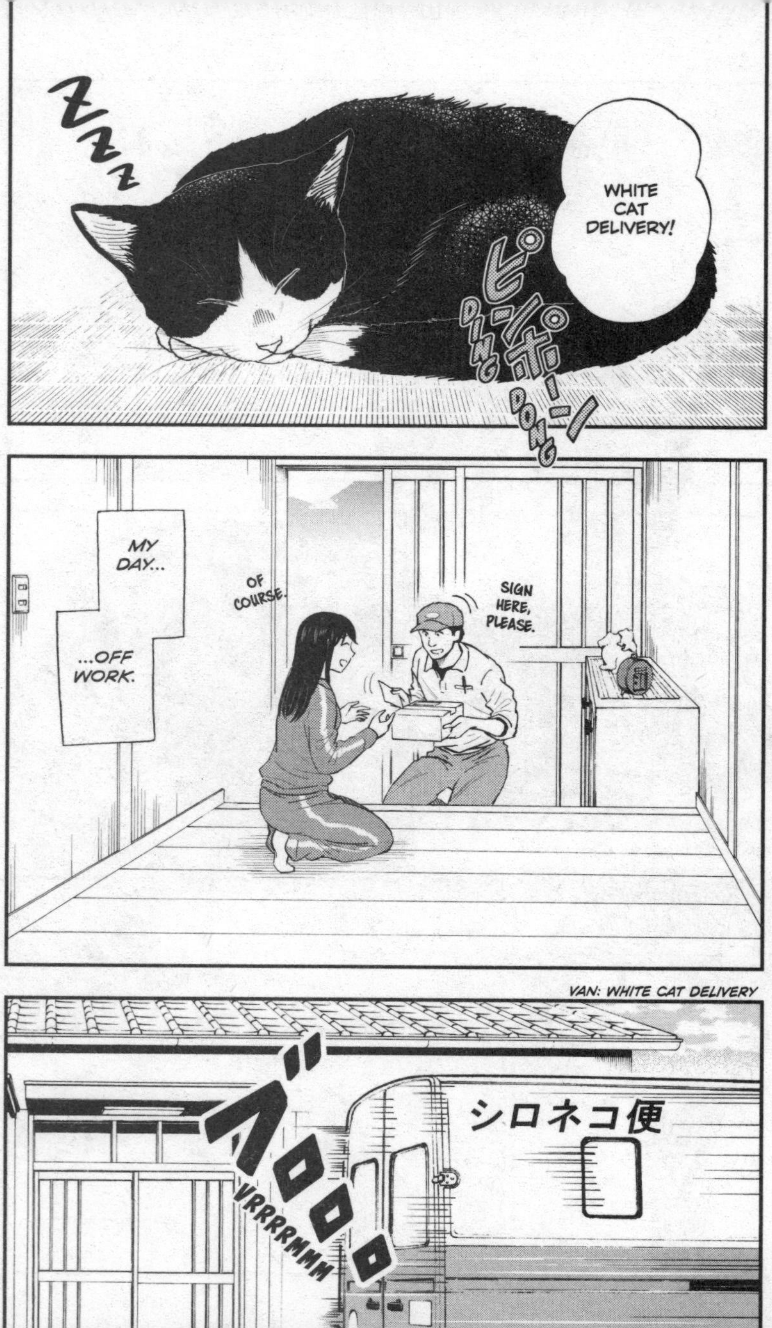
ZZZ
WHITE CAT DELIVERY!
ピンポーン
DING DONG
SIGN HERE, PLEASE.
OF COURSE.
MY DAY...
...OFF WORK.
VAN: WHITE CAT DELIVERY
シロネコ便
ブロロロロ
VRRRRMMM

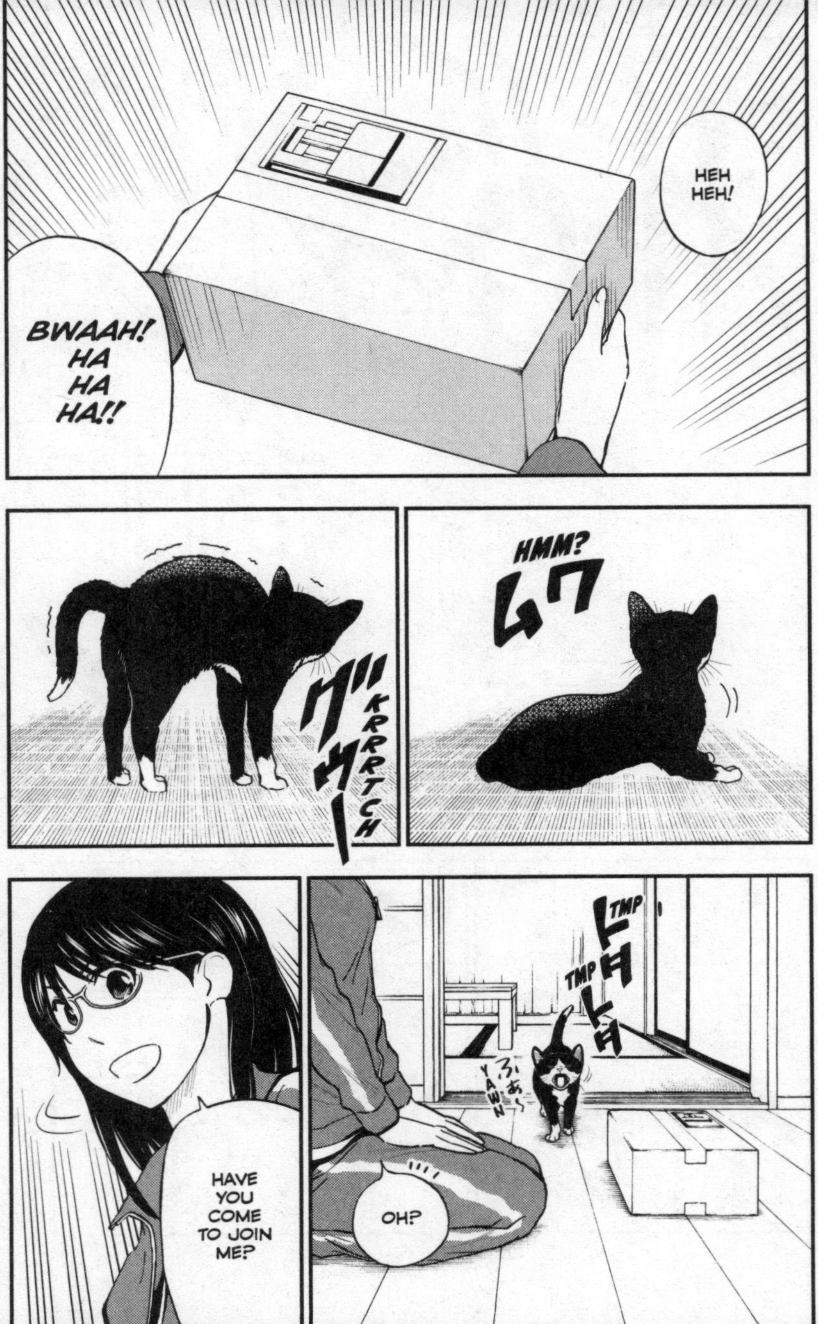
HEH HEH!
BWAAH! HA HA HA!!
HMM?
KRRRTCH
TMP
TMP
YAWN
OH?
HAVE YOU COME TO JOIN ME?

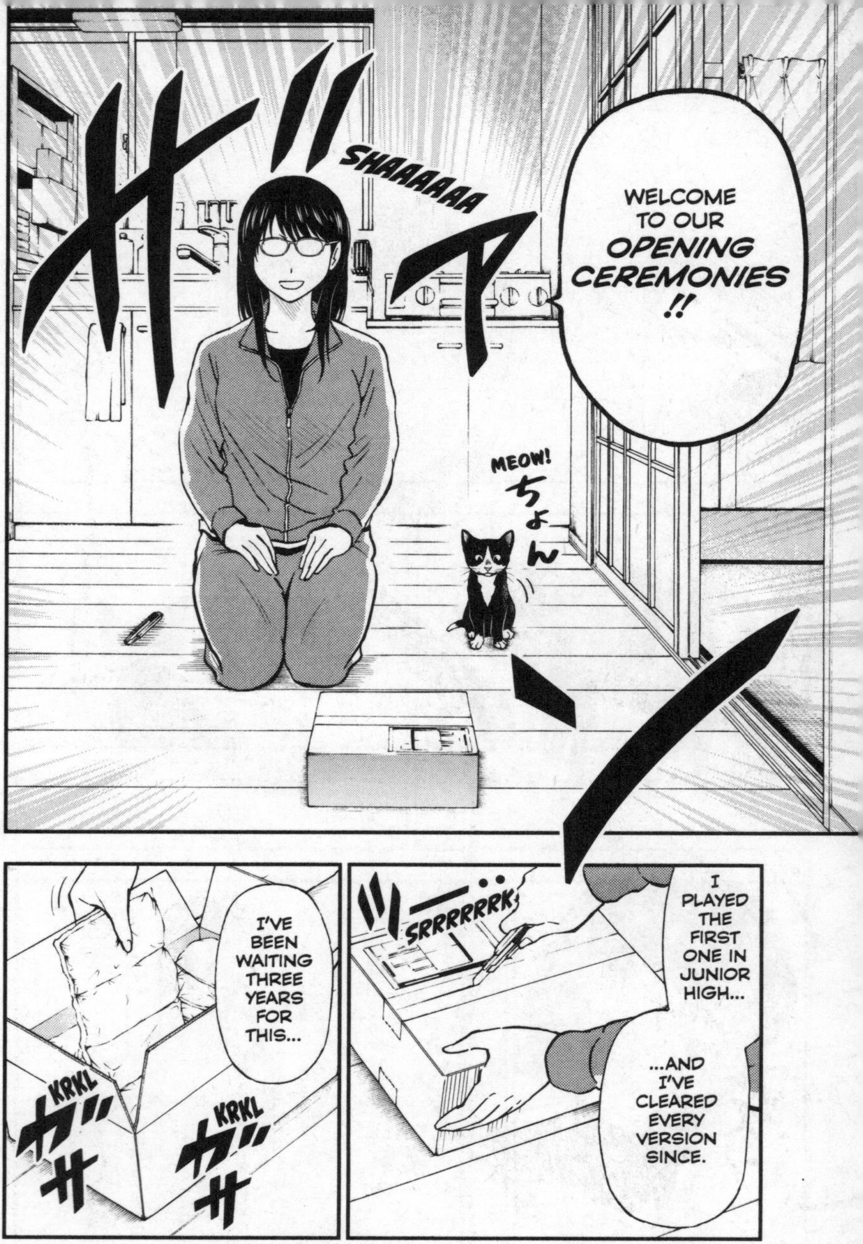
SHAAAAAAA
WELCOME TO OUR OPENING CEREMONIES!!
MEOW!
ちょん
SRRRRRRK
I PLAYED THE FIRST ONE IN JUNIOR HIGH...
...AND I'VE CLEARED EVERY VERSION SINCE.
I'VE BEEN WAITING THREE YEARS FOR THIS...
KRKL
KRKL

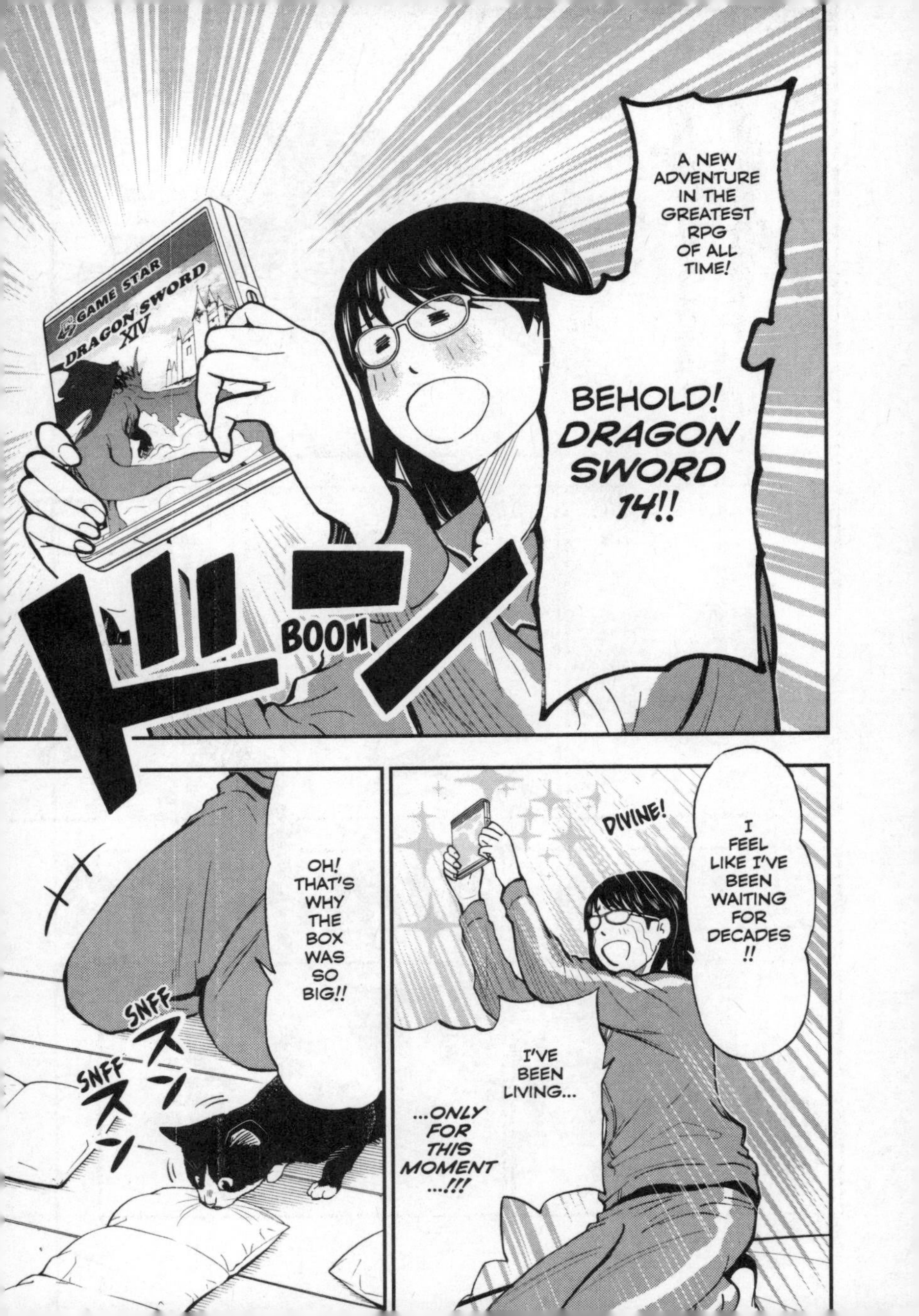
A NEW ADVENTURE IN THE GREATEST RPG OF ALL TIME!
BEHOLD! *DRAGON SWORD 14*!!
GAME STAR
DRAGON SWORD XIV
ドーン
BOOM
I FEEL LIKE I'VE BEEN WAITING FOR DECADES!!
DIVINE!
I'VE BEEN LIVING...
...ONLY FOR THIS MOMENT...!!!
OH! THAT'S WHY THE BOX WAS SO BIG!!
スーッ
SNFF
スーッ
SNFF

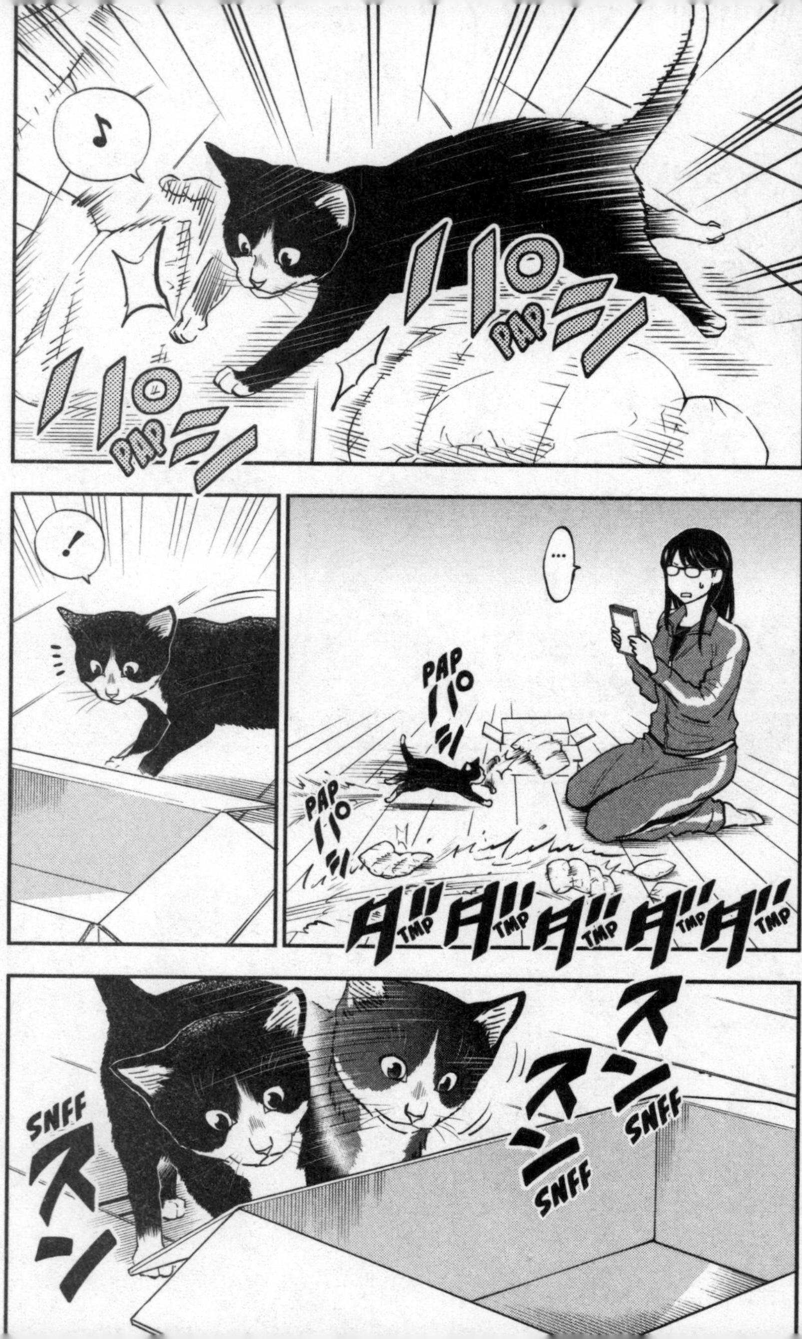
♪
PAP
PAP
...
PAP
PAP
TMP
TMP
TMP
TMP
TMP
!
SNFF
SNFF
SNFF
SNFF

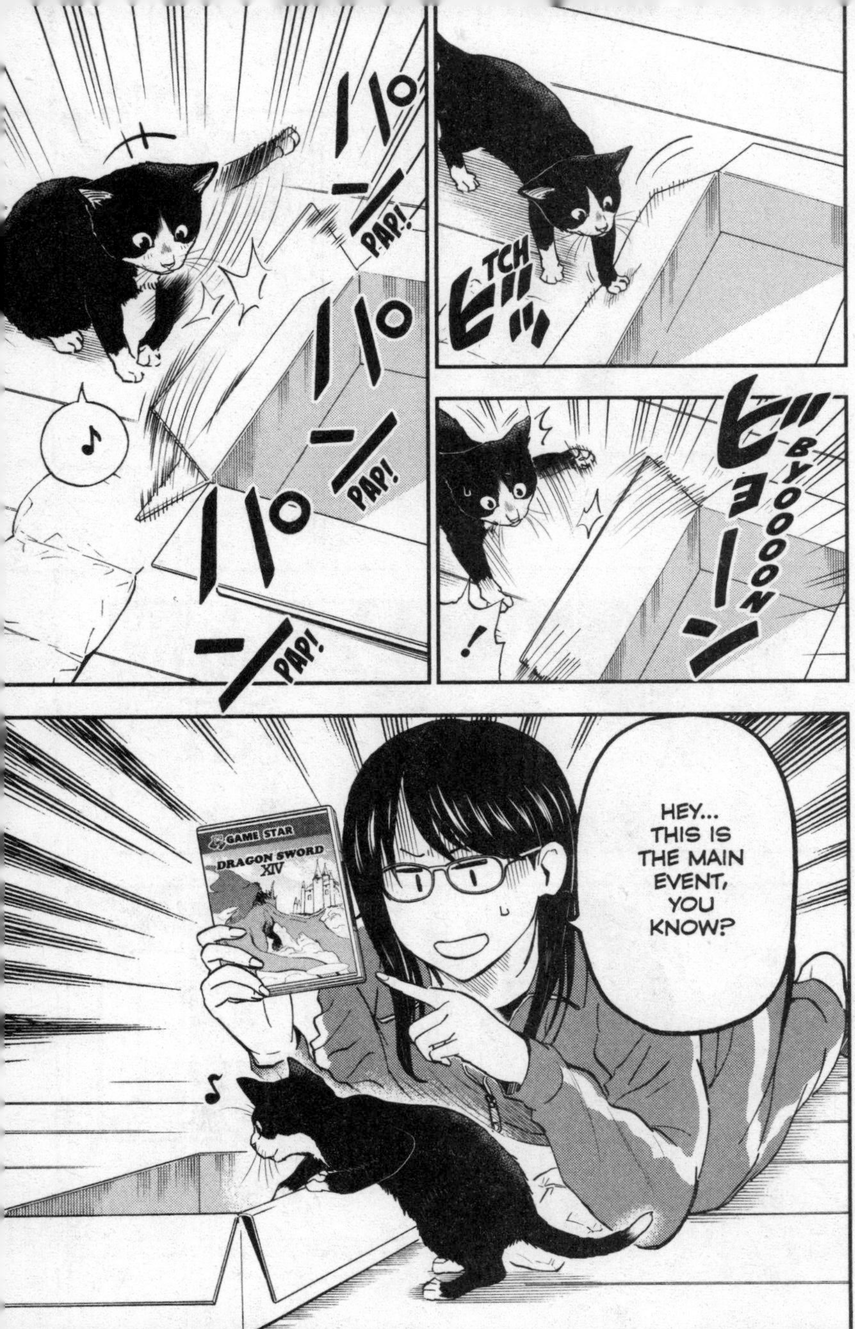

ビッ
TCH
ビョーーン
BYOOOOON
パーン
PAP!
パーン
PAP!
パーン
PAP!
HEY... THIS IS THE MAIN EVENT, YOU KNOW?
GAME STAR
DRAGON SWORD XIV

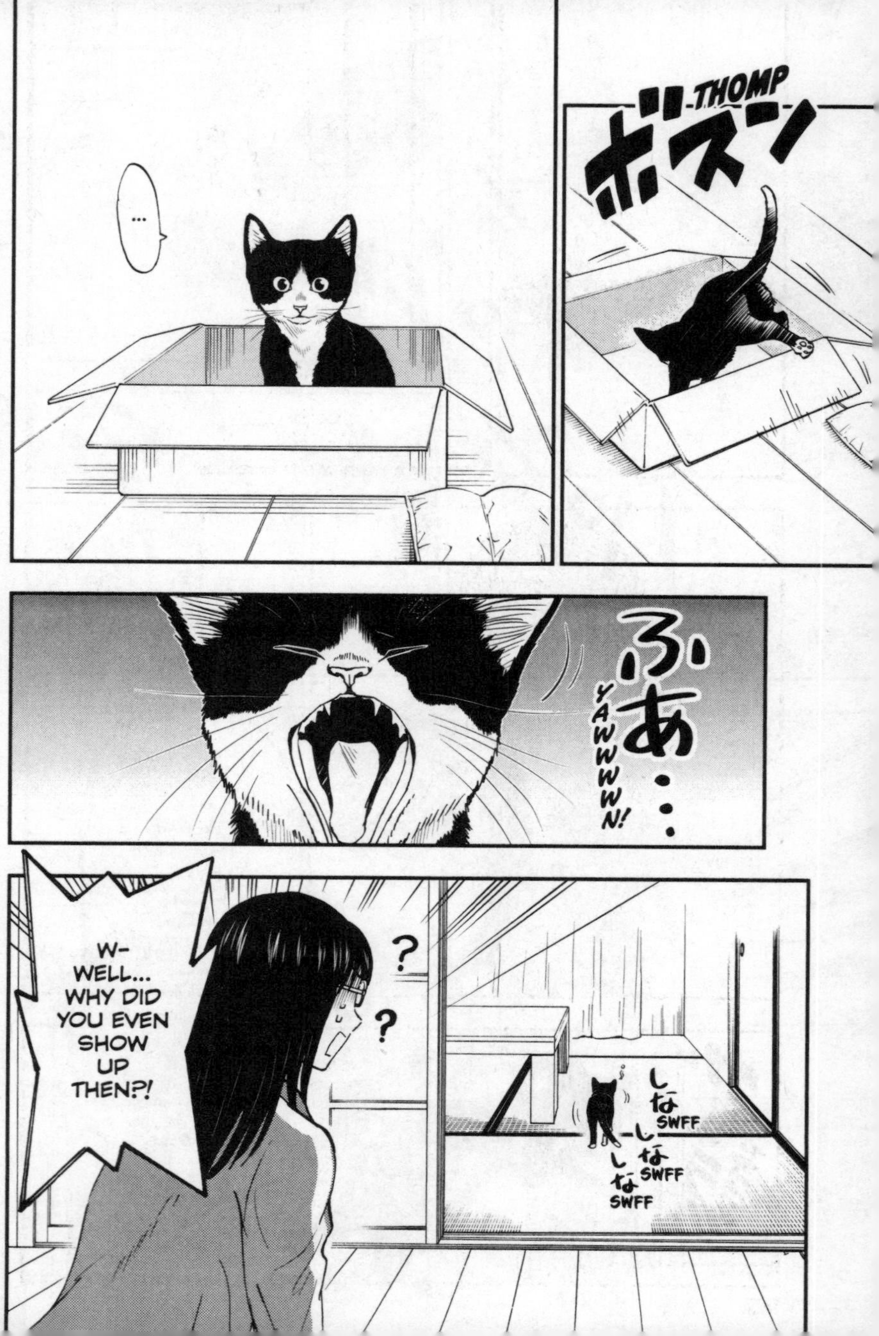
ボスン
THOMP
...
ふあ・・
YAWWWWN!
しな
SWFF
しな
SWFF
しな
SWFF
?
?
W-WELL... WHY DID YOU EVEN SHOW UP THEN?!

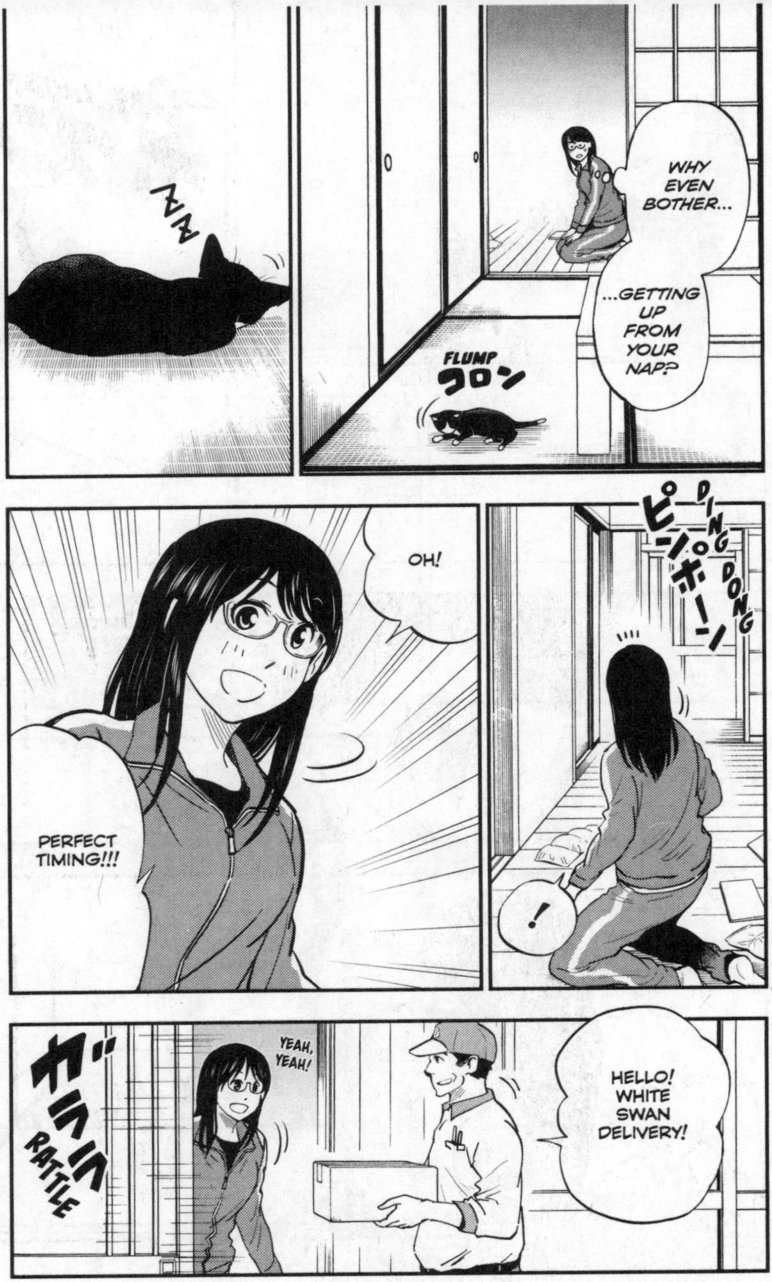
WHY EVEN BOTHER...
...GETTING UP FROM YOUR NAP?
FLUMP
コロン
ZZZ
DING DONG
ピーンポーン
!
OH!
PERFECT TIMING!!!
HELLO! WHITE SWAN DELIVERY!
YEAH, YEAH!
ガラ
RATTLE

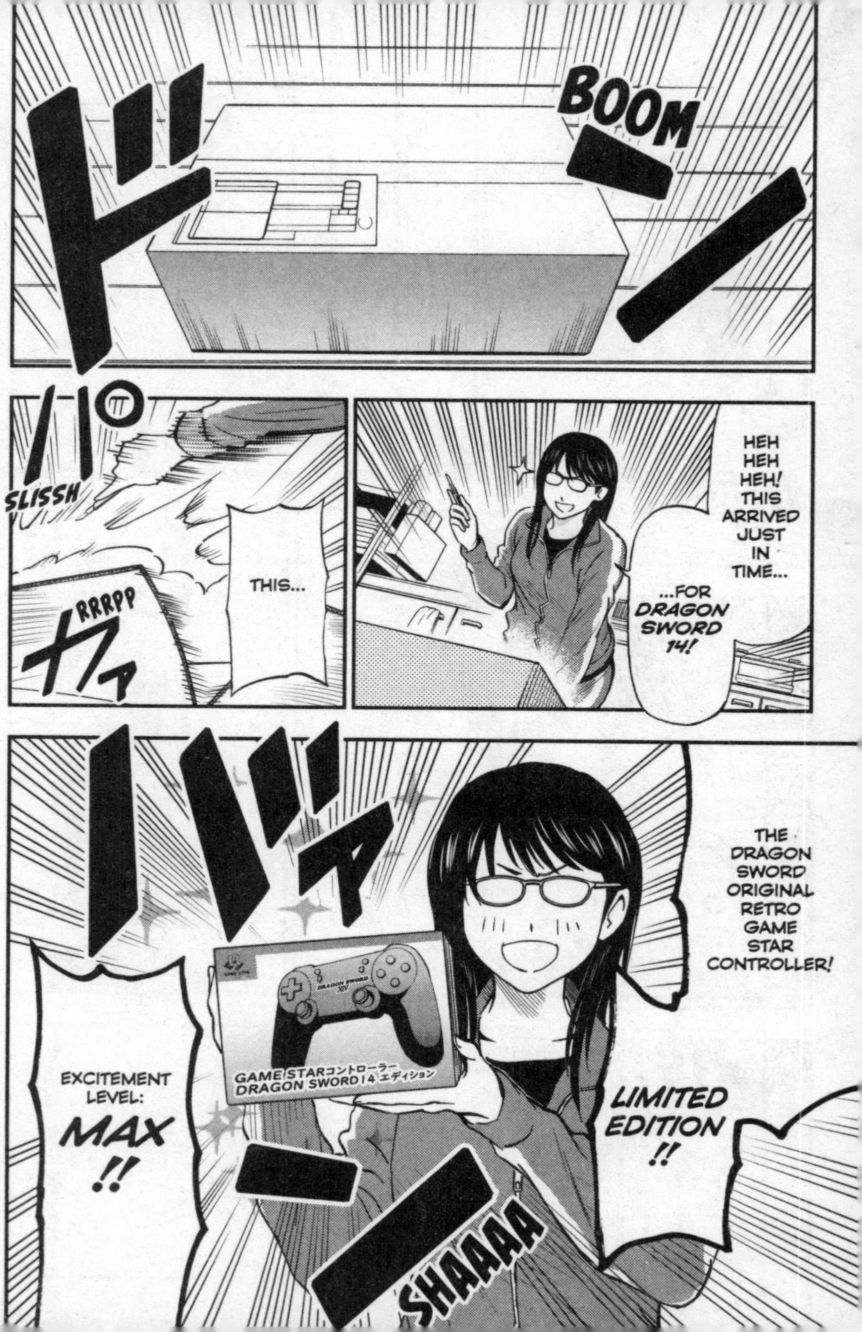
BOOM
HEH HEH HEH! THIS ARRIVED JUST IN TIME...
...FOR DRAGON SWORD 14!
SLISSH
THIS...
RRRPP
THE DRAGON SWORD ORIGINAL RETRO GAME STAR CONTROLLER!
LIMITED EDITION !!
GAME STARコントローラー
DRAGON SWORD14 エディション
EXCITEMENT LEVEL: MAX !!
SHAAAA

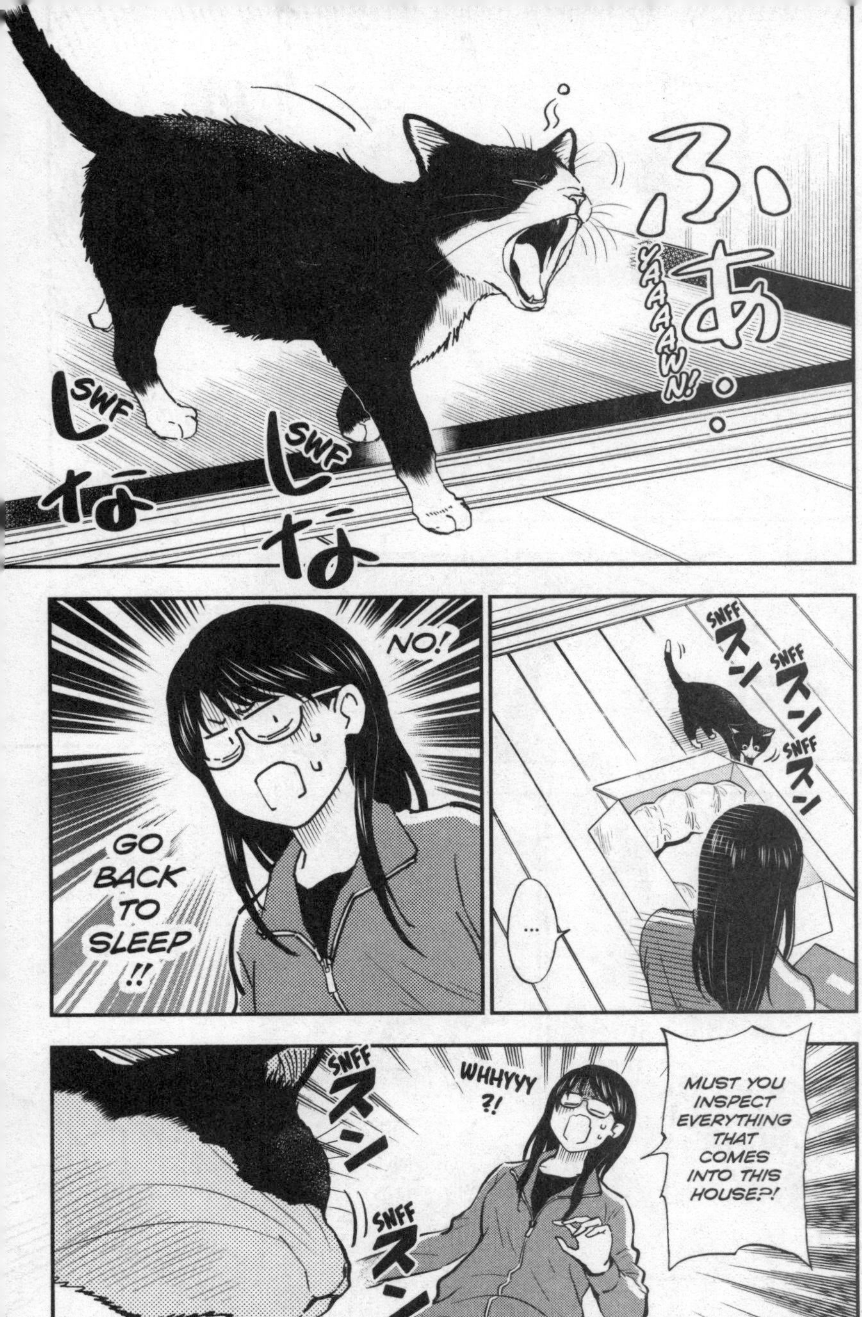
ふあ。。
YAAAAAWN!
しな
SWF
しな
SWF
SNFF
スン
SNFF
スン
SNFF
スン
...
NO!?
GO BACK TO SLEEP!!
MUST YOU INSPECT EVERYTHING THAT COMES INTO THIS HOUSE?!
WHHYYY?!
SNFF
スン
SNFF
スン

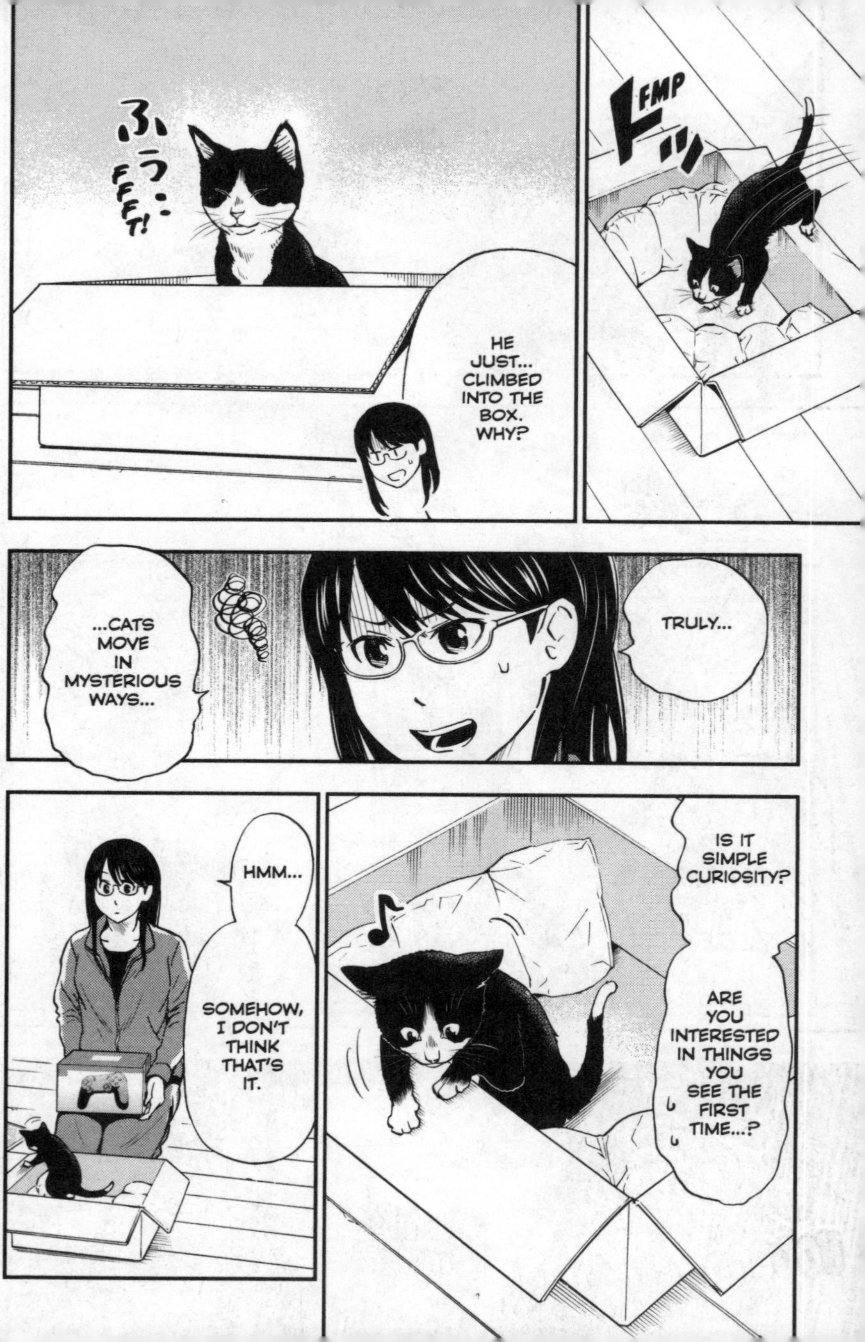
ドッ
FMP
ふぅ…
FFFT!
HE JUST... CLIMBED INTO THE BOX. WHY?
TRULY...
...CATS MOVE IN MYSTERIOUS WAYS...
IS IT SIMPLE CURIOSITY?
ARE YOU INTERESTED IN THINGS YOU SEE THE FIRST TIME...?
HMM...
SOMEHOW, I DON'T THINK THAT'S IT.

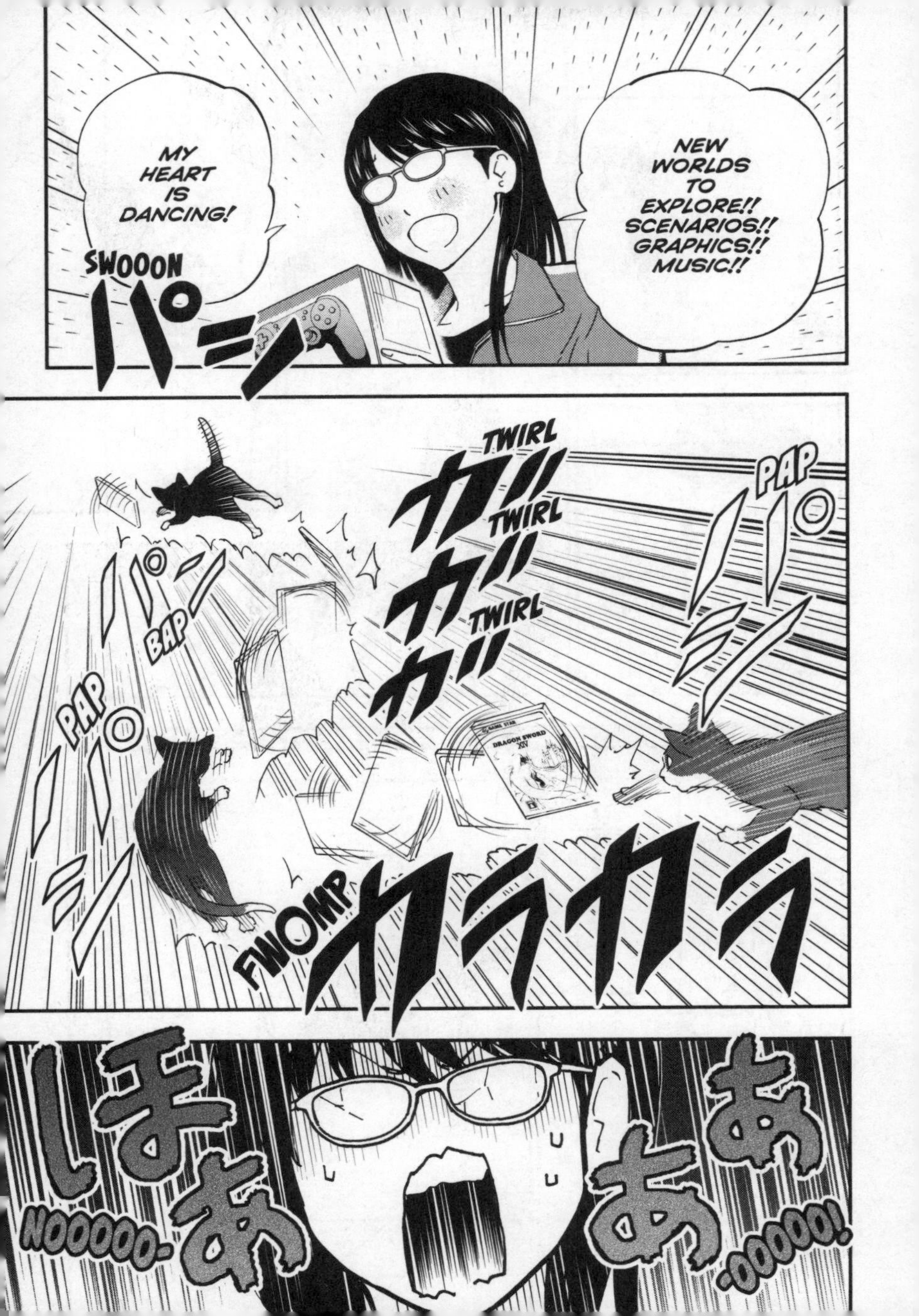

NEW WORLDS TO EXPLORE!! SCENARIOS!! GRAPHICS!! MUSIC!!
MY HEART IS DANCING!
SWOOON
PAP
TWIRL
TWIRL
TWIRL
BAP
DRAGON SWORD XIV
PAP
FWOMP
NOOOOO-
-OOOOO!

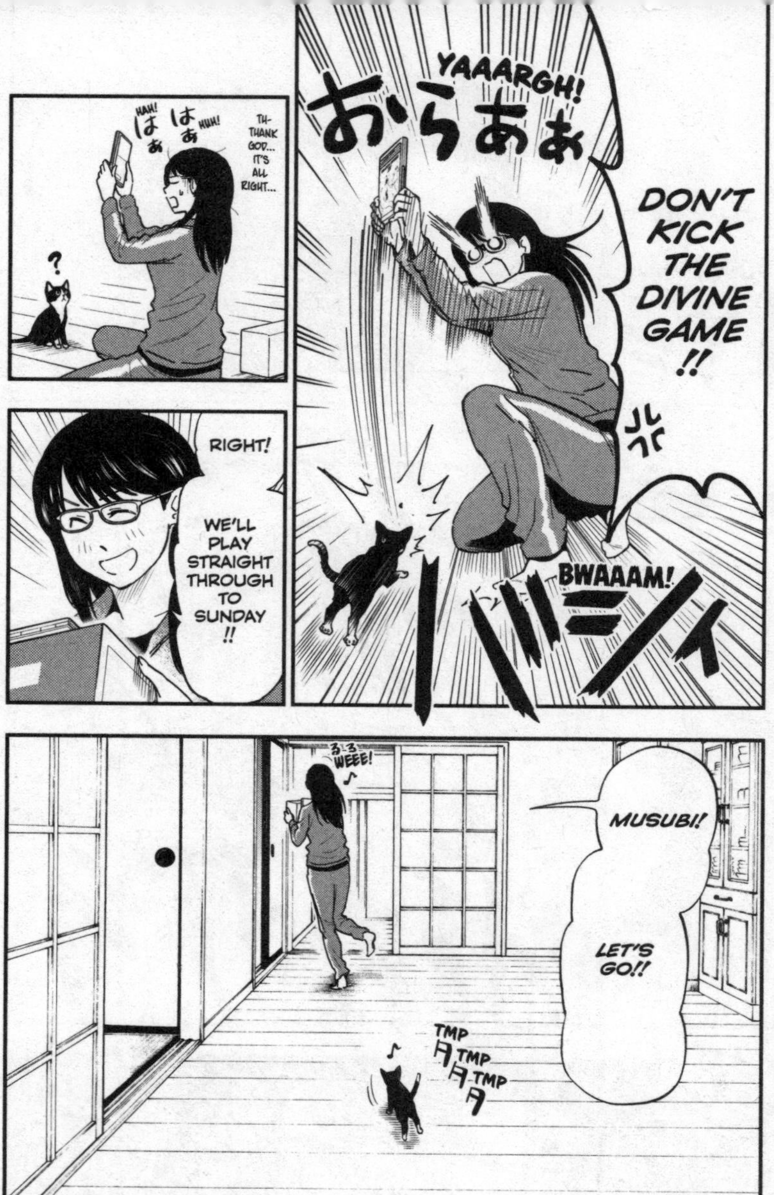
YAAARGH!
おらあぁ
DON'T KICK THE DIVINE GAME !!
BWAAAM!
バシィ
HAH! HUH!
TH-THANK GOD... IT'S ALL RIGHT...
?
RIGHT!
WE'LL PLAY STRAIGHT THROUGH TO SUNDAY !!
WEEE!
MUSUBI!
LET'S GO!!
TMP TMP TMP

Chapter 7: Bonus Stage

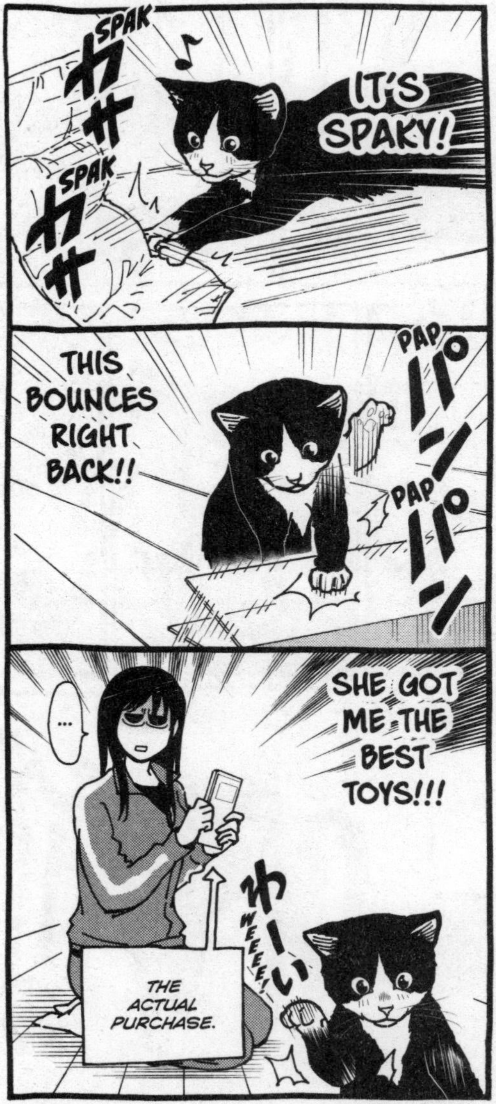
IT'S SPAKY!
SPAK
SPAK
PAP
PAP
THIS BOUNCES RIGHT BACK!!
SHE GOT ME THE BEST TOYS!!!
...
WEEEE!
THE ACTUAL PURCHASE.

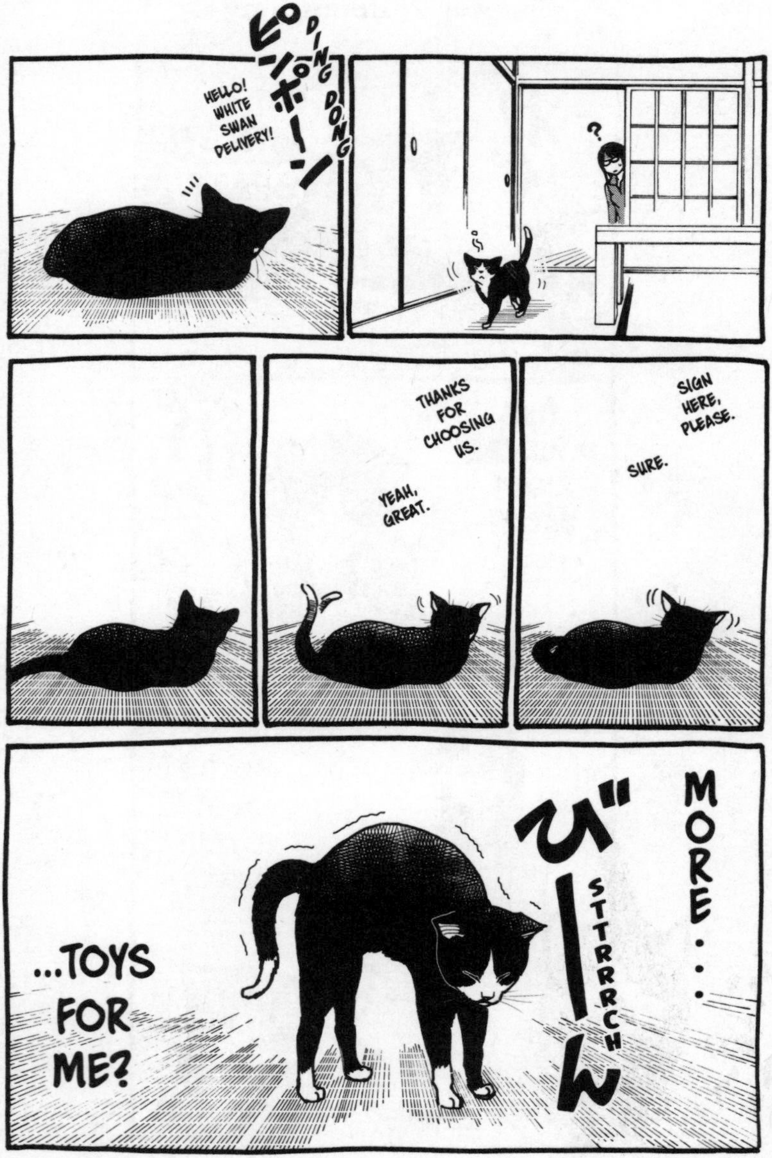
?
ピンポーン
DING DONG
HELLO! WHITE SWAN DELIVERY!
SIGN HERE, PLEASE.
SURE.
THANKS FOR CHOOSING US.
YEAH, GREAT.
MORE...
びーん
STTRRRCH
...TOYS FOR ME?

ふぁ～
Y.AWN

CAT +
GAMER

Chapter 8: Cat + Gamer + Tweeter

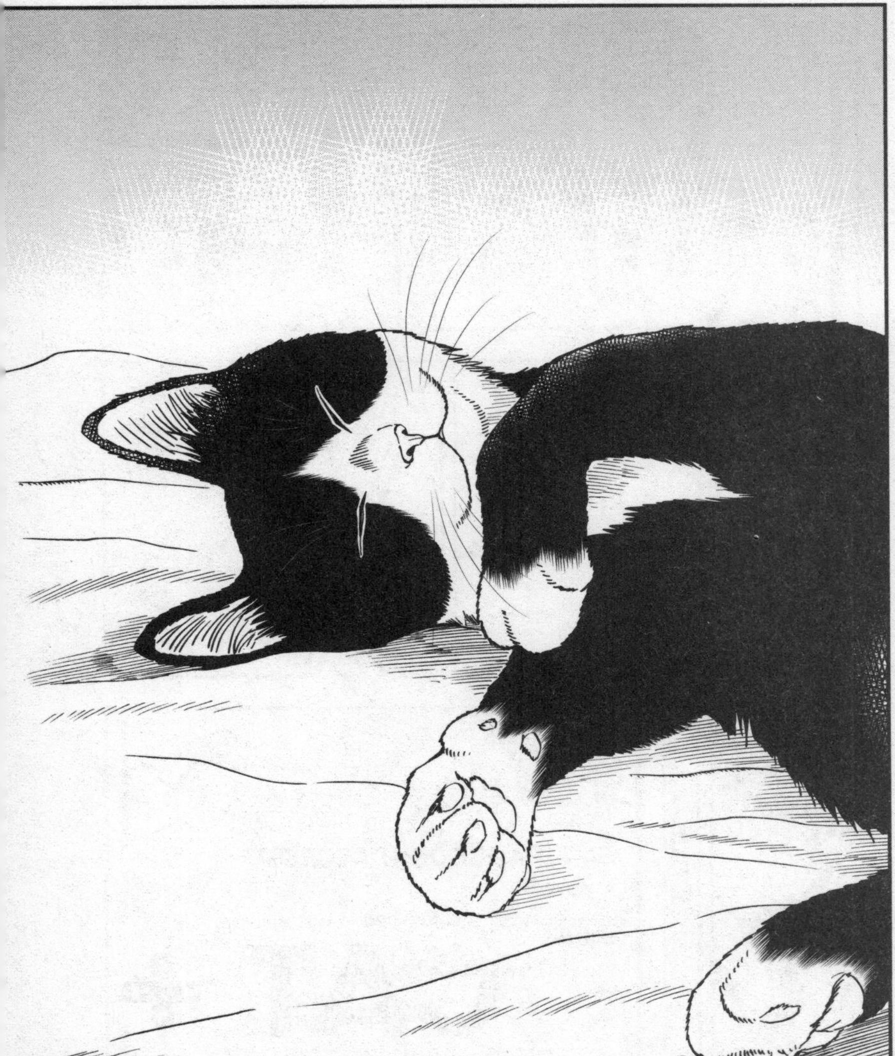

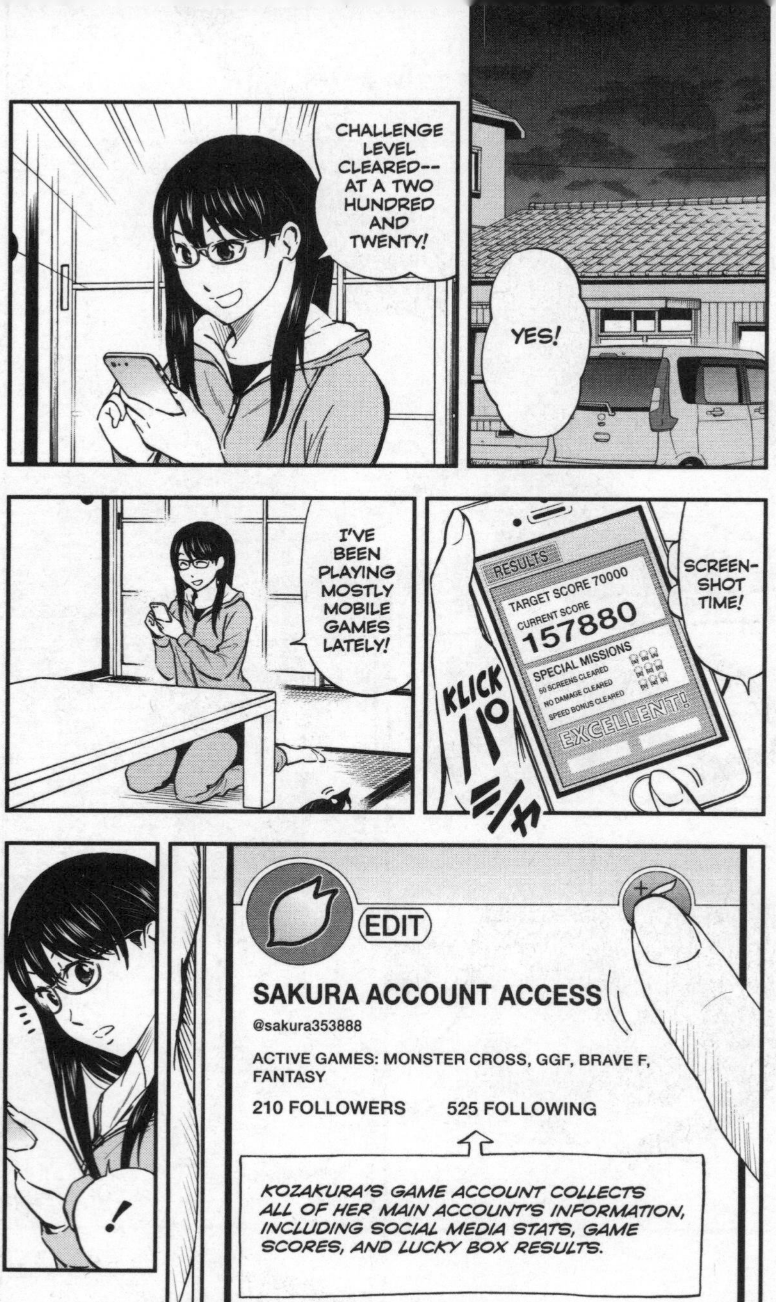
YES!
CHALLENGE LEVEL CLEARED-- AT A TWO HUNDRED AND TWENTY!
RESULTS
TARGET SCORE 70000
CURRENT SCORE
157880
SPECIAL MISSIONS
50 SCREENS CLEARED
NO DAMAGE CLEARED
SPEED BONUS CLEARED
EXCELLENT!
SCREEN-SHOT TIME!
KLICK
I'VE BEEN PLAYING MOSTLY MOBILE GAMES LATELY!
EDIT
SAKURA ACCOUNT ACCESS
@sakura353888
ACTIVE GAMES: MONSTER CROSS, GGF, BRAVE F, FANTASY
210 FOLLOWERS
525 FOLLOWING
KOZAKURA'S GAME ACCOUNT COLLECTS ALL OF HER MAIN ACCOUNT'S INFORMATION, INCLUDING SOCIAL MEDIA STATS, GAME SCORES, AND LUCKY BOX RESULTS.
!

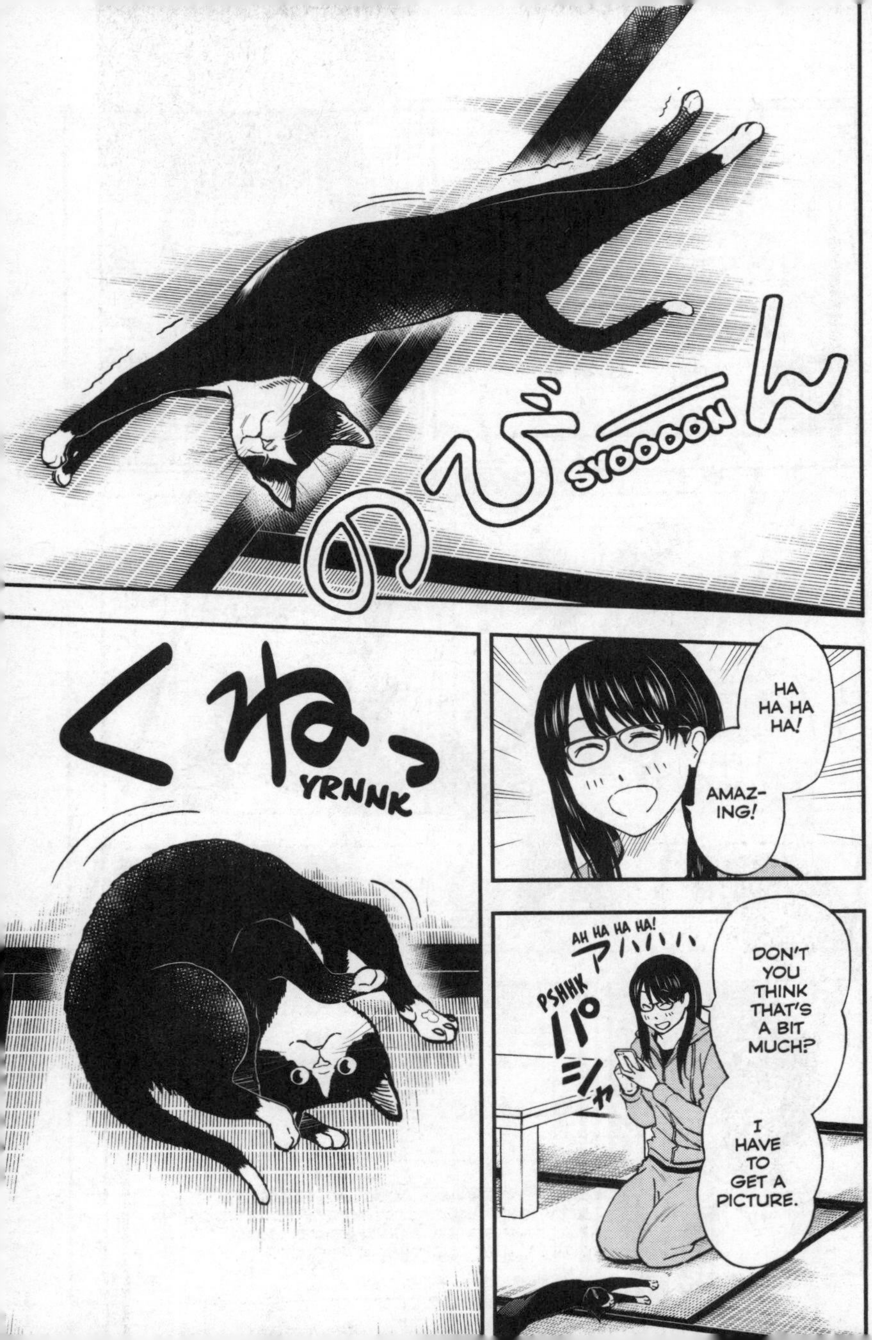
のびーん
SYOOOON
HA HA HA HA!
AMAZING!
DON'T YOU THINK THAT'S A BIT MUCH?
AH HA HA HA! アハハハ
PSHHK パシャ
I HAVE TO GET A PICTURE.
くねっ
YRNNK

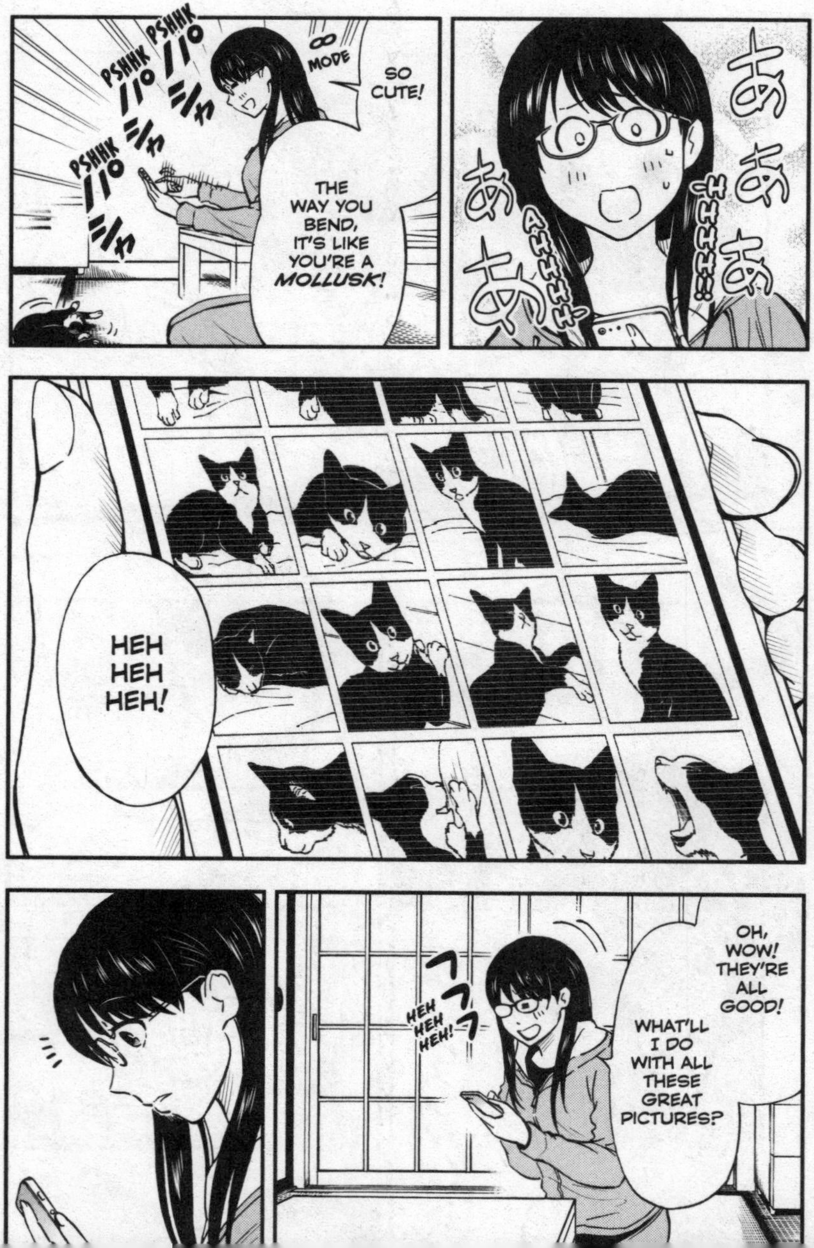

あああああ
AHHHHHH!!
PSHHK
パシャ
PSHHK
パシャ
PSHHK
パシャ
∞ MODE
SO CUTE!
THE WAY YOU BEND, IT'S LIKE YOU'RE A *MOLLUSK*!
HEH HEH HEH!
OH, WOW! THEY'RE ALL GOOD!
WHAT'LL I DO WITH ALL THESE GREAT PICTURES?
フフフ
HEH HEH HEH!

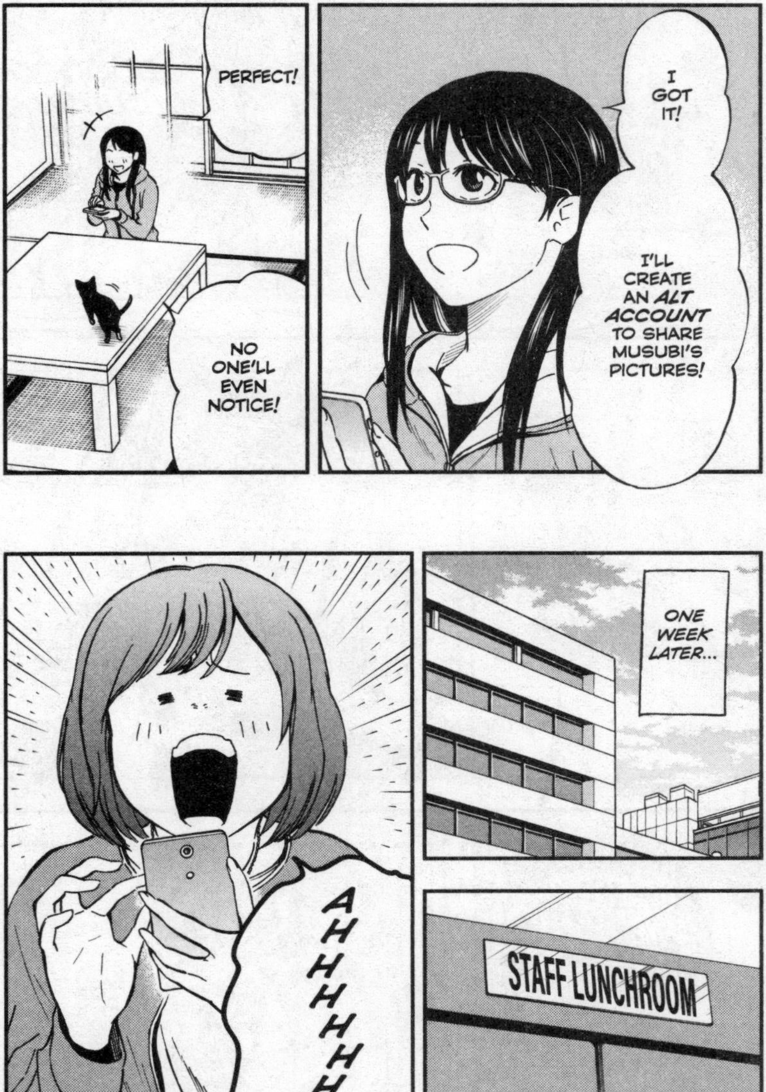
I GOT IT!
I'LL CREATE AN *ALT ACCOUNT* TO SHARE MUSUBI'S PICTURES!
PERFECT!
NO ONE'LL EVEN NOTICE!
ONE WEEK LATER...
STAFF LUNCHROOM
AHHHHHHHHHHH...

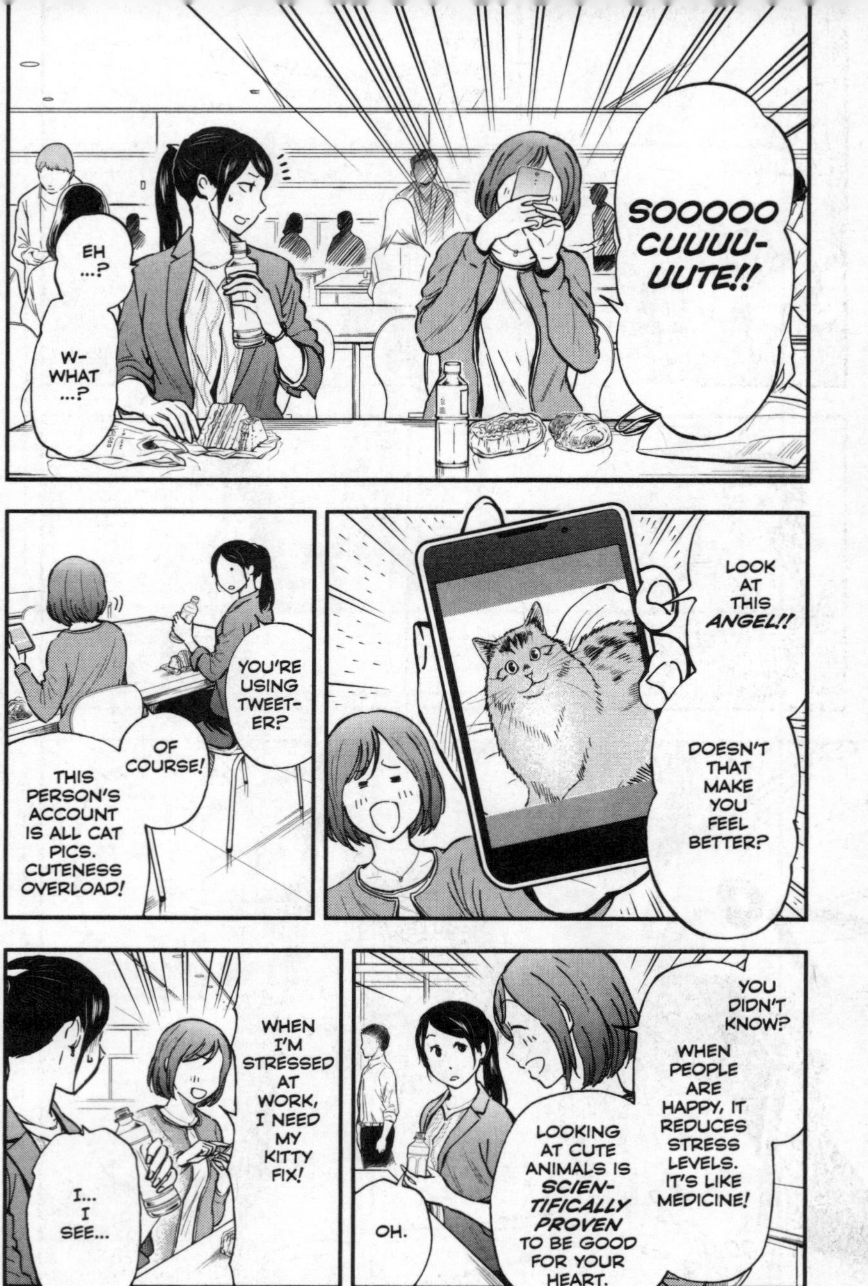
SOOOOO CUUUU-UUTE!!
EH ...?
W-WHAT ...?
LOOK AT THIS ANGEL!!
DOESN'T THAT MAKE YOU FEEL BETTER?
YOU'RE USING TWEETER?
OF COURSE!
THIS PERSON'S ACCOUNT IS ALL CAT PICS. CUTENESS OVERLOAD!
YOU DIDN'T KNOW?
WHEN PEOPLE ARE HAPPY, IT REDUCES STRESS LEVELS. IT'S LIKE MEDICINE!
LOOKING AT CUTE ANIMALS IS SCIEN-TIFICALLY PROVEN TO BE GOOD FOR YOUR HEART.
OH.
WHEN I'M STRESSED AT WORK, I NEED MY KITTY FIX!
I... I SEE...

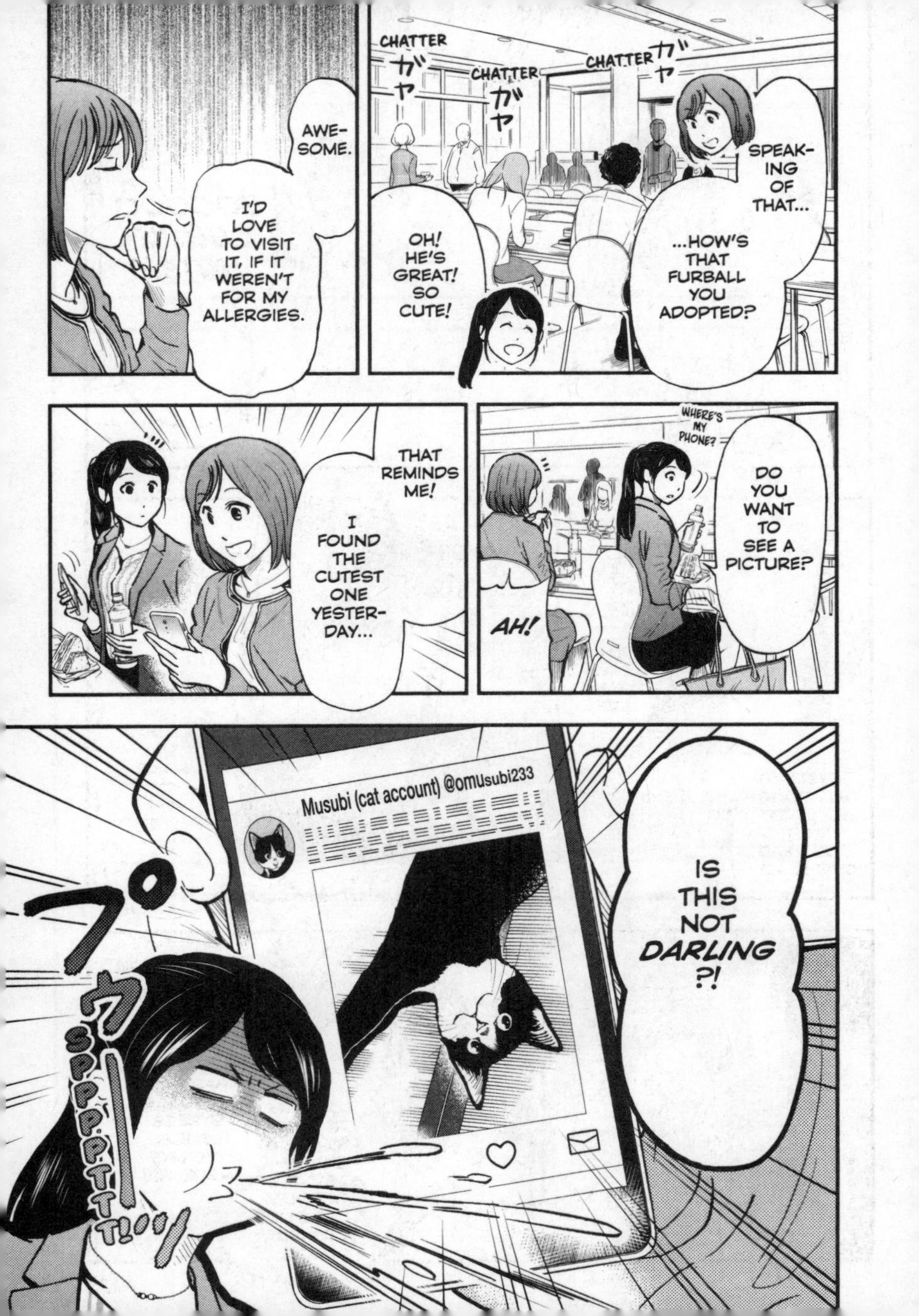
CHATTER ガヤ
CHATTER ガヤ
CHATTER ガヤ
SPEAK-ING OF THAT...
...HOW'S THAT FURBALL YOU ADOPTED?
OH! HE'S GREAT! SO CUTE!
AWE-SOME.
I'D LOVE TO VISIT IT, IF IT WEREN'T FOR MY ALLERGIES.
WHERE'S MY PHONE?
DO YOU WANT TO SEE A PICTURE?
AH!
THAT REMINDS ME!
I FOUND THE CUTEST ONE YESTER-DAY...
Musubi (cat account) @omusubi233
IS THIS NOT DARLING?!
プ
ウ
SPPPTTT!!

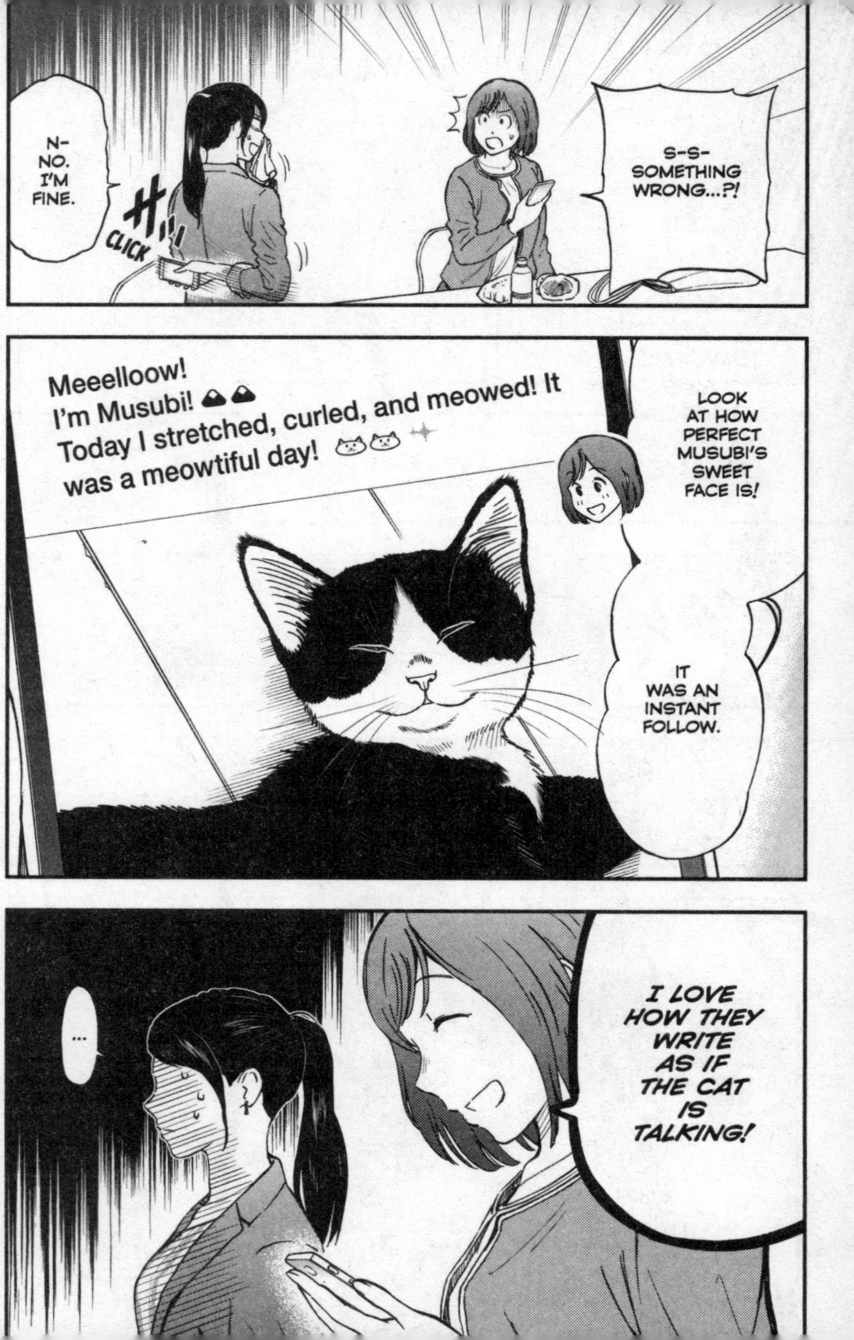
S-S-SOMETHING WRONG...?!
N-NO. I'M FINE.
CLICK
LOOK AT HOW PERFECT MUSUBI'S SWEET FACE IS!
Meeelloow!
I'm Musubi!
Today I stretched, curled, and meowed! It was a meowtiful day!
IT WAS AN INSTANT FOLLOW.
I LOVE HOW THEY WRITE AS IF THE CAT IS TALKING!
...

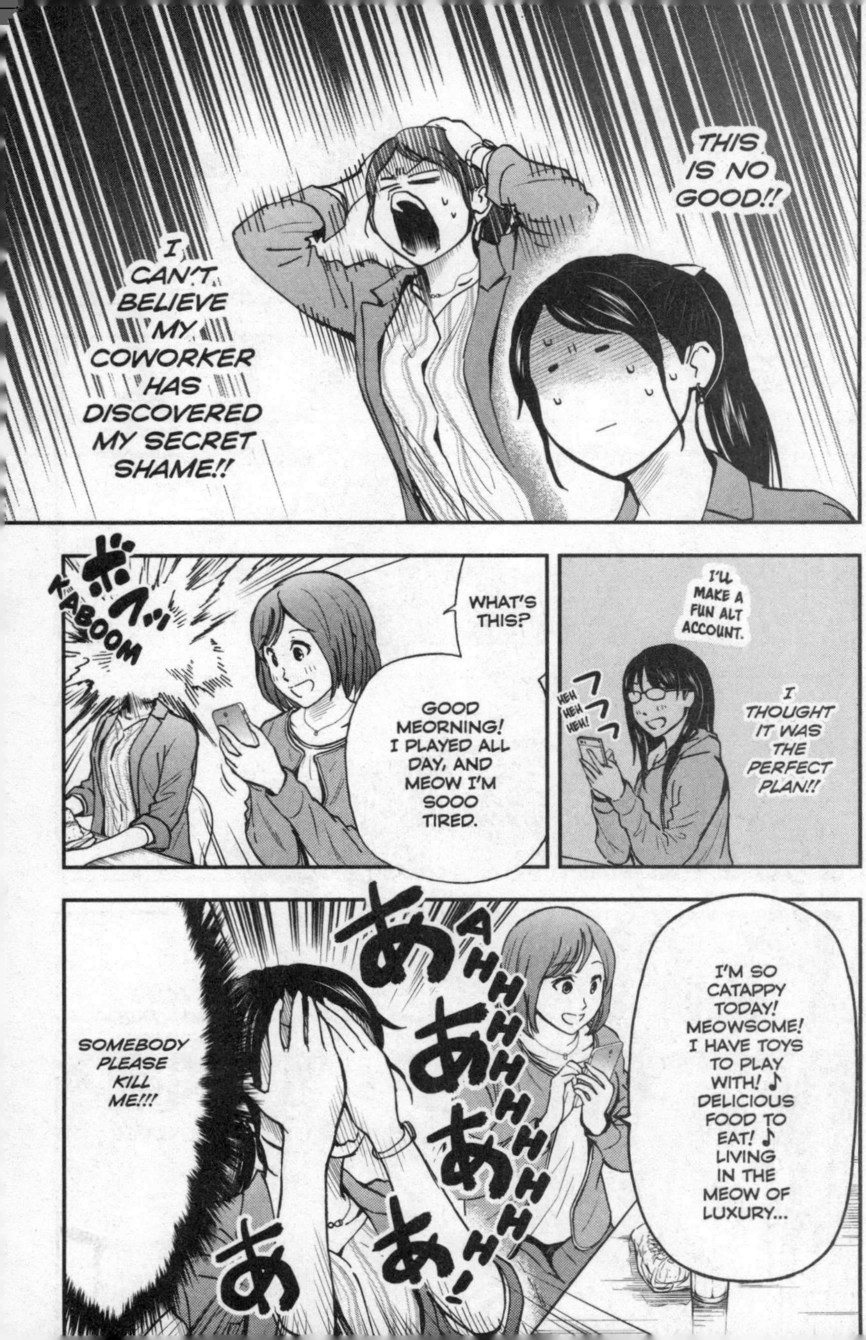
THIS IS NO GOOD!!
I CAN'T BELIEVE MY COWORKER HAS DISCOVERED MY SECRET SHAME!!
I'LL MAKE A FUN ALT ACCOUNT.
I THOUGHT IT WAS THE PERFECT PLAN!!
HEH HEH HEH!
WHAT'S THIS?
GOOD MEORNING! I PLAYED ALL DAY, AND MEOW I'M SOOO TIRED.
KABOOM
I'M SO CATAPPY TODAY! MEOWSOME! I HAVE TOYS TO PLAY WITH! ♪ DELICIOUS FOOD TO EAT! ♪ LIVING IN THE MEOW OF LUXURY...
AHHHHHHHHHHHHHHH!
SOMEBODY PLEASE KILL ME!!!

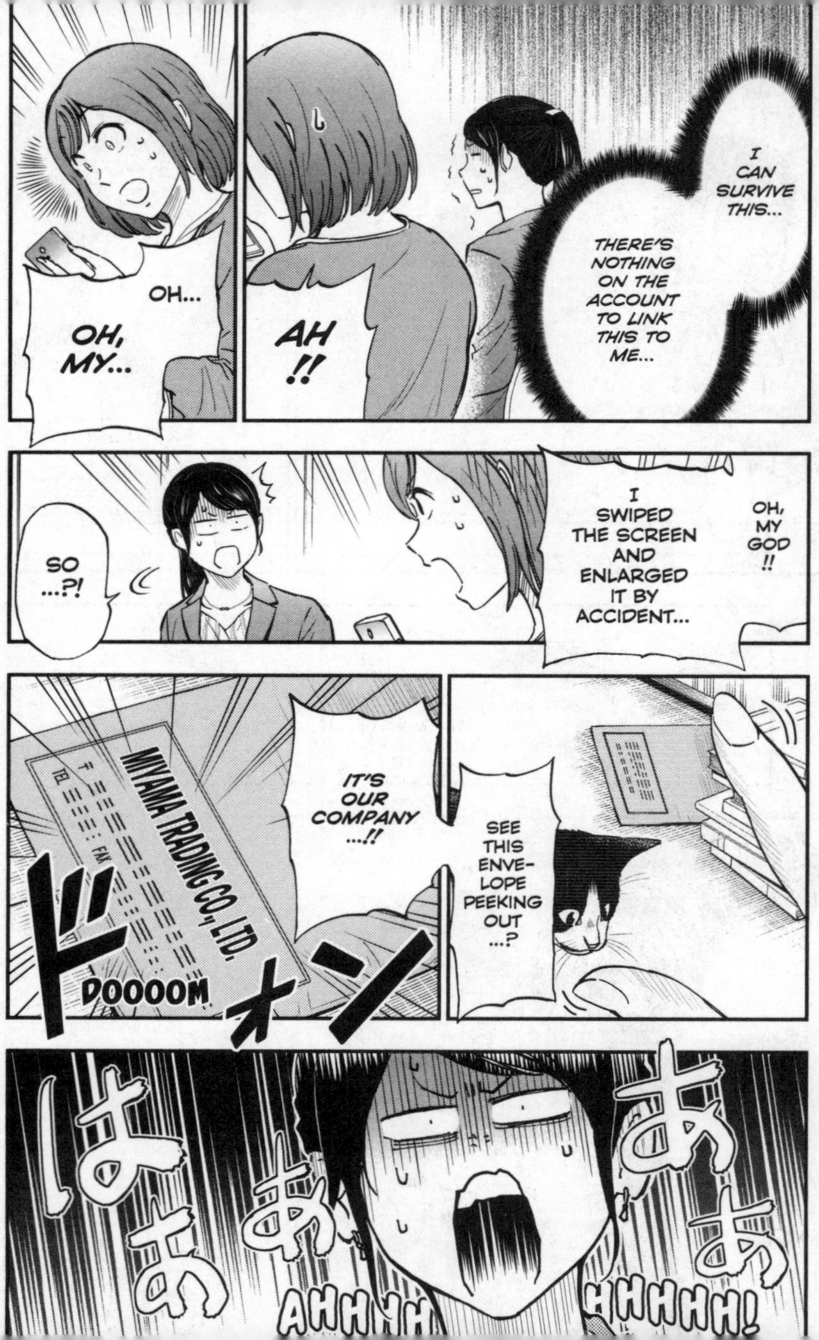
I CAN SURVIVE THIS...
THERE'S NOTHING ON THE ACCOUNT TO LINK THIS TO ME...
AH !!
OH...
OH, MY...
OH, MY GOD !!
I SWIPED THE SCREEN AND ENLARGED IT BY ACCIDENT...
SO ...?!
SEE THIS ENVELOPE PEEKING OUT ...?
IT'S OUR COMPANY ...!!
MIYAMA TRADING CO., LTD.
TEL
FAX
ドオン
DOOOOM
はあああああ
AHHHH HHHHHH!

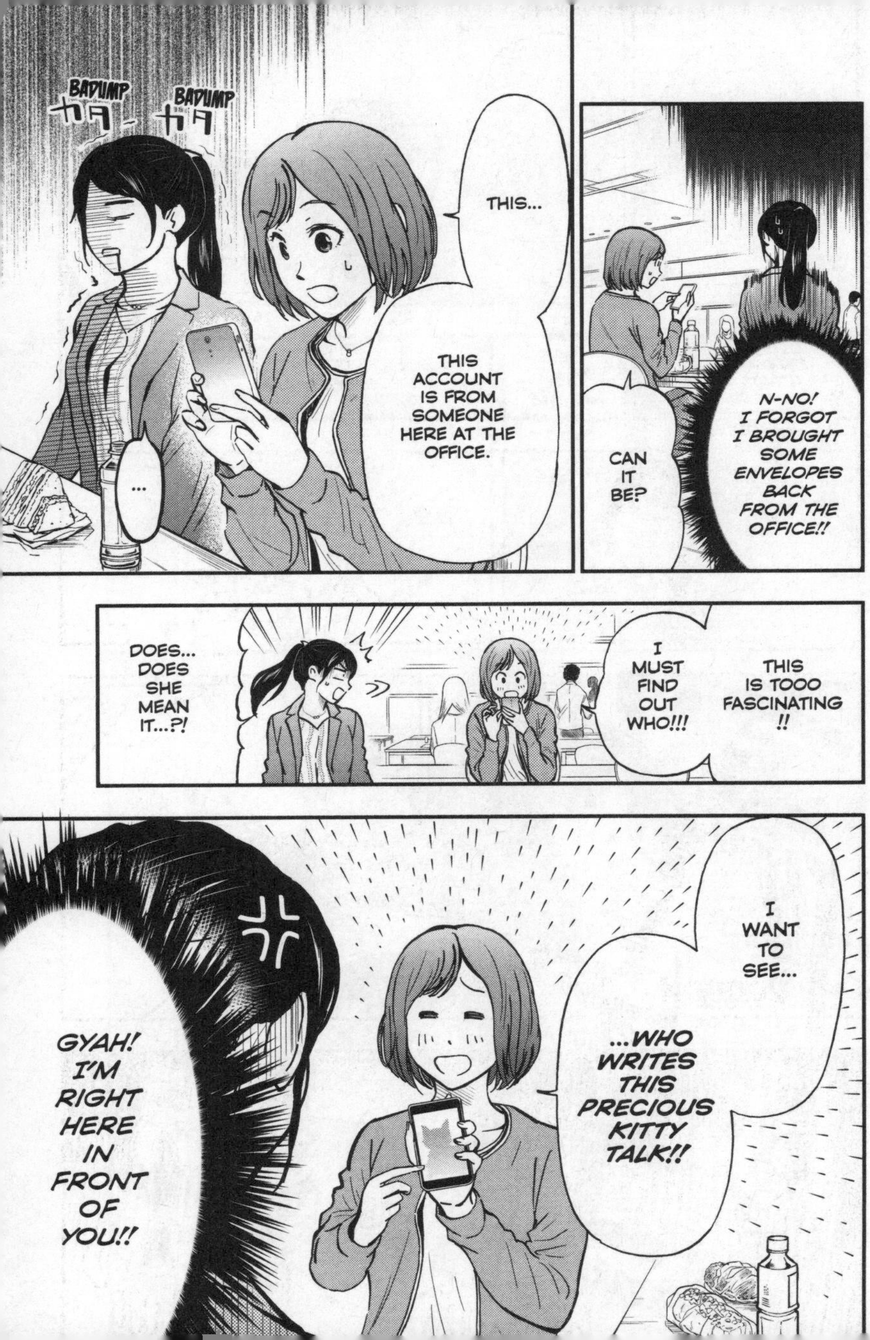
N-NO! I FORGOT I BROUGHT SOME ENVELOPES BACK FROM THE OFFICE!!
CAN IT BE?
THIS...
THIS ACCOUNT IS FROM SOMEONE HERE AT THE OFFICE.
BADUMP
BADUMP
...
THIS IS TOOO FASCINATING!!
I MUST FIND OUT WHO!!!
DOES... DOES SHE MEAN IT...?!
I WANT TO SEE...
...WHO WRITES THIS PRECIOUS KITTY TALK!!
GYAH! I'M RIGHT HERE IN FRONT OF YOU!!

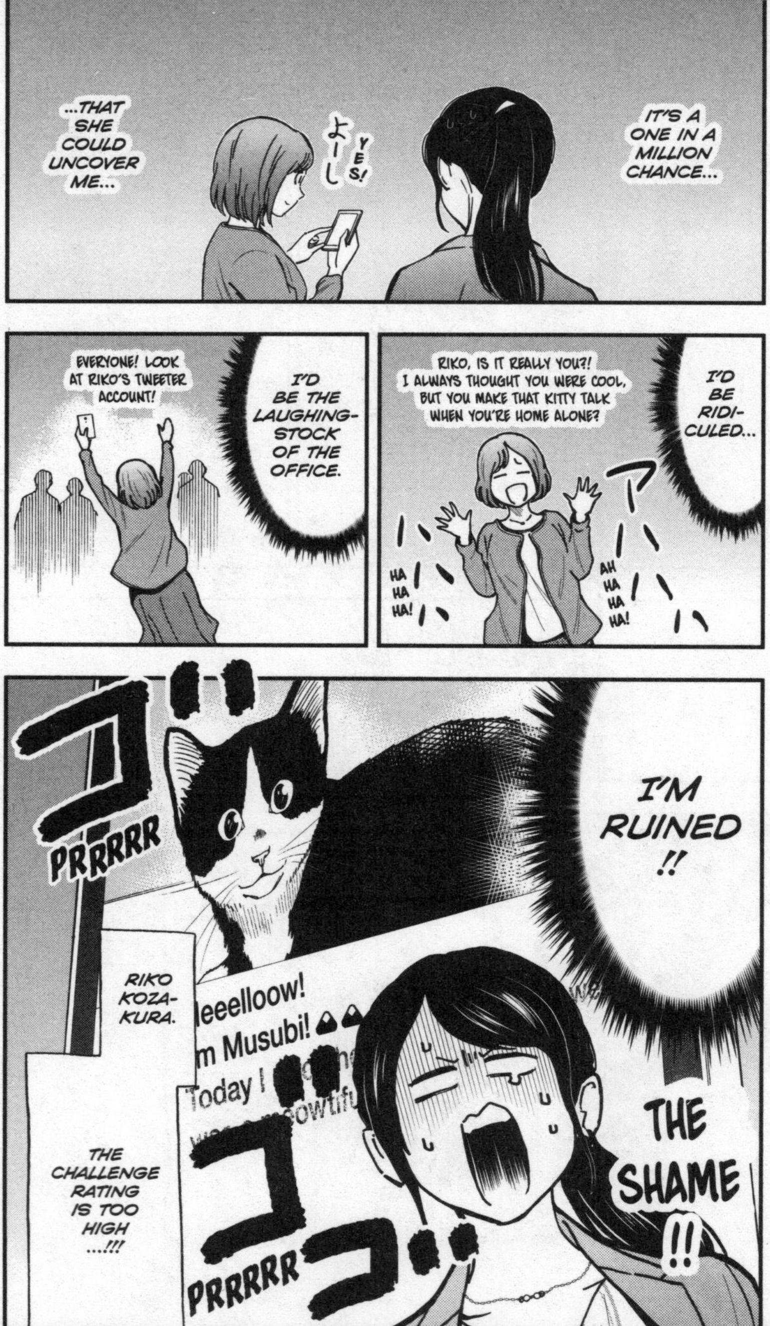
IT'S A ONE IN A MILLION CHANCE...
よし
YES!
...THAT SHE COULD UNCOVER ME...
RIKO, IS IT REALLY YOU?! I ALWAYS THOUGHT YOU WERE COOL, BUT YOU MAKE THAT KITTY TALK WHEN YOU'RE HOME ALONE?
I'D BE RIDICULED...
AH HA HA HA!
HA HA HA!
I'D BE THE LAUGHING-STOCK OF THE OFFICE.
EVERYONE! LOOK AT RIKO'S TWEETER ACCOUNT!
I'M RUINED!!
PRRRRR
RIKO KOZA-KURA.
THE SHAME!!
THE CHALLENGE RATING IS TOO HIGH....!!!
PRRRRR

END OF CAT + GAMER VOL. 1!

Chapter 8: Bonus Stage

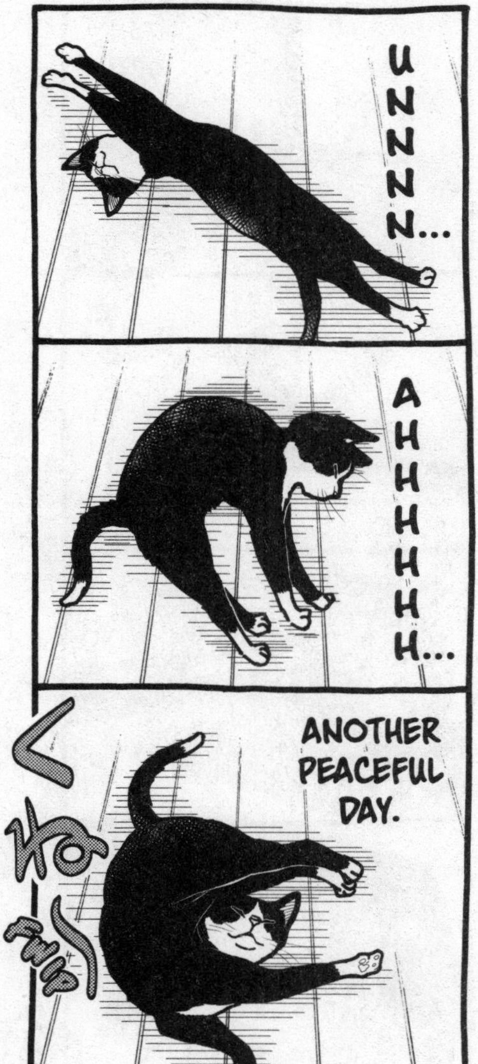

UNNNN...
AHHHHHHH...
ANOTHER PEACEFUL DAY.
FWIP

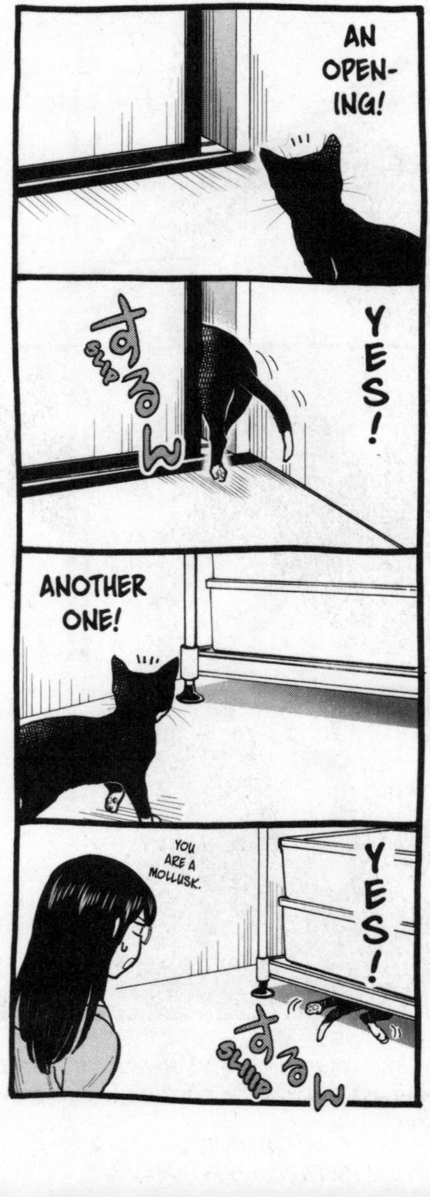

AN OPENING!
YES!
するん
SLIP
ANOTHER ONE!
YES!
YOU ARE A MOLLUSK.
するん
SLIIP

To be continued in *Cat + Gamer* Volume 2—
coming soon, so please keep reading!

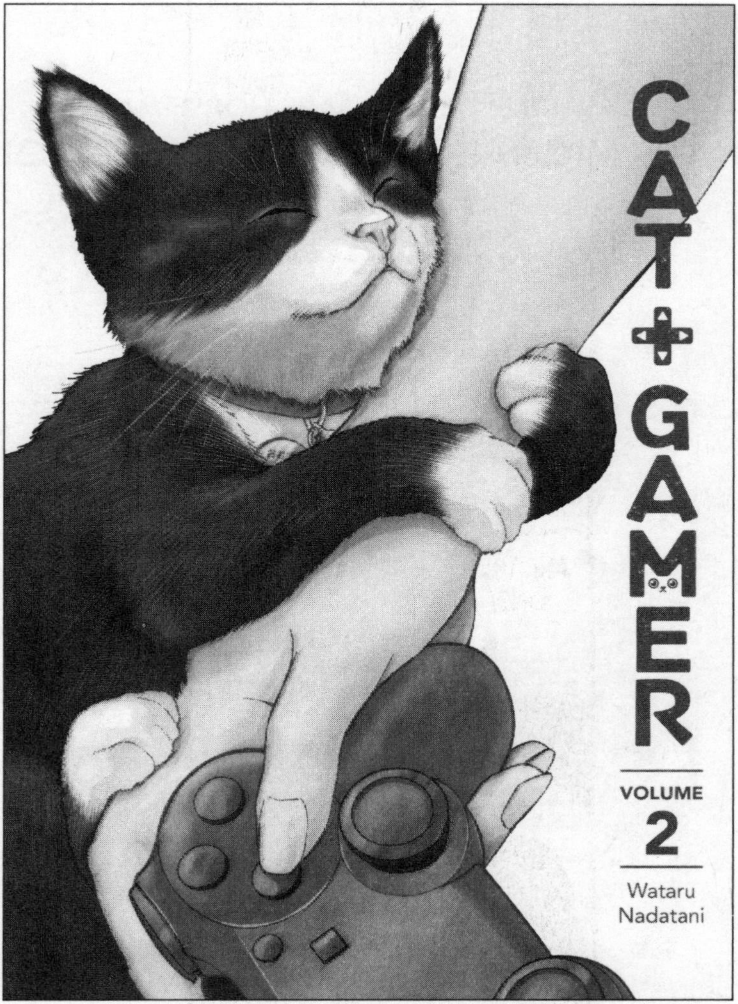
CAT+GAMER
VOLUME
2
Wataru
Nadatani

"Leveling up" in skills, surprises, and adventures extends to real life, as Riko continues to discover what it's like living with a cat!

VOLUME 2

ISBN 978-1-50672-742-4

FLCL

STORY BY GAINAX
ART BY HAJIME UEDA

OMNIBUS

The complete *FLCL* manga adaptation—
now with bonus color illustrations and
remastered story pages!

"This show will change your life."
—Adult Swim

ISBN 978-1-59582-868-2
$19.99

FROM THE STUDIO THAT BROUGHT YOU *EVANGELION!*

灘谷 航

WATARU NADATANI PRESENTS

At the start of this series, I got myself a real-life cat! It's a black-and-white tuxedo cat just like in the manga. Sometimes it gets in the way of my work, but it makes up for that by being my model! Thanks, kitty!
—Wataru Nadatani

PUBLISHER **MIKE RICHARDSON**

SENIOR EDITOR **PHILIP R. SIMON**

ASSOCIATE EDITOR **JUDY KHUU**

ASSISTANT EDITOR **ROSE WEITZ**

DESIGNER **SARAH TERRY**

DIGITAL ART TECHNICIAN **ANN GRAY**

CAT + GAMER Volume 1

NEKOGURASHI NO GAMER-SAN Vol.1
by Wataru NADATANI
© 2019 Wataru NADATANI
All rights reserved.
Original Japanese edition published by SHOGAKUKAN.
English translation rights arranged with SHOGAKUKAN
through Tuttle-Mori Agency, Inc.

Dark Horse Manga, a division of Dark Horse Comics LLC
10956 SE Main Street
Milwaukie, OR 97222
DarkHorse.com

First English-language edition: March 2022
ISBN 978-1-50672-741-7

3 5 7 9 10 8 6 4 2
Printed in the United States of America
To find a comics shop in your area, visit comicshoplocator.com

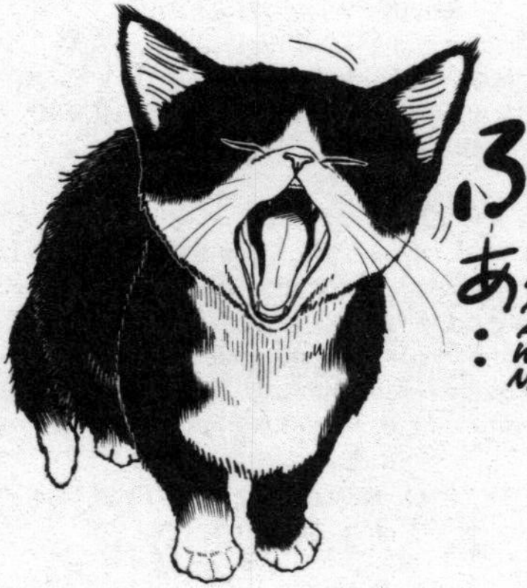
ふあ‥
YAAAAAWN!